BERLIN TO LONDON

An Emotional History of
Two Refugees

Esther Saraga

VALLENTINE MITCHELL
LONDON • CHICAGO, IL

Parkes–Wiener Series on Jewish Studies

ISSN 1368-5449

The field of Jewish Studies is one of the youngest, but fastest-growing and most exciting areas of scholarship in the academic world today. Named after James Parkes and Alfred Wiener, this series, created by David Cesarani and Tony Kushner, aims to publish new research in the field and student materials for use in the seminar room, to disseminate the latest work of established scholars and to re-issue classic studies that are currently out of print. The selection of publications reflects the international character and diversity of Jewish Studies; it ranges over Jewish history from Abraham to modern Zionism, and Jewish culture from Moses to post-modernism. The series also reflects the inter-disciplinary approach inherent in Jewish Studies and at the cutting edge of contemporary scholarship, and provides an outlet for innovative work on the interface between Judaism and ethnicity, popular culture, gender, class, space and memory.

Other Books in the Series

Schulz, Levi, Spiegelman and the Memory of the Offence
Gillian Banner
Remembering Cable Street: Fascism and Anti-Fascism in British Society
Edited by Tony Kushner and Nadia Valman
Sir Sidney Hamburger and Manchester Jewry: Religion, City and Community
Bill Williams
Anglo-Jewry in Changing Times: Studies in Diversity 1840–1914
Israel Finestein
Double Jeopardy: Gender and the Holocaust
Judith Tydor Baumel
Cultures of Ambivalence and Contempt: Studies in Jewish–Non-Jewish Relations
Edited by Siân Jones, Tony Kushner and Sarah Pearce
Alfred Wiener and the Making of the Wiener Library
Ben Barkow
The Berlin Haskalah and German Religious Thought: Orphans of Knowledge
David Sorkin
Myths in Israeli Culture: Captives of a Dream
Nurith Gertz
The Jewish Immigrant in England 1870–1914, Third Edition
Lloyd P. Gartner
State and Society in Roman Galilee, A.D. 132–212, Second Edition
Martin Goodman
Disraeli's Jewishness
Edited by Todd M. Endelman
Claude Montefiore: His Life and Thought
Daniel R. Langton
Approaching the Holocaust: Texts and Contexts
Robert Rozett
Campaigner Against Antisemitism: The Reverend James Parkes, 1896–1981
Colin Richmond

For Lotte and Wolja
and all those refugees whose stories go
untold and unheard

First published in 2019 by Vallentine Mitchell

Catalyst House, 720 Centennial Court, Centennial Park, Elstree WD6 3SY, UK	814 N. Franklin Street, Chicago, Illinois, 60610, USA

www.vmbooks.com

Copyright © Esther Saraga 2019

British Library Cataloguing in Publication Data
A catalogue record has been applied for

ISSN 978 1 912676 16 3 (paper)
ISSN 978 1 912676 17 0 (ebook)

Library of Congress Cataloging-in-Publication Data:
A catalog record has been applied for

Contents

Foreword

There are more autobiographical writings from the refugees from Nazism than any other group of forced migrants in world history. This quantity is matched by the amount written *about* them in the academy and beyond. On the surface the question of 'why another refugee life story?' appears to have validity. Esther Saraga's laser-sharp analysis of her parents' lives shows the superficiality of this critique. The book is subtitled 'An Emotional History of Two Refugees'. Its dissection of the lives and relationship of her mother Lotte and father Wolja reveals (and this still needs to be understood), how difficult being a refugee is – even for those from relatively privileged backgrounds.

There is an ongoing debate of whether the study of refugees should be subsumed within forced migration studies. For those who are concerned to keep the specific dynamics of the former, the key issue is that 'the centrepiece of refugee studies should be the persons and not just the phenomenon, and that the specificity of the refugee's circumstances does and should matter'.[1] In *Berlin to London* the individuality of the two refugees, as well as their complex relationship, is always to the fore. That it is based on a close reading of their personal documents, especially correspondence between the two, ensures that this is the case.

For the forcibly displaced, communication with family and friends is of crucial importance. It can be a matter of life or death and more mundanely of keeping up morale when so much has been lost, especially a place called 'home'. Today, for those escaping to Europe through desperately inadequate vessels, and those left behind, the days and weeks without mobile phone contact is the most dislocating and frightening. For Jews in Nazi Europe, especially in the 1930s but even into the early years of the Second World War, letter writing was equally essential. Slow and not always reliable, delays either in receiving correspondence or in replying caused anxiety and unhappiness. Esther Saraga's forensic analysis of her parents' letters to one another provides a brilliant analysis of this genre in helping us to understand what it was (and is) to be a refugee. It is part of a new wave of such studies but a particular and remarkable one at that.[2]

This study, following the pioneering work of French historian Lucien Febvre in the mid-twentieth century and what has become a growth industry in recent decades, is a history of emotions.[3] Another dimension, however, is added to it by the interjection of the author herself. Esther Saraga's parents had neither re-read their correspondence nor had they thrown it away. Its voluminous survival posed a practical, ethical and psychological dilemma for Esther. This book provides a painfully honest account of her engagement with this correspondence over many decades leading now to its final publication. This has not been an easy process.

It has become fashionable for historians and other scholars to insert themselves into their work, even when its subject matter has little or nothing to do with their own biography.[4] At its worst, it can be an exercise in narcissism. At best, it can provide self-reflexivity about research technique, the problematic nature of the archive, and the challenge of representing the full complexity of the past and its ongoing impact. There is no doubting of the quality of Esther Saraga's creative and exhaustive research. By placing herself firmly in the process, it not only helps understand the dynamics of the Saraga family but also illuminates the slippery, multi-layered nature of the documents she has interrrogated and laid open to the public realm. The process of examining and re-examining the archive reveals memory processes at work and how they continue to shape the historic record and give it different meanings.

It is not only personal correspondence that forms the Saraga archive. There are official documents that either hindered or enabled their and their family's arrival in Britain and beyond, Wolja's internment in Britain, naturalisation, and the agonisingly slow and often humiliating experience of getting post-war compensation. If the twentieth century was 'the century of the refugee', it was also the one of increasingly restrictive 'paper walls' and the invention of the 'illegal immigrant'. Indeed, Esther Saraga's narrative does not shy away from making connections to contemporary migrant crises and the tyranny of documentation – most recently in Britain with the Windrush scandal.

Lotte and Wolja were, as their daughter notes, in the scheme of Nobel Prize winners, just 'ordinary refugees' – though it remains that it was Wolja's engineering talent that enabled his (temporary) entry to Britain through the untiring efforts of refugee activists and campaigners. Their lives in Britain were not especially remarkable but that is not the point. It has been said of the much-loved children's author, Judith Kerr (who died a few months before this book was published), that had she 'never written anything longer than a note to the milkman it would still have been right to shelter her family from the Nazis'.[5] So too, Lotte and Wolja. They were ordinary people to whom something extraordinary and damaging happened. Yet what is rare in the realm of refugee studies is that their daughter has managed to convey in

Berlin to London that hardest task of the imagination – how it feels to have your home taken away from you and to start life afresh.

Tony Kushner
Parkes Institute
University of Southampton

Notes

1.   James Hathaway, 'Forced Migration Studies: Could We Agree Just to "Date"?', *Journal of Refugee Studies,* vol.20 no.3 (2007), p.1.
2.   Mark Roseman, *The Past in Hiding* (London, 2000); Joachim Schloer, *'Liesel, it's time for you to leave'* (Heilbronn, 2015); and Shirli Gilbert, *From Things Lost: Forgotten Letters and the Legacy of the Holocaust* (Detroit, 2017).
3.   For an overview and defence, see Rob Boddice, *The History of Emotions* (Manchester, 2018).
4.   See, for example, Matt Houlbrook, *Prince of Tricksters: The Incredible True Story of Netley Lucas,* Gentleman Crook (Chicago, 2016).
5.   Gaby Hinsliff, 'Judith Kerr: a life to celebrate in dark times', *Guardian,* 25 May 2019.

List of Illustrations

Acknowledgements

A project that has lasted so long has inevitably relied on support from many people, with only the occasional questioning of why it was taking so long!

I am immensely grateful to Peter, my brother. He not only supplied some helpful alternative perspectives and slightly different memories, but most significantly gave me free rein to work on the papers in my own way.

When we first found the papers my therapist, Rosalie Kerbekian, told me that what I chose to do with them might be very significant for me. Although it took me eighteen years to get started, I discovered that she could not have been more right. When I did start I was working at the Open University, where many of my friends and colleagues played an important role in helping me to develop my approach to the papers. I am particularly grateful to Gail Lewis who first encouraged me to think of it as an 'academic' project, to Felicity Edholm who worked very closely with me in the first few years, offering many helpful insights, and to Janet Fink who acted as a wonderful research mentor. Other OU colleagues – John Clarke, Janet Newman, Sarah Neal, Jean Carabine, and Megan Doolittle – all gave me important support and ideas.

Thanks are also due to Ruthie Petrie, Mike Newman and Jane Caplan who at crucial moments read chapters and offered me very helpful feedback, advice and encouragement.

At a later stage Tony Kushner gave me invaluable help and support. I had always admired his research and his approach to writing about refugees, which now provided a backdrop for my own work. I could not have completed this project without his belief in the importance of what I was doing.

It has been a great joy to re-establish contact with two friends, Clare Ungerson and Miriam Glucksman, with whom I share my German refugee family history, something that had not seemed to be at all significant when we had known each more than 30 years earlier. I am grateful for their feedback and support. I also developed very special friendships with two women originally from Germany – Gisela Albrecht and Margret Cochrane. They helped me with German from time to time but, more importantly, our friendships helped me to think about my relationship to my German past and were, I think, as significant for them as for me. It is a great sadness to me that both died before the book was completed.

Five archives gave me access to papers with information about my parents. Without the papers in the archive of SPSL, now the Council for At-Risk Academics, a large section of my father's story would have been missing. Additional bits of helpful information came from records in the Wiener Library, the Albert Einstein Archives [AEA] at the Hebrew University, Jerusalem, World Jewish Relief, and the papers of S. M. Rich held at the University of Southampton Special Collections. Thanks are also due to Jean Ridings for a few papers that she translated for me, to Simon Crab for providing additional information about Wolja's electronic musical instrument and to Cristina Fischer for further information about Lotte's expulsion from Berlin University.

I am very grateful to all my close friends who sustained their interest in my work and helped to keep me going. Finally, my partner Liz Reed worked on the illustrations and cover design. She has lived all these years with my ambivalence and anxiety. She has been my greatest supporter and sometimes a much needed severe critic. Thank you.

Preface

18 April 2017. I'm on my way to the German Embassy. I have an appointment at the consulate. I am going to explore the possibility of claiming German citizenship as the daughter of someone who had his citizenship taken away. I feel very anxious, identifying with Wolja's experiences of never being recognized. He was only a citizen for three years and the letters I have about it are all copies. I can't find his name in any of the lists of people who lost their citizenship under the Nazi law of 1933.[1] Born before 1953, I am not entitled to apply on the basis of my mother's lost citizenship.

When I get to the embassy I don't notice the queue on the other side of the road and feel embarrassed when I am asked, very politely, to join the queue. But it isn't long before I go through security and wait inside. As soon as I am there, it feels wrong. This seems to be a place where you go for a passport. When my number comes up I say immediately to the woman behind the counter, I think I have made the wrong appointment – and indeed I have. She gives me a card with the name of the person I should email and I go away again, feeling cross with myself and upset. I had made the appointment two months earlier and have wasted all this time. I feel very depressed and I realize that I am now exactly as old as Wolja was when he died, 71 years and 165 days. In February I had passed the same milestone in relation to Lotte – 71 and 101 days – and also felt depressed. I am astounded by my strength of feeling, and the fact that as soon as each deadline passes I feel better. Is this telling me something about my over-involvement in my parents' history?

My parents died more than thirty years ago and their experiences as refugees go back even further, so why is it interesting to tell their story? My mother often said that she feared that the world would become ever more frightening and dangerous during my lifetime – even more frightening and dangerous than it had been for her. I was sceptical; she had fled from the Nazis and escaped the Holocaust. But I am frequently reminded of her fears as millions of people across the world are forced to flee, imprisoned for their beliefs, tortured, murdered or left to starve.

My parents' story is important because so many of their experiences continue to have echoes today. The personal letters they left behind, which

I am using to construct their stories, tell us more than 'what happened'; they offer moving insights into the emotional journeys of two refugees.

Note

1   Law on 'Revocation of Naturalisations and Deprivation of German Citizenship of 14 July 1933', https://uk.diplo.de/uk-en/02/citizenship/restoration-of-citizenship (Accessed 27 April 2019). See also Friedländer, *Nazi Germany and the Jews. The Years of Persecution 1933–39* (London: Weidenfeld & Nicolson, 1997), p.27.

1

Introduction: Through the Lens of Ambivalence

I grew up in a very untidy family. My mother often apologized for the mess she would be leaving after her death, so my brother Peter and I knew that there would be a lot to clear up. But we had no idea that we would find so many boxes and envelopes full of papers and photographs. They were in sideboards and cupboards, in the loft and in the garage. Some were simply stuffed at the back of drawers. There were personal and official letters, unfinished drafts and carbon copies, legal documents, bills, receipts and my father's childhood poems in a school exercise book. They span more than 80 years from my grandmother Esther's student records in the early 1900s to post-war restitution claims, which continue until 1982.

Both my parents were born in Berlin. They came to this country as Jewish refugees – my father Wolja in May 1938 and my mother Lotte four months later at the end of August. When Lotte died, nearly five years after Wolja, she had lived in the same house – our childhood home – for almost 40 years. Whenever they went away, Lotte left an envelope on the sideboard marked 'to be opened in the event of our deaths'. It not only told us where to find their wills, but was full of apologies about the mess.

I have no idea why my parents kept these papers, nor why we were not told of their existence, but it was clear from the labels on some of the envelopes that Lotte had started to sort them. Sometimes this was by topic, as with the restitution claims, but often her label would describe the nature of the correspondence, for example 'Private Letters' or 'Personal Letters – Lotte to keep'.

Did she want us to read them? These labels, and names written on the back of a few photographs, suggest that she did think about a time when we would find them. I remember my mother as someone who avoided or denied emotional difficulties. Was she unable to dispose of them because it meant throwing away her past, or was it a refusal to say 'it's over', even though the way they brought us up suggested that they tried to live in the present? Was she relying on us to finish the process for her?

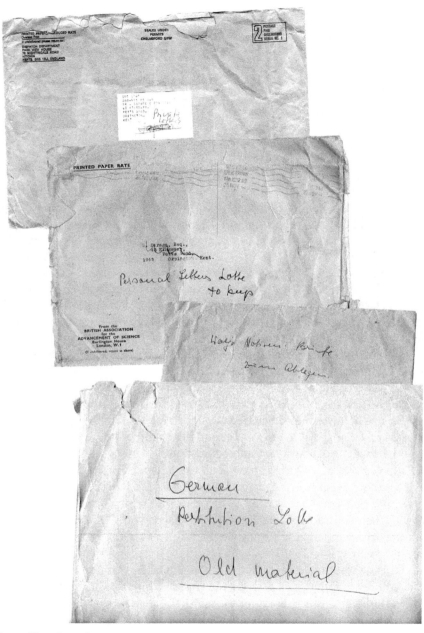

Four of Lotte's envelopes.

Finding the papers was emotionally overwhelming; we kept coming across them in different places during the process of clearing the house for sale. As we dipped into them, Peter said it made him feel guilty because he had not known what they had been through. I responded very fiercely: 'They wouldn't have wanted us to feel guilty; we're not responsible for their experiences; would you want your children to feel like that about your life?' But now I know that the strength of my response was a defence against exactly those same feelings in me – a sense that somehow we should have known.

Finding the papers also meant keeping them; or more specifically it meant not throwing them away – to do so would have felt like an act of denial or betrayal, even of violence. In line with the role I had played as a child, as mediator in an emotionally volatile family, there was a tacit understanding that they were my responsibility. We boxed them up and they travelled with me through three house moves over the next eighteen years.

During this time I had short forays, doing bits of reading and sorting, but I used my limited capacity to read German and lack of time as excuses for not taking it further. I promised myself that it would be a 'retirement project'. However it slowly became clear that the biggest obstacles were emotional. About eight years after my mother's death I had a real 'go' at reading some of the letters, and recorded my thoughts on tape. Another ten years on, in November 2002, when I had begun to work on the papers in earnest, I came across this tape and listened to it. I wrote in my notebook: '... how hard it was, how much I cried, how unhappy and lonely I was. I had forgotten. No wonder I couldn't do it then.' Reading the papers at that time had been too painful. I was on my own following the break-up of a long term relationship. The letters are suffused with anxiety about loss and separation and this triggered my own feelings of loss – about my parents, and about their stories, which we had only ever known in fragments.

Several things eased my way in. In 1995 Liz, my new partner, offered me a trip to Paris as a 50th birthday treat. As we had both been to Paris with other people, I suggested that we go somewhere new. Berlin, my parents' birthplace, seemed appropriate for such a significant occasion. It was only two days before the trip that it occurred to me to search the papers for some addresses to take with me. We walked down streets where my parents and grandparents had lived. Many of the houses had been destroyed during the war, but enough remained to have a sense of what it might have looked like, although Liz had to remind me that many of the trees were not seventy years old. I felt 'at home' in Berlin and the impact of being physically in space that Lotte and Wolja had occupied gave me a powerful sense of connection to them and I could imagine their lives in a different way. Most importantly I knew that I wanted to embark seriously on what I was beginning to call 'my project'.

A few bits of serendipity helped to solve the practical problems. The Open University, where I worked, started a series of German courses. I enrolled and after three years obtained a 'Diploma in German'. As a child growing up in the wake of the Second World War, I had hated the sound of the German language, even though my parents sometimes spoke to each other in German. I have a memory of putting my hands over my ears and saying 'I won't listen if you speak that horrid language' when my mother suggested that we could easily be bilingual if we spoke German at home. 'You'll regret it when you're older', she said. In one sense I do, but learning German in my 50s and 60s has been liberating and fun, and I often imagine how amazed and pleased my parents would be.

I had seen the papers as a personal legacy, but the turn to biographical and autobiographical work within the social sciences gave me permission to do this work formally as part of my job.[1] This not only made it practically possible, in terms of time, but the need to think about the material academically also helped me to establish some emotional distance.

Perhaps most importantly, I was now in a stable relationship and twelve years of psychoanalysis had helped me both to reflect on my feelings and to develop strategies for dealing with them. I recognized a buried feeling I didn't like to face – I was frightened I would die without having done the work.

Getting Started

But I still had no idea how or where to start. A social historian friend and colleague[2] advised me simply to 'immerse myself in the material'. I began to sort the letters, skim-reading them and making notes as I went along. I constructed categories partly chronologically and partly based on the context in which they were written and by whom. There were letters in German, English, French, Romanian and Italian and I had soon reached over twenty separate categories. But it was a useful exercise; I became very excited as I discovered what was there, so much that they had not told us.

The papers helped me to elaborate the story with which I grew up.

At the end of August 1938, four days before her twenty-fifth birthday, my mother arrived at Liverpool Street station in London to join my father. They were both born in Berlin to non-observant Jewish families. Lotte's parents, Erna and Hermann, both came from families that had lived in Germany for generations. Hermann fought for Germany in the First World War and was decorated. By contrast Wolja's parents (Avram and Estera, known as Ado and Eti) were both immigrants to Germany – from Romania and Russia/Poland respectively. In 1932 Lotte started to study medicine at Berlin University, but she was thrown out after Hitler came to power. She went to Milan where, unable to continue her studies, she did clerical work and looked after children. In 1935 a telegram called her back to Berlin when her father died of a heart attack. Wolja was five years older than Lotte. He had a PhD in physics and worked as a research scientist at the Heinrich Hertz Institute. But he too was thrown out by the Nazis and was unable to get another job. He lived with his parents on their savings. By the time Lotte and Wolja met, they and their families had already decided they had to leave Germany, but it was not easy to find a country to take them. Lotte lived with her widowed mother, Erna, in Berlin; they planned to join her older sister and her husband in Palestine. Wolja had particular difficulties. He was stateless, had very little money, and was virtually blind in one eye. The Swiss would not allow him in because he was stateless and the USA refused him a visa because of his eyesight, despite the affluent relatives who were willing to vouch for him. Eventually in May 1938 he was given permission, as a scientist, to enter the UK on a temporary basis to look for work. To join him, Lotte had to obtain a 'domestic permit'. Her mother did go to Palestine. Lotte worked in London for a family of communists, with whom she remained friends for several years. Wolja's parents had to return to Romania.

Lotte and Wolja married in July 1939 and settled in a middle-class suburb south east of London. In 1940 Wolja was interned; in 1941 they tried unsuccessfully to emigrate to America. My brother was born in 1942 and I followed in 1945. Both grandmothers died during the war from natural causes. After a long struggle with the Home Office, my grandfather Ado was allowed to come to England in January 1947. He died ten months later, three days before my second birthday. Lotte and Wolja were naturalized as British citizens in 1947.

They both died at 71 – Wolja in February 1980 and Lotte in December 1984.

We knew that Wolja's father came from a bourgeois, well-educated family in Romania, but I had no idea that a book had been written about their bookselling and publishing business. A second-hand bookseller, invited in when we were clearing the house, pulled it off the shelf saying 'I expect you would like to keep this'. Wolja had told us that Ado and Eti had come from Berlin to London to get married because Ado was still a student, financed by his parents who might cut off his financial support if they knew about his marriage. In London they needed fewer documents. Eti's wedding ring, later

Wolja Saraga and Lotte Isenburg, Berlin 1938. Photos in the possession of the author.

The most significant people in this story can be shown in a short family tree:

FAMILY TREE

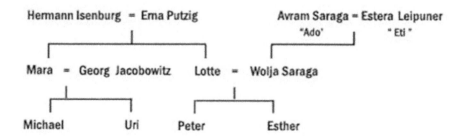

worn by my mother and since her death by me, has 'Ado 15.7.07' engraved inside. Wolja and Lotte chose the same date for their wedding – 15 July 1939. We did not know until we found their marriage certificate that Eti and Ado actually married in April 1908, five months before Wolja was born.

These discoveries were enjoyable and interesting. It was a shock and upsetting to learn that several of Eti's sisters did not survive the Holocaust and to realize that Wolja had never spoken about it.

Whenever I felt overwhelmed by the emotions, which happened frequently at the beginning, I wrote down my feelings as a free association.

> I've been working on these papers on and off for one month now…it is so painful reading letters of people I know so well – but I know them as 'parents'. I can feel their pain, particularly the loss and separation. I have so many regrets – I wish we had spoken of all these things while they were alive – I knew some/most of it a bit, but not the detail. Perhaps they tried to tell us and I/we didn't want to hear. Perhaps they told me more than I can remember. But why didn't I ask? Why didn't I use those 5 years after my father died to get my mother to tell her story? Had they assimilated us so well that the story would be unsettling?
>
> There is so much more here about my father, his father, his father's father…than any of the other parts of my family. I know very little at all about my mother's family.
>
> But they kept it all – they couldn't throw it away. Was it for us, or because they couldn't say 'it's over'? Yet what they went through was as nothing compared to the horrors of the Holocaust. Lotte in particular felt that way, and I feel it, especially when I read about the Holocaust in Romania. My father's letters say his parents escaped being shot in Bucharest 'by a miracle' – how? I wish I knew.
>
> …Many of the letters are not important, I don't know who they are from, I can't read the writing…but I can't throw them away – not yet anyway.
>
> I feel voyeuristic reading the love letters between my parents – especially the early ones in 1938 when he was already here – clearly they loved each other greatly, were already lovers…am I supposed to read these…how does it fit with the people I remember…with the later letters about his affairs?
>
> It is so different to think of them as people, as adults rather than parents.
>
> The pain/loss/regret for me can seem overwhelming…why am I engaged in this project? It feels it needs to be done. (7 July 2002)

In the early stages of the project, even in these private notes, I have often written 'my mother' and 'my father', when I am describing a time before I was born. In later notes I more commonly wrote 'Lotte' and 'Wolja', which seemed to give them an identity independent of their parenthood. This was also the way in which we addressed them once we were grown up. My memory is that we started to call them Lotte and Wolja during our adolescence, but letters in the collection that we wrote to them as young adults belie this. I have now discovered that Peter's memory was the same as mine – and also wrong.

Exploring Ambivalence

The first time that I prepared a presentation of this material for an outside audience, I experienced great anxiety and resistance. I kept finding something else that I needed to do first. Then one beautifully sunny day I treated myself to a cappuccino in the courtyard of the British Library, asked myself what this resistance was about and wrote down my thoughts.

> I approach this with great ambivalence – as someone who has resisted 'Jewish' as a major feature of my identity, yet enjoying a sense of difference it has given me, and fascinated by the extent to which 'I' have been formed in the context of 'foreignness' and 'Englishness'. The ambivalence also comes from the emotional pain generated by working on these papers. For eighteen years I couldn't. But they are there – and I can't ignore them. Finally the ambivalence is about a sense of self-indulgence, a resistance to discourses of victimhood and recognition of the ease with which I can slip into that and feel comfortable and validated, although I have had a relatively privileged life. (5 March 2003)

My parents' denial, or at least avoidance, of the past seemed to be connected to where we lived, a middle-class suburb south east of London, rather than in the refugee enclave of north west London. We knew we were Jewish, but lived in a way that none of the traditional characteristics of being Jewish, such as food, observing holidays or speaking Yiddish applied to us. We celebrated Christmas, but were not allowed a Christmas tree as my father considered it too 'Prussian', and we often had roast pork for Sunday lunch. My father asked for bacon for breakfast on the morning of my Israeli cousin's wedding in Cardiff in the early 1970s, where he was standing in for Uri's father who had died. My mother had to stop him as they were in a hotel with other wedding guests. When I visited Lotte in the Royal Marsden Hospital in 1974 after her first breast cancer operation, she told me she had come round from the anaesthetic to see a rabbi approaching her bed. The story I remember went like this:

Lotte: How did you know I am Jewish?

Rabbi: I look at names, ages and places of birth and put two and two together. You are Jewish, aren't you?
Lotte: Yes, but not at all religious.
Rabbi (with a sigh): Hitler has a lot to answer for.
Lotte: No, I had no religion before Hitler came to power.

He asked her the names of her parents and wanted to say a prayer for her. She asked him not to. When he left the other women in the ward, surprised, asked her whether he was Jewish. 'Yes', she replied in a tone that implied 'so what?'

My mother told the headmistress at my secondary school that although I was Jewish she wanted me to attend religious assembly and scripture classes to learn about what she thought of as English culture. We did go very occasionally to a Passover or Friday night celebration with one set of my parent's old friends, but I also went to the children's class on Sunday mornings at Quaker Meeting with my friend Janet, the daughter of a neighbour who befriended my mother. My parents made a lot of good English friends locally, mainly through Wolja's work, the Labour Party and the Workers' Educational Association (WEA). They did not change their names, although few English people could pronounce my father's first name.

Looking back, Jewishness for me was primarily about being different. The key markers of that difference were my parents – their names, the fact that they spoke German, or English with a funny accent, and the food we ate, which was German rather than Jewish. As a family we also enjoyed and felt superior about some of the differences; we felt 'continental', which gave us a particular kind of cultural capital.

With these memories, I was surprised to find a letter from Wolja to Lotte, written in England before they were married, while she was looking after children for a family. He tells her he has been invited to a Passover celebration, wishes she could be there, and remembers the previous year when they were together and with his parents. 'Seder has such a beautiful meaning and really, it was our ancestors who were set free at that time and those who were set free were the first people in history to develop the ethical code which in the non-fascist states is recognized, officially at least, as the goal' (1 April 1939). This letter suggests a complex and many-layered Jewish identity, with a deeper attachment to Jewishness than I ever thought he had. How much of this was strengthened through his experiences of the Nazis I don't know.

There is also evidence in the papers of a bit more Jewishness in my childhood than I remember, though it is still infused with ambivalence. I found a certificate showing that Peter was enrolled for Hebrew classes at the nearest synagogue (fifteen miles away). He attended one class! A letter to my mother from the Liberal Jewish Synagogue in St John's Wood in 1953, told her about 'correspondence lessons for your little girl', which would stress 'the religious and scriptural side of the instruction', with an option for me to learn Hebrew as well. It was a shock to find this. I have no memory of it at all. But I do remember going with the daughter of friends of my parents to a Liberal Jewish holiday camp when I was eleven years old. My abiding memory is of being an outsider – not only did I not know the songs or the prayers, but all the girls were comparing their developing breasts. I did not have those either. At school I never told anyone I was Jewish, but I also knew I should not deny it. I still feel guilty that I remained silent when the scripture teacher explained the meaning of the word gentile, saying 'I imagine we are all gentiles here'. The following year when I was twelve my friend Mary, who was proud to have a Jewish friend, told everyone. Slowly I learned to accept and even be proud of it myself. More recently Mary has told me she thinks of me as the least Jewish of all her Jewish friends!

This sense of difference that my background gave me has been at various times a source of either fear or strength. At school I desperately wanted to belong and not to be different, something that was very difficult in middle-class suburbia where everyone voted Conservative and went to church. But from the 1960s I enjoyed the sense of being an outsider, which found expression mainly through political radicalism from CND to anti-Vietnam War protests, feminism and lesbianism.

Being Jewish

Since working on this project I have engaged in far more activities with other Jews, as Jewish people, than I had ever done before. I learned for the first time that there was a Jewish Museum in Camden Town, which in another piece of serendipity had an exhibition on 'Continental Britons', documenting the experiences of Jewish refugees in the 1930s, just as I was beginning my work. It was a strange but familiar setting. A video played continuously with people talking on it who sounded just like Wolja and Lotte; but it also made me aware of a refugee Jewish community in north west London to which we did not belong. I joined the 'Second Generation Network', an organization of the children and grandchildren of survivors and refugees from Nazi persecution and found out that every year a Jewish Book Week was held in central London. But I continued to feel and be seen as an outsider. On my first visit to the Book Week, I was greeted by a woman I had known more than twenty years earlier in a feminist anti-racist group, with the words 'you're the last person I would have expected to see here'. And when I told her that I had joined the group 'Jews for Justice for Palestinians', she remarked 'so you have found an outsider way of being Jewish'.

As a result of all these activities I have inevitably had to think about my own Jewishness, an identification that is unusual for me except in relation to my parent's history. I continue to feel ambivalent. I enjoy the feeling of self-recognition when I read other people's stories[3] but I also want to resist the sense of 'We' that goes with such an engagement. Sometimes the 'We' has been as a 'Jew', sometimes as a person described as 'second generation'. I recognize that people get together on the basis of shared identities or in relation to common experiences and I have gained a sense of belonging and strength this way myself, particularly through the Women's Movement. But I am also aware of the dangers of such uses of 'We', the way it can homogenize people, making it harder to see nuances, ambiguities of meaning and differences. It assumes not only that we have similar experiences, but also that our emotional responses to those experiences are similar, reducing us to whichever 'We' is being invoked at that time.

In 1963, after I left school, I spent four months in Israel, two of those months on a kibbutz. Amongst the papers I found the letters I wrote to my parents during this time. When I went to Israel I knew nothing about Zionism and I couldn't understand why people asked me whether my family planned to move there. These letters give me insights into my feelings at that time about being Jewish as well as about my struggle to understand the relationship between Jews and Arabs in Israel. The kibbutz was debating its move away from its strict socialist principles by employing Arab labour and I also experienced some of the 'class distinctions' amongst Jews. On 24 June 1963 I wrote:

> Mummy, do you remember I told you that there was trouble here between the Moroccans and the European-Americans. Well it's really getting bad now...the two groups just do NOT mix. The other day a group of E-As were complaining about the Moroccans in German (by chance their common language) and the teacher came in – was furious and accused them of Anti-Semitism- most of them are Jewish!! Anyway that's typical of the situation here – it's pretty awful.

And on 5 July:

> Next weekend we want to have a barbecue. I am afraid it will be exclusively English and American – "No Sephardic Jews allowed!!!!!" Though seriously it's because of the language – all the people who

speak English are coming…You know one thing I like here is that for the first time in my life really it means something to me to be Jewish – Do you understand what I mean – and I like it? Here you're one of them if you're Jewish - not the exception – it's difficult to explain what I mean!

Little did I know that I would discover from the papers that my paternal grandfather's family were Sephardic! On 17 July I described going to Nazareth with a Canadian and an English boy: 'We had a wonderful time – met an Arab boy who showed us around and invited us back to his house to meet his family and have Arab coffee – wonderful!' And on 23 July: 'On Friday afternoon I WAS FED UP (we had another of those pointless arguments on the Arab-Jewish situation and I was feeling upset…)'

My parents were never Zionists. Lotte and Wolja worried about the fate of Lotte's sister and her family in Palestine/Israel, but they were often critical of Israeli policy. When I learned from these papers that my grandmother Eti had been a member of the Bund, a left wing organization opposed to Zionism, it seemed to give me access to a Jewish heritage with which I could identify. As I enter the Jewish worlds associated with my project I meet so many apologists for the actions of the Israeli government – 'we mustn't forget what the Jews have suffered', as if somehow the Holocaust can justify or condone what has been done to the Palestinians. I was delighted to be able to join the organization 'Jews for Justice for Palestinians', in which I feel comfortable, although I still struggle with statements about 'we Jews'.

Holocaust Survivor or Refugee?

Although this book is not about the Holocaust, inevitably it intrudes and knowledge of the Holocaust makes it easy for my interpretations to be affected by my fears about what could have happened to my parents if they had not been able to get out in time. This is important because within much of the 'Holocaust survivor' literature there is a strong idea of who is a legitimate person to write about. Crucial differences are made between survivors (those who suffered in camps) and refugees (those who got away). Vansant describes the way refugees may have to 'gain the sense that their stories are worth telling', since 'they may also have suffered from the feeling that "nothing exceptional" has happened to them in comparison to the pain and suffering of those in concentration camps'.[4] My therapist, Rosalie Kerbekian, once said to me quite sharply, 'the Jews are not the only people who have suffered'. I guessed from her name that she had Armenian origins, but only discovered many years later, from an obituary, the extent of her own parents' suffering as a result of the Armenian genocide.[5]

In contrast to the stories of the Holocaust, there is another story – a success story – of refugees. Many of the studies focus on 'famous' refugees emphasizing, sometimes in their titles ('Hitler's Gift', 'Hitler's Loss') as well as their content, the wide ranging intellectual contributions to the UK and USA, made by Jewish refugees of the 1930s.[6] The danger with these books is that they reinforce a view of the Jews of the 1930s as 'ideal immigrants' who were willing to assimilate and contributed so much, in contrast to negative views of asylum seekers and refugees today.[7] It also ignores the fact that many refugees from Nazism were refused entry. Those that were well-qualified were only allowed in temporarily and only on the basis that the Jewish organizations took responsibility for supporting them.[8] These books make me angry because I do not believe that the right to be here as a refugee should depend upon the contribution a person can make to British society. But my feelings are also personal – my parents are not recognized by these books and I have found myself searching in vain for some reference to them. Lotte and Wolja were not special or famous, but I was to learn from the papers how much their class and educational background, and the informal and formal networks this gave them access to, were crucial for the successful outcome to their story.

Gendered Assumptions

After eighteen months I had only scratched the surface of sorting and categorizing the literally thousands of letters and documents. In 2002, when asked to present a seminar at work, I decided to focus on the 'public story', describing how my father got out of Germany. His story seemed more 'academic'. I was shocked and upset when a colleague said she would also like to know about my mother. Defensively I told her that Wolja's story was more interesting because of his statelessness, and easier to tell because of the materials that were available and because he spoke so much more about his family than Lotte had done. She was not persuaded.[9] Reflecting on this, I recognized that Lotte's story, her decision to come to the UK to be with Wolja rather than to travel with her mother to Palestine, was always presented to us as the only option for them to be together. This sense of inevitability was reinforced by the teasing story my father told - that he had said to Lotte 'Please come to England with me – I don't know whether I want to marry you, but I want to have the option of doing so.'

My father's academic and professional losses dominated the family stories. He always talked about how he could or should have been an academic, a great scientist, but he had lost ten years because of Hitler, and then in this country he had to take and hold on to a frustrating job because he had to earn money to support us, his children. I grew up with a sense of guilt – feeling that my parents' lives had been ruined, or at least made a lot worse, by their experiences as refugees. It meant that I had to be 'good', so that I did not give them any further problems. We knew that my mother had lost her chance to become a doctor when she was thrown out of university in 1933, but this was less of a family theme. She would always dismiss it, saying 'I would probably have been a bad doctor anyway'.

Various experiences led me to question my assumptions both that the reason I had started with my father's story was pragmatic, and also that 'the story' was as inevitable as we had been told. Two were pivotal: I read a memoir by Reinhard Bendix in which he justifies not attempting a 'full portrait' of his mother 'because the book is an intellectual biography, and my mother played a secondary role in these intellectual concerns'.[10] Reading this angered and shamed me. Finally I was able to recognize my own defensiveness when a friend asked me in July 2004: 'Why do you and Peter only speak about your father? I never hear you talk about your mother'.[11]

I realized that the family story was always presented hermetically – my father at the centre, my mother defined in relation to him. While there do seem to have been very good, practical reasons for Lotte to follow Wolja to England, it was the usual story – his career had primary importance, reflecting the 'normal' pattern of gendered relationships. I began to reflect on ways in which gender operated within our family. On the surface it was a traditional division of labour for a middle-class family in the suburbs in the 1950s – breadwinner father, mother responsible for the housework and childcare. But there were important exceptions. My father was very emotional and incompetent practically. My mother took charge of money matters, repairs, maintenance and redecoration. On the other hand she was not a 'good housewife' in comparison with her English friends and neighbours, and seemed to be tolerated for this because she was 'foreign'. They were less tolerated for having an untidy front garden, perhaps because well-kept front gardens are quintessentially English and publicly visible.[12] As a woman who had started to study medicine, Lotte was atypical for suburban England in the 1950s. There were of course other women who also resisted the 'domestic ideal'; some did not marry, others were perceived as 'eccentric'. I vaguely remember Lotte's attempts in the 1950s to find employment, a memory confirmed by the discovery of a series of letters of application for jobs. She practised her shorthand and typing at home, but could not find a job. Her shorthand was rusty and of course based on German rather than English. Perhaps it was just as well, as it led to her pursuing adult education instead. Following years of classes put on by the WEA and London University

Extramural Department, she became one of the first students on the part-time University of London external sociology degree at Goldsmiths College, graduating in 1969 at the age of 55. From the papers I learned that she had gained a distinction in her social history diploma and, following her BA, was invited to do postgraduate work, which she postponed as she got a teaching job. She taught liberal studies in a Technical College for nearly ten years until she retired.

I have always been enormously proud of Lotte getting this degree; but only now do I recognize the collusion in which we all, including Lotte, engaged as a family in denying her educational and professional losses in the 1930s. As a child I had always planned to become a doctor, but I saw this as following in the footsteps of my grandmother Esther, after whom I had been named. It was not until I was engaged in this project that I connected this idea in any way with my mother, a startling realization. I gave up the idea of medicine once we started biology at secondary school. I was far too squeamish. I studied mathematics and physics instead, as my father had done. Much later I moved via psychology to becoming a social scientist like Lotte. Lotte's experience probably influenced my own career, teaching mature students in higher education, and perhaps also my desire, as I approached retirement, to continue studying.

Having re-found my feminist consciousness, I went back to the papers to look at them in a new light, from Lotte's perspective rather than Wolja's. This led me to select different letters and to tell a very different kind of story. Whereas the story that I had been telling about Wolja is a story of the big events in life – the struggle for identities concerned with male and public matters, particularly those of nationality and professional status – Lotte's story took me straight into the realm of what is traditionally seen as private – the everyday, the domestic and the intimate.

It was not until even later that I realized I could tell a different story about Wolja too.

I have described this experience because it raises questions about my different relationships to the material, as daughter, researcher and author and recognizes that different kinds of stories can be told. It also made me aware of the way in which my emotional responses to the papers could block my thinking. This led me to consciously use my reflections as a resource.

History, Memory and Testimony

By immersing myself in the material and allowing the papers to lead me, I had developed a particular method of working: reading the letters triggered memories of family stories which then informed my interpretations, which were in turn influenced by what I learned from historical research and archives as well as by links to wider social and political issues. My memories and reflections often led me to change my original interpretation or to find a whole new layer of meaning that I had not seen before. Other people also suggested interpretations or made associations that had not occurred to me, and this reminded me that I was reading the papers through the lens of being their daughter, which has several different implications for my work. My knowledge and experience of Lotte and Wolja help me to understand their letters and to recognize continuities in their experiences later in their lives. But I may also take for granted aspects of the stories that I have known all my life or avoid material that is personally too painful.

By this time the process of working on the papers had become as important to me as their content, and I knew I wanted to go beyond simply 'telling the story'. Moreover I empathized with Atina Grossmann who wonders why anyone should want to read yet another story of German Jews[13]. Jeremy Popkin makes an interesting distinction between first person narratives written by professional historians who are also survivors and the vast majority of survivors' memoirs. Although I am not a historian, my project fits more with the former, for which telling the story is less important than raising the kinds of questions that I am posing in relation to my parents' papers.[14] In the introduction to her book on women refugees, Sybille Quack writes: 'The eyewitness reports are unique documents of individual experiences and stand for themselves.'[15] By contrast, although not concerned with the Holocaust per se, my approach to these papers is consistent with the 'critical historical approaches' to the Holocaust advocated by Donald Bloxham and Tony Kushner, which recognize that survivor testimony, often considered sacred, must be problematized like all other testimony.[16]

The emotional impact on me of Lotte and Wolja's letters led me to focus on emotions as an overall theme for my work – using the letters to gain an understanding of how it felt to live through these historical events. In order to do this, I had to read more history. To an academic historian my choices will I imagine seem arbitrary and unsystematic. Sometimes my reading helped me to understand or contextualize my parents' experiences: life in Nazi Germany in 1938, the response of the British state to the situation of Jewish refugees, and their internment in 1940. Other reading arose from reflections. My responses to Wolja's letters from internment on the Isle of Man led me to explore ideas about the importance of letters for emotional survival in conditions of imprisonment and, following the arrival of my new e-passport in 2010 when I was reflecting on the impact of my father's statelessness, I read about the history of the passport and ideas on nationality, citizenship and belonging.

Different sets of letters triggered different themes and the following chapters are organized around these letters and themes, rather than following a straightforward chronology of events. However they do more or less fall into three distinct sections: getting out of Nazi Germany and into the UK; being a refugee, and coming to terms with the past. In all the chapters I have selected extracts from the letters and other papers to help me to explore these themes. Where they were originally written in German or French, the translations are mine unless otherwise stated. Some of the letters written by Lotte and Wolja are carbon copies; I have indicated where they are drafts and therefore perhaps not identical to the version that was sent. Once they were living in this country, Lotte and Wolja chose whenever possible to write in English. I have not changed their (few) spelling and grammatical mistakes, nor their various different spellings of Romania.

But I still had a big gap – no detailed information about how Wolja was able to come to the UK. In 2004 I wrote to the Home Office to see whether they had his papers. I was unsuccessful. They informed me that: 'A search has been made of the appropriate Home Office Records but it has been established that your father's file S13414 has not survived. I am sorry to have to send you such a disappointing reply.'[17] I had a similar response from the archive in the Isle of Man, where Wolja was interned: 'Unfortunately I cannot find any references in the internee database to your father.'[18] Not surprisingly, these responses came back to me in 2018 when the Windrush scandal broke.

But another unexpected rich source of evidence did become available to me. I knew that Wolja was allowed into the UK to look for work, and that he had been helped by an organization called the Society for the Protection of Science and Learning (SPSL) and in particular by a woman called Esther Simpson with whom he stayed in contact. Her name remained with me, as she wrote to Lotte when Wolja died in 1980. In 2009 I learned that SPSL had an archive at the Bodleian Library in Oxford. The online catalogue told me there was a file of personal correspondence with Wolja and additional papers filed under 'internment' and 'naturalisation'. On my first visit to the Bodleian I sat in the Special Collections Reading Room with a large box folder on the desk in front of me. It contained the personal files of four different refugees. I did not open it immediately, I was too apprehensive, fearing there would be very little there. To prepare myself I wrote in my notebook:

> 71 years ago yesterday Wolja arrived in Britain. I'm in the Bodleian Library, about to look at Wolja's correspondence in the SPSL archive. What will be there, am I about to be disappointed again?… It is a huge collection – Folio 269 – 407, 137 pages…It feels strange to be in the

Bodleian crying. (8 May 2009)

Notes

1. I am immensely grateful to Gail Lewis who persuaded me that I could do this.
2. This was the beginning of Janet Fink's invaluable help and support.
3. Two books from which I had experiences of self-recognition are: A. Karpf, *The War After, Living with the Holocaust* (London: Heinemann, 1996) and G. Rosenthal (ed.), *The Holocaust in Three Generations. Families of Victims and Perpetrators of the Nazi Regime* (London: Cassell, 1998).
4. J. Vansant, *Reclaiming Heimat. Trauma and Mourning in Memoirs by Jewish Austrian Reémigrés* (Detroit: Wayne State University Press, 2001), p.31.
5. H.High, 'Rosalie Kerbekian – an Appreciation', *Educational Therapy and Therapeutic Teaching*, 15 (2007), p.80.
6. This issue will be discussed further in Chapter 2. Examples of this literature include: J. Medawar & D. Pyke, *Hitler's Gift. Scientists who fled Nazi Germany* (London: Piatkus, 2001); T. Ambrose, *Hitler's Loss. What Britain and America gained from Europe's cultural exiles* (London: Peter Owen, 2001); D. Snowman, *The Hitler Émigrés: The Cultural Impact on Britain of Refugees from Nazism* (London: Chatto & Windus, 2002).
7. A. Kushner, 'Remembering to forget: racism and anti-racism in post-war Britain', in B. Cheyette and L. Marcus (eds.), *Modernity, Culture and 'The Jew'* (Cambridge: Polity Press, 1998), pp. 226-214, p.236.
8. See, for example, L. London, *Whitehall and the Jews 1933-1945. British Immigration Policy and the Holocaust* (Cambridge: Cambridge University Press, 2000). This issue is discussed more fully in later chapters.
9. I am now very grateful to Megan Doolittle who was the first person to push me on this issue.
10. R. Bendix, *From Berlin to Berkeley. German-Jewish Identities* (New Brunswick, NJ: Transaction Books, 1986), p.x.
11. Thanks to Ros Kram who finally shamed me.
12. An interesting observation from Gail Lewis.
13. A. Grossmann, 'Versions of Home: German-Jewish Refugee Papers out of the Closet and Into the Archives', *New German Critique*, 90 (2003), pp. 95-122, p.103.
14. J. D. Popkin, 'Holocaust Memories, Historians' Memoirs. First-Person Narrative and the Memory of the Holocaust', *History & Memory* 15, 1 (2003), pp. 49-84.
15. S. Quack, *Between Sorrow and Strength. Women Refugees of the Nazi Period* (Cambridge: Cambridge University Press, 2002).
16. D. Bloxham and T. Kushner, *The Holocaust. Critical historical approaches* (Manchester: Manchester University Press, 2004).
17. Letter to author, Home Office, 26 July 2004.
18. Email to the author, Yvonne Cresswell, Curator: Social History, Manx National Heritage, Douglas, Isle of Man, 21 January 2009.

2

'Ach, Wenn es Klappen Wollte!'

(If Only It Would Work Out)

Between 7 May and 31 August 1938, while Lotte was still in Berlin and Wolja was in London on a temporary visa, they wrote to each other very frequently, sometimes twice in one day, and sometimes with gaps of several days. Ninety letters and postcards and one telegram have survived, most of which were written by Lotte. For the first three months (May, June and July) I only have her letters; from 1 August I have Wolja's letters as well. The original letters are all in German and the translations are mine. As I worked on the papers it became clear that Lotte had been the collector and keeper. I imagine that she had packed Wolja's earlier letters with their household goods, which were never delivered – a story that appears in Chapter 8.

At this distance four months seems like a very short time, but reading their letters gave me a sense of their experience in 'real time' – I lived their story day to day as it happened. I felt overwhelmed by the complexity of their circumstances and by their expressions of emotion. In August 2004 I wrote in my notebook:

> …it is very strange and upsetting to be reading and recording these last letters at the same time of year that it was happening…I feel so involved, and anxious about whether she will actually get out – even though I know the end of the story – indeed I am one of the ends of the story!

This reflection alerted me to the implications of reading with hindsight. Frustrated by what seemed like a lack of urgency for Lotte to leave, I wrote in my notebook: 'clearly war and genocide were not in their minds'. But when a friend described my parents as 'fleeing genocide', I recognized how this misrepresents their experience. Colin Holmes calls the use of knowledge of what happened later to interpret or understand earlier events the 'sin of presentism' and Michael Bernstein refers to 'backshadowing' – the tendency to attribute a 'gift of historical prophecy', which is then followed by judgements of people's actions at the time – 'Why didn't they leave?'[1]

These 1938 letters tell several stories: there is a personal story of forced migration that despite its successful ending was not smooth and which went wrong several times. Lotte's only way out of Germany was through a domestic permit and it took Wolja three attempts to find a position for her. In mid-June Erna (Lotte's mother) was knocked over by a cyclist and badly hurt. This not only added greatly to Lotte's distress, but delayed her departure for at least a month. On 16 August her mother left for Palestine – to join Lotte's older sister; on 19 August Lotte finally got her permit to come to England; on 23 August she obtained her visa; on 30 August Wolja's parents sent him a postcard: 'At Zoo Station. 23.20pm. Dear Wolja. So, the train has just left. Tomorrow evening Lotte will be with you…soon we shall leave ourselves'; and on 31 August she arrived at Liverpool Street station in London.

I can also construct a more general story about the circumstances for Jewish refugees from information about Wolja's uncertain position in the UK, the permits and documentation that Lotte needs both to leave Germany and to enter the UK, and the rules and regulations governing export of their possessions.

Finally, the letters tell the story of a relatively new personal relationship conducted, for these four months, only through this correspondence. Lotte and Wolja were clearly lovers, but not yet married. Their letters had to fulfil multiple purposes – to convey information, negotiate decisions, and express conscious and unconscious feelings. They were also a physical manifestation of contact between people who are separated.

I am aware that I am choosing which story to tell and on which of the multiple purposes to focus. I wanted to capture the tension between the personal and the social in a way that recognizes that they are inextricably linked. The strongest impact of the letters was the complexity of the emotions that Lotte expresses, so I decided to use this as my way in – to explore how it felt at the time to live through these events and to identify the strategies they used to cope with and manage their feelings.

Optimism and Reassurance

In the early letters Lotte was very optimistic. She constantly reassured Wolja of her love and tried to ease his anxiety, offering him both emotional and practical support. Her first letter, written on 7 May, starts: 'Isn't it strange, the first day alone in such a young marriage.' She imagined Wolja having arrived in England, told him how 'beautifully distinguished' he looked when he left and reported conversations with her aunt and cousin, who had both described him as someone who would succeed. She spoke to Wolja's parents every day, saw them regularly, and tried to protect them from worrying about Wolja. 'If you write something that your parents shouldn't know, then write on two separate pieces of paper, one private and one for general reading. And you know that I still see myself as your secretary and can type things for you that you don't need in a hurry.'

The following day (8 May) she was visiting a family who had a typewriter she could use to type some affidavits for Wolja:

> I miss you everywhere. On every street corner we once stood, here we had a row, there we drank Ahorn.[2] But I am so pleased that you have gone, that something new is beginning, that we live in the future, and I feel terribly optimistic about it…Dita [daughter of the house] says she wouldn't let herself be exploited in this way; in the twentieth century a woman doesn't have to work so hard for her husband. When I said that I also want you to be successful there, then she nodded her head very seriously. I think that if one spoke to her seriously more often she would be less arrogant. But this topic is unimportant.

So why did she tell him what Dita had said? Did her comment touch a nerve for Lotte? Did she feel ambivalent about how much she was doing for Wolja?

As the months passed Lotte became more and more anxious and developed stomach problems. From her letters I surmised that Wolja was also very anxious and he was lonely, despite having some refugee friends already in London. This was confirmed by his letters in August, which express his longing for Lotte to join him; indeed he did not seem to understand why she was taking so long to come. Alongside her own fears Lotte continued to reassure Wolja, whilst denying her own needs; she coaxed and pleaded with him, addressed him in affectionate diminutives ('little monkey', 'little one') and used their private names for each other 'Peter' and 'Teddy'. She often told him that she could cope with anything so long as he was OK.

From Lotte's letters I learned that Wolja was being financially supported by the refugee organizations – on 13 May she asked him 'Are you managing on the money from the committees?' In the same letter she told him how hard she was working, and that her boss was very pleased with her work and very sorry that she was leaving. The letter ends: 'So you are not allowed to make your revenge come true, but must write to me immediately if you have any prospect of staying. For my part I won't shed any bitter tears…' Lotte uses the German word *Zähren* for tears, a word described as obsolete and poetic which appears in Bach, both in his St Matthew and St John Passions. It is difficult to know how to translate it in a way that preserves Lotte's style of communication. More significantly, I had no idea what her last two sentences referred to. Were they a response to something in his letter, or did they relate to conversations they had had before Wolja left? I wondered whether it was a way of handling the fear. This was one of the many times I regretted not having Wolja's letters.

On 18 May Lotte tried to reassure Wolja: 'Don't be too downhearted that everything is taking so long. It is hard to get close to English people. I think as a consequence, they are very reliable when you do get there.' And on 20 May: 'Darling, darling Peter, don't write such sad letters to your parents, write them instead to me.'

Frustration, Longing, Anxiety and Reproaches

Four days later (24 May), commenting on the efficiency of the post, she told him: 'Your very big cross letter with its frowns and furrowed brow arrived on Saturday and was sent on Friday – a marvel of speediness.' Here the power of the letter as a material object that embodied Wolja's feelings is also apparent. It was also the first indication of Wolja expressing himself as 'cross' rather than anxious. The following day he was clearly feeling a bit better. Lotte wrote:

> I see myself smiling proudly as I get out of the train in the London station…Fate definitely means to be kind to us. I am so happy that you seem to be calmer and more optimistic. I wish that everything goes sooooooooooo well for you. Any day something can happen for you, and it is still a very short time that you have been there. (25 May)

However three days later on 28 May Lotte was saddened by Wolja's letter, which she described as being full of reproaches or accusations, even though it was also full of love. Wolja had complained that she wrote 'nasty letters', did not write often enough and did not sign one of her letters. She replied that she wrote as often as she could to ensure he had post every day. She wrote fast in the office, but had to hide the letter when someone came in.

> …and then the unforgivable sin of not signing the letter happens – is it so important? And do you think I only write to <u>you</u> in order to send good wishes to <u>other people</u>…If you think I only say things to be nice, that I do not long to be with you, then go on thinking it. I think that when you know someone, you can read letters a bit differently from the way that you are doing.

My indecision about whether to write 'reproaches' or 'accusations', alerted me to the way in which my emotional responses to the letters had an impact on my translations. Lotte refers to Wolja's *Vorwürfe*, which I had originally translated as 'accusations'. My identification with Lotte's anxiety had made me feel angry with Wolja. Later, when I had read his letters too and felt more sympathetic towards him, I used the milder (and better) term 'reproach' instead.[3] Conveying style through translation is never easy and in these letters Lotte uses a range of styles, including slang, idiom, humour and irony, to express her feelings. On 14 June, in response to further reproaches, she complained that he had *geschimpft wie zwei Rohrspatzen*, an idiom that I translated as 'fussed like a mother hen', only recognizing later that Lotte had amended the usual version; I should have written 'two mother hens'.

Wolja's criticism and anger increased Lotte's anxiety. In a postcard on 2 June she told him: 'I know I am being too sensitive, but at the moment I can't help it, it will certainly be better when I am with you and find peace again. And this sitting and waiting also affects my nerves. But it will pass...' And the following day in a letter, she wrote: 'I have just read your lovely long letter again. It was so wonderful that it came and was so loving. But you have shouted at me a little and I have already written that I can't help it...As soon as anyone says anything I don't like I explode...this sitting and waiting and trembling makes one sensitive.'

Lotte used the identical phrase *sitzen und warten* [sitting and waiting] in both the postcard and letter and I realized that she was doing two kinds of waiting – to get out of Germany and for Wolja's letters. It reads like an expression of powerlessness.

On 11 June Lotte responded directly to Wolja's query about whether she was cross with him for criticising: '...but in the end as we can't speak to each other, we have to do it in letters as best we can. No, I am only sad and hurt when you make moralistic judgements as you once did in long forgotten times. But factual criticisms? No.' Another technique for dealing with Wolja was to tease him: 'Which page will you ignore when you are reading this? Do you sometimes forget 5 minutes later what you ate for lunch?' (4 July)

The most powerful emotion expressed in Lotte's letters is her longing for everything to be resolved. Variations of the phrase *'Es muss klappen'* [It must work out] are a constant refrain throughout the correspondence. On 3 June she wrote: *'Ach, wenn es klappen wollte!!!!!!!!!!!!!'* [If only it would work out] and on 24 July: *'Aber es wird, u. es muss u. es soll klappen!!!'* [But it will and it must and it has to work out]. She made comments of this kind so often that I wondered whether she was trying to defend herself against the fear of it not doing so. These examples also show how she used exclamation marks to express her feelings.

On 8 July she wrote two letters. In the first letter she expressed and then seemed to deny her own feelings in her concern to care for Wolja.

> Beloved little monkey,
>
> I've been incredibly worried about you, because today is Friday and we last had news of you on Monday. And then I always think that you'll suddenly collapse from exhaustion and overwork, and then you won't be there anymore. But your parents have had a peep from you. Thank God…Are you unhappy, Wolluk? Please, please don't be. What are you worrying about? Don't always speak about problems, little one. It sounds as if everything is very difficult, and it can all be solved, and everything isn't so crazy, is it? Anyway don't worry about me…If only something would work out for you, and you can remain strong, everything else is bearable. If only the business with Mutti's arm had not got in the way…Darling, darling Peter, I made myself anxious. I hear your voice in the letters – whether you're loving, whether you're worked up, whether you're angry. But I can understand that you couldn't write – you are so alone.

For Lotte, Wolja's letter embodied his voice and I too can hear their voices when I read their letters – especially in their use of language and their style of writing, which I recognize from my experiences as their child. This raises questions about whether I can capture the language and style in my translations, as well as reminding me that the translations are also part of my interpretations.

In her second letter of 8 July, written after a letter from Wolja had arrived, Lotte was more assertive. She believed it was very important to try to discuss everything in their letters and she was explicit about the value of irony.

> In relation to what you write about in principle, I say to you that you apparently don't yet know me very well if you think I am not taking your suggestions seriously. Up to now I have thought about all your suggestions very carefully, but given that this is <u>our joint</u> life that we are planning, you have to allow me sometimes to criticize as well…I can't say anything about your tone. I think one can sometimes deal with certain questions more easily through irony than to construct them as problems. Sadly everything is bloody serious and therefore not a joke.

She was exhausted, there was tropical heat at work, and she had a bad stomach. She pleaded with him not to tell her off in letters: 'I find that terribly sad'. She wrote a final bit the following day, acknowledging she did not like the tone of her own letter, but asking him to read 'the facts'. 'With a (no many) warm kisses, and don't be such a nervous Wolja anymore. I have such anxiety that one day you'll fall apart. PS this time I have numbered the sides in your way?? (If I can't be cheeky, then I might as well hang myself.)'

This use of irony is something I associate with my mother and something I loved about her. At my father's secular funeral, as we walked into the crematorium, she said to me 'I'm glad they've put the hymn books out; that will be so useful'.

Although her situation in Germany was very precarious and the future as uncertain for her as for Wolja, Lotte was often apologetic about expressing her own needs. On 28 July she wrote:

> Darling Frog, I long for news from you. This whole emigration grind, which has become 100% more complicated since you left, is more than two poor women like us can cope with. We're done in! I can't wait for the moment when I am sitting in the train. But how much has to be done before then!!!! No, but it isn't any easier for you, I am bad that I complain so much.

By mid-July the uncertainty, disappointments and fear caused them to row. In his letter of 1 August (the first of his letters that I have) Wolja told Lotte he had been so nervous about the domestic positions for Lotte falling through, that he was unable to work or sleep. Across the top of this letter he wrote: 'First the most important thing – we have a position for you.' He tried to explain why they were quarrelling:

> Dear little Lotte, you have written me incredibly loving letters. Why didn't they arrive sooner, then I wouldn't have written you an 'angry' letter yesterday.' ...And when your first letter came without a single loving word, completely cold I had to be 'angry' again. Lotte, you good, dear, darling, beloved Lotte. I was so happy to get your loving letter...It has been very difficult recently dealing with our loving and angry letters. Having written you an angry letter, I then wrote you 3 loving ones, then I got your angry reply to my angry letter, which made me reply angrily to you, and then came several loving letters from you.

Responding on 3 August Lotte wrote: 'Thank goodness this period is over.' But disappointingly the rows continued. On 18 August she tried again to end them:

It is hopefully not long until I come, and then face to face we can communicate much better. Of course at times I am imprecise. I don't have your masculine logic. But do you really believe that it is always so easy to write clearly?...if something new occurs to you, write to me immediately. But I don't think we need to write about the old things any more.

Towards the end of their separation, worried whether Lotte would get all the paperwork in time, their communications took yet a different form. On 16 August Lotte tells Wolja that because he doesn't write often enough she won't even phone him when she gets to London, she'll find another man to meet her. In his reply Wolja says that if she really is coming he'll have to get rid of his new girlfriend; after all, he can't abandon Lotte in Germany. This style of writing, which initially horrified me, later intrigued me. I wondered whether they were expressing resentment about not meeting each other's needs, or perhaps it is a way of managing the anxieties both that something can still go wrong and also about seeing each other after a four month separation. Crucially, this pair of letters demonstrated the importance of having both sides of the correspondence.

Gendered Communication

Extracts from Wolja's letter of 9 August show that he was able to express his feelings directly:

I am so terribly alone despite all the people I know. I mean this superficially. Of course I know enough people to be able to invite myself to someone so long as I plan it days in advance...I am beginning to get sick and tired of the asking and applying for jobs...I can hardly believe that you will be here soon. And I am already angry that you sometimes won't have much time.

Wolja's style of writing, in this and other letters, was very different from Lotte's. He tended to write mainly from his point of view, usually without the subsequent apology, denial or concern about the impact of his letters that was characteristic of Lotte.

The importance for both of them of receiving letters became apparent: for Lotte through her fantasies of disaster when she had not heard from Wolja for a few days, feelings that may have been accentuated by the sudden loss of her father three years earlier; for Wolja through his complaints that she did not write often enough. They responded to the fear in very different ways.

Lotte became very sensitive and Wolja reacted with anger, usually at Lotte, which of course made her feel even worse.

Their styles of communication seem implicitly gendered, with significant differences in the kind of 'emotional work' each of them was doing. Lotte was the emotional carer who policed her own emotions in order not to stress or distress Wolja.[4] But I am also aware that this kind of interpretation is very much influenced by my own experience of Lotte and Wolja. I recognize Wolja's tendency to criticize and Lotte's need to defend herself and, because I am very like Lotte, it makes me respond angrily to Wolja's letters; how can he behave like this when she is the one still in danger in Nazi Germany?

We have also seen explicitly gendered aspects of their communication, when Lotte referred to Wolja's 'masculine logic' or to herself and her mother as 'two poor women like us'. I do not know whether such phrases are ironic or an indication of how she constructed herself in relation to him. Lotte herself had referred to her use of irony as a way of deflecting difficulties, so this may have been a safe way of challenging his assumption that he knew best, even though he had been away for a long time.

Looking again across the whole correspondence I found further examples of gendered language. The most striking of these is the way in which they both described Lotte as '*dumm*' [silly]. In early June she responded to his complaint that she did not understand about his work: 'Isn't it lovely to have such a silly wife?'[5] On 16 August she told Wolja that her mother had gone to the Dolomites to recuperate; she had had a dreadful day, made worse by the fact that she had not heard from him and believed he simply had not written. She concluded: 'Peterchen, it's now 11.30pm. I want to lie next to you, and tell you so much, and just be a totally silly woman. It must be soon.' I presume that 'going to the Dolomites' was code for Erna's emigration. Lotte once told me the story of putting her mother on the train. I do not know who else was with her, but her mother asked to speak to her alone. She told her she must not cry, but go home immediately and pack everything and get to England to join Wolja as quickly as possible. Instead Lotte spent the day with a friend getting drunk. She must have felt so alone, exacerbated by not hearing from Wolja.

Although Lotte sometimes also referred to Wolja as 'silly', or 'a silly sheep', it was rarely used in an explicitly gendered context.[6] Was her description of herself as a silly woman a defence against his 'bullying' or a way of saying that she did not want to take any more responsibility, even though in her letter of 8 July she was also exasperated by Wolja 'knowing best' and reminded him that they were a planning a joint life together?

His cleverness and her silliness were also part of their sexual relationship. On 18 August Wolja responded to Lotte's desire to lie next to him and be a 'totally silly woman':

Do you really want to lie next to me in bed? Lotteli, today for the first time I wanted to say sweet Lotte, to you. May I?...Lotteli, if we had more money I would send you a present every day, and flowers. I think you had better bring some armour with you, so that I don't crush you with joy.

In many of his letters, as on 1 August, Wolja addressed Lotte as *Du Dummes Ding* [you silly thing] and he started his final letter of 25 August: 'You rascal, you silly thing, you, little you, you, you, you, it is so wonderful to scold you, my darling little wife. Outside in the street, I say to myself all the time 'you silly thing, you' only out of love.'

This use of the word 'silly' reminds me of ways in which my parents related to one another when I was a child. My brother, my father and I were constructed as the 'clever' ones in the family, interested in science and mathematics. My father would say 'do you think Mummy would understand?' Years later, with shame, I recognized my collusion in this myth, and the way that I had enjoyed being categorized as 'clever' with my father and big brother, and I feel that shame now. Although Wolja used 'silly' in an affectionate way, it is hard not to experience it as having derogatory undertones, and operating as a way of keeping Lotte in her place.

Possessions as the Focus of Emotions

A central concern of their correspondence was the discussion, sometimes in great detail, of what Lotte should bring with her, what should be shipped, and what had to be left behind or sold. Clearly these were important practical decisions, made much harder by the ever-changing regulations. My reading of their letters suggests that their discussion of possessions was about much more than this; it was also a place in which their desires, fear and uncertainty were played out.

In an early letter on 30 May Lotte described an imaginary conversation she had had with Wolja while she was eating her lunch:

And then I wondered whether we would have enough money to furnish 2 rooms and how we would do it. And then I said I'd like a beautiful sofa, but with drawers for linen, and you were so silly and didn't understand why that's important. Ach, Wolluk, something must be resolved soon! I don't mean the sofa and the drawers, but for us two.

And real sofas also appear in a postscript to Lotte's first letter of 8 July: 'Do you still remember Mutti's sofa in her room in Franzensbader? Where your

Miaou stood, in front of the radio. Shall I bring that one and my small one, or that one and your old one, or my small one and your old one? (My small one is the one from my alcove.)'

At the end of his letter on 1 August Wolja wrote: 'don't forget the dictionary, the big English one, please in the transport. I need it very quickly for the article and publications that I should write. It is already a problem not having them. I am sad about the fiction, but if it is doesn't work, it doesn't.' On 24 August, in response to her letter in which she said she had been asked by someone to bring a present for her daughter: 'I think it's preposterous to bring a bulky vase, when you aren't bringing my fiction books, because you haven't got enough money.' The next day he explained in English that if she was bringing his large Cathode Ray Tube with her, 'it is for indicating and measuring electric currents. It is a single model for a special scientific experiment, of no commercial value'. He continued in German: 'I could make good use of my two old pairs of black shoes.' Two days later, on 26 August, Lotte told him: 'I am bringing some of the novels. Your father will sell the rest, mainly several classics. They will hopefully bring in a bit of money.'

It is clear from the letters that Lotte was organising the transport of Wolja's possessions as well as her own. I presume that he took very little with him when he left Germany, not knowing whether he would be allowed to stay in the UK. He had left his home, his parents, everything that was familiar to him and he was separated from Lotte, not knowing when she would be able to join him. It was probably very important for him in this lonely, uncertain position to imagine being reunited with his own possessions, especially those connected to his work. At the same time he did not seem to be aware that he was adding to Lotte's stress by the demands that he was making.

This discussion of possessions became one of their main areas of conflict. Their quarrels focused on one item, not necessary for Wolja's work, the *Staubsauger* [vacuum cleaner]. On 28 June, describing the furniture she was planning to bring, Lotte explained: 'The vacuum cleaner is a problem. Apart from anything else, Wolluk, we don't have any carpets; there won't be that much to vacuum for us...I have real romantic desires for you. Every beautiful evening, every couple I see make me burst with anger.' Wolja must have queried her decision as, on 3 July, she wrote: 'for your latest suggestions thank you...by the way in relation to the vacuum cleaner you are being illogical. If you live in a furnished flat, the people see to the cleaning of the carpets etc. themselves.' But in his letter of 1 August Wolja continued to insist that it was vital to bring a vacuum cleaner: 'The dust here is unbelievable and it is pointless to beat the carpets.'

The vacuum cleaner even became an issue for Lotte's mother when, at the end of July, she wrote to Wolja to ask him to stop upsetting Lotte. In response Wolja also discussed the vacuum cleaner:

> You have used the issue of the vacuum cleaner as a particular example. So, I will do this too, just as an example. And I have to say to you that all your experience as a housewife has nothing to do with it. There are housewives here too who one can ask. The bottom line is that both the way of living together in a flat or house, as well as the amount of dust here, is so different from that in Germany, that the experience from Germany is worthless.

The dust refers I believe to coal fires. Wolja's low opinion of English heating systems will appear again in Chapter 7 in a letter to his father in 1946. More generally, I began to recognize a pattern of Wolja making comparisons between England and Germany. His pedantic style is also one that is familiar to me. On 11 August Lotte expressed her frustration through humour: 'You describe to me all the 'multicoloured' advantages of vacuum cleaners. I have no aversion to vacuum cleaners. I have already written to you several times that any new purchases made after 1933 carry a 100% surcharge on export from Germany.'

The Nazi Context

Apart from such evidence of the ever-increasing difficulties created for emigrating Jews, I was at first amazed at the normality of life. Lotte met friends, went to the cinema and was employed throughout, voluntarily leaving her employment at the Italian Bank a month before she emigrated. The Nazi context is of course apparent in Lotte's letters through phrases such as 'since 1933', and in her accounts of the changing regulations. Later I recognized ways in which she described the emotional atmosphere: 'This sitting and waiting and trembling makes one sensitive' (3 June); 'It's not just me. Everyone is complaining now. It's probably in the air' (4 July); and 'Everything is sadly bloody serious and therefore not a joke' (8 July). Was she consciously understating or avoiding what was happening around her or did she not say very much because they had become so used to it?

Both interpretations are possible. In her memoir, Lily Pincus describes how careful people had to be, and the fact that there were 'spies' everywhere.[7] On the other hand, in his diary entry of 29 June 1938, Victor Klemperer wrote: 'We are so accustomed to living without rights and to waiting apathetically for further disgraceful acts, that it hardly upsets us anymore.'[8]

Lotte's phrases triggered my imagination, wondering how it felt to be living in Berlin at this time. As I re-read the letters, looking specifically for evidence of Nazism, I realized that I had missed or avoided many examples – sometimes because the German was difficult for me, but perhaps too because I did not want to have to think about the content. Lotte's letter of 31 May provides a good example.

> Dearest boy
> It is again two days without news of you. Hopefully there is nothing wrong. Here there is nothing new…I spent yesterday with Heinz. He sat here and waited for a telegram, that would tell him that the embarkation deposit had been paid, for which he has no money here. If it hasn't been done by today, which is very likely, then he must wait again until the end of August for a ship. He is very depressed, because he feels so useless without anything to do and apart from that he has no money. Two weeks ago, he told his father that he was going to Africa. Since then they haven't spoken at all. A nice state of affairs! He probably won't come to London, because of lack of money. We then went to the cinema for a bit of mutual cheering up, 'Night Club Scandal'.

[She told him about the film and continued]

> Today my boss took a photograph of me. I was terrified, but nothing happened. He had to try out a camera, and therefore took various photos in different light. That is after all so important!! In lightning speed I had to sit at a desk, couldn't even comb my hair, had to look at him, and then it was done. If there's anything worth seeing I'll definitely send you a copy (he didn't say that, but I am saying it).

[And towards the end]

> There's nothing new, sadly always nearly – things.

She ended the letter playfully with a very long signature to tease him about his complaint that she did not sign one of her letters.

This description of her boss taking the photograph gave me one of my most chilling moments. In this short paragraph we see how the social atmosphere can be conveyed so powerfully within tiny fragments of communication about simple, everyday events, as well as through phrases like 'always nearly – things'.

I tried to imagine the circumstances of the photograph; I have no idea whether Lotte's fear was a specific or a general one. It makes great sense that a Jew would be terrified of being photographed in 1938. As part of the investigation of racial characteristics many children were photographed by so-called 'race-hygienists'.[9] Referring in her memoir to an event that occurred in June 1938, Inge Deutschkron describes this in more detail:

> A seemingly meaningless experience disturbed me much more. I sat at the photographer's. Like every 16 year old I was vain. When the photographer told me to push my hair behind my left ear, I was completely distraught and close to tears. He had spoken neutrally, without any scorn, a business-like instruction, nothing more. Nevertheless, I experienced the humiliation like the lash of a whip. But I had learned self-control. This photo must not give away what was going on in me...Racial origin could be identified from the shape of the left ear. National Socialist race scientists had discovered this. The left ear of a Jew betrayed Semitic origins, and therefore Jews' passport photos had to be taken with the left ear clearly visible.[10]

What could I learn from the history books about daily life for Jews at this time? Mid-1938 is not a period written about specifically. It is after the early waves of emigration by German Jews which took place in 1933, when Hitler came to power, and in 1935 after the Nuremberg laws were passed. But it is just before the state-organized pogroms and destruction of synagogues, shops and houses on 'Kristallnacht' (9-10 November 1938) which led to the arrest and imprisonment of thousands of Jews and a rapid increase in the numbers trying to get out. Yet there were many significant events in 1938: Austria was annexed in March and there were preparations throughout the year for war against Czechoslovakia; laws requiring Jews to carry identity cards and to add Israel or Sara to their names were passed in July and August respectively, both to come into effect on 1 January 1939.[11] And three days before the photograph incident with Lotte's boss, all Russian Jews were arrested and sent to concentration camps, including women, children and old men. Their property was confiscated and they were only to be released on condition that they emigrated. It is not surprising that Lotte's initial response was to be terrified.

On 18 July, in a letter mainly concerned with describing her visits to the clinic with her mother, Lotte asks Wolja if he has heard from their friends Hans and Jael, who were of Russian origin. 'I have heard they are in two different camps, c'est tout.' I was relieved; I knew these two people; they had survived.

On 10 August 1938 Victor Klemperer recorded in his diary that it was a period during which there was 'intensified Jew-baiting again and drastic new measures all the time'.[12] On 11 August, in her letter to Wolja, Lotte also referred to how much things had changed and how much harder everything had become since Wolja left. She was frustrated that he did not understand this. 'Peterlein, you must believe me, when I write that all the regulations have changed enormously since you left, and when you don't understand something, receive it patiently and trust me, and rely on us. Please please.' Lotte's experiences are consistent with Wolfgang Benz's description of the contradictions in Nazi policies to Jews at this time. They wanted to be rid of them – it was a policy of forced emigration, not yet genocide – but they put every possible obstacle in their way.[13]

On 23 August Lotte sent Wolja a telegram: 'HURRAH VISUM KUSS = TEDDY'.

In a letter the same day, she tells Wolja how she only just got her visa: 'I rushed on Monday straight to the consulate. It was terribly nerve-racking. Most people were turned down. Also for me it hung by a thread…But he let himself be moved. And Hurra!! For a year.'

Wolja knows that decision making may also be arbitrary in England. In response to the telegram, he advises her how to behave as she arrives in England.

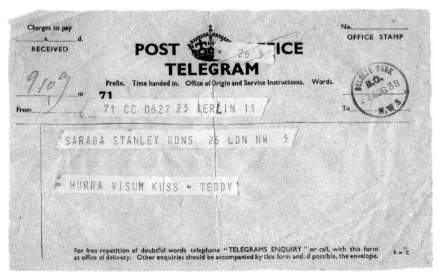

Telegram from Lotte to Wolja, 23 August 1938 – she has her visa!

Don't forget that you must show the immigration officer your permit
as well as the Passport with the visa. Apart from that you must give a
trustworthy impression, so that he lets you in. And you must be very
'correct' with the English customs. Don't risk anything…(23 August).

Benz argues that even in the early years of the Nazi regime, when people
apparently left of their own free will, the emigration of Jews from Germany
should be seen as 'both flight from persecution and also expulsion'.[14] I
wondered whether it would be possible to discover from their letters how
Lotte and Wolja themselves saw their situation. Was it for them a flight or
an emigration? Lotte always used the expression 'thrown out'. In her letter of
28 July she refers to *Auswanderung* [emigration]. They believed they had no
future in Germany, and feared for themselves and their parents. On the other
hand they thought they had time to plan and prepare Lotte's departure. In
their discussions towards the end of this correspondence, they decided that
Wolja's parents, who had Romanian nationality and therefore did not qualify
as refugees, should go to Romania while Lotte and Wolja settled in England,
before they tried to get his parents to join them. Their detailed discussions
about what to bring, including presents for friends and Lotte's concern to
have the right clothes which appears in many of her letters, make it feel like
an emigration – albeit a forced one – rather than a flight. In his letter of 1
August Wolja appeared to believe that the situation in Germany would not
last for ever, when he asked Lotte 'What are you doing with your books and
silver? Also sell them? Or in the meantime leave my and your fiction with
Lil until better times come?'

A Return to Gender

When focusing on Lotte and Wolja's personal relationship, I explored the
gendered nature of the 'emotional work' in which they were each engaged.
Reading the letters again through a social lens made me acutely aware of
gendered aspects of other kinds of 'work' too. Wolja was actively trying to
secure his residency in the UK or to obtain a visa for the USA, to find a
domestic situation for Lotte and to look for scientific research work. In 1932
Lotte had started to study medicine. After two semesters she was thrown
out for being friendly with communists; this was a few months before she
would have been expelled as a Jew. She immediately learned shorthand and
typing. In 1934 she went to Milan where, she writes, she worked as a
'governess', but in 2018 Peter found yet another box of papers we had not
looked through. It contained a student book from the University of Milan,
showing her registration in the Faculty of Jurisprudence. She had to return

Lotte's Milan University student book, 1934-35.

to Berlin when her father died suddenly in May 1935. She then worked in a range of clerical and secretarial jobs, and was preparing to take on domestic work.

In contrast with the predominant picture given in the history books, Lotte was employed almost continuously until she left Germany. At the time of these letters, she had been working for two years as a secretary and translator for the *Italienische Nazionale per I Cambi con l'estero* [Italian

National Institute for the Exchange of Foreign Currency]; she described it as a bank. She was earning money to support both of them, caring for her own mother, seeing Wolja's parents regularly and helping them with their plans to emigrate, as well as organising her own and her mother's emigration, including the transport of their possessions. She was networking widely on Wolja's behalf, taking advice and getting hold of a *Gutachten* [expert opinion] about his sight, which would confirm that it was not going to deteriorate further. She also drafted letters in English for him for another visa application for the USA. Despite the amount of work that Lotte was doing, the responsibility she was taking on, and the fact that she was at that time the only earner, in her letter of 11 June she was clear that Wolja was in charge and would eventually be the breadwinner. 'Look, if you suddenly get a swanky job, so that we can get married, I won't have any more problems.' It seems both that a range of employment possibilities were always available to women, irrespective of class, and also that she was more prepared than Wolja to take on such work.

The most explicit operation of gender and also of class can be seen in relation to the structures of immigration into the UK. Wolja was allowed to enter the UK temporarily to seek work, but only because he was scientifically qualified. Lotte was persecuted in Germany as a 'Jew', not as a woman; but as a woman, a 'domestic permit' offered her the only way out of Nazi Germany. Tony Kushner shows how the concept of 'domestic service' itself is constructed through both class and gender.[15]

In many letters Lotte expressed her feelings about housework. On 10 June: 'In practice I understand nothing about housework, whereas I am good at languages and also have experience with children.' With this letter she enclosed the photograph taken by her boss in May 1938, commenting 'I think it's quite cute. Perhaps you can show it to families with lots of children, in case they might need me. You can tell them that I would comb my hair if I was living with them.' Four days later (14 June) she complained that Wolja had not mentioned the photograph. Another week later on 21 June she told him: 'My heroic attempts to learn to sew have failed…On 1 July I am taking a few cookery lessons, so that the housewives don't shake their heads at me too much' and on 26 August (her penultimate letter): 'In relation to me, don't worry that I can do some cooking and sewing. I cannot do either.'

In November 2005 I found the photograph.

Lotte is sitting at a desk and, although it is cut off half-way up, there is clearly a photo of Mussolini behind her. I must have seen it before, but without the letter I had not realized its significance. How much it represents: a moment of fear; both flirtation and disappointment in her relationship with Wolja; her status as a professional woman; and also an advertisement of

Photo of Lotte taken by her boss, 31 May 1938. In the possession of the author.

suitability for domestic work. Excited about finding it, I carried it around with me, frightened of losing it! When I looked again at the letter of 10 June, in which Lotte sent it to Wolja, I discovered I had missed out a sentence: 'I and my photo kiss you many many times.' So it was also important for her as a physical object to connect them and convey her love. This photo must also have become significant for Wolja. On 2 August 1940, when he was interned on the Isle of Man, he wrote to Lotte: 'Why don't you send me a photo of you, the one you sent two years ago'.

The original photo is very small. When enlarged I could see that Lotte is wearing a bracelet that she later gave to me. I still had it, thus connecting me in turn to her and to her experiences at that time. In October 2009 my brother's first grandchild was born – a girl they decided to call Lotti. I gave the bracelet to Lotti.

Notes

1. C. Holmes, *John Bull's Island: Immigration and British Society, 1871 – 1971* (Basingstoke: Macmillan, 1988), p. 148; M. A. Bernstein, *Foregone Conclusions. Against Apocalyptic History* (Berkeley, CA and London: University of California Press, 1994), p.26.
2. *Ahorn* is German for 'maple', but I have been unable to find out, even from people who lived in Berlin at that time, what kind of drink it was. I imagine it was maple syrup.
3. Although some dictionaries offer 'accusation' as a translation of *Vorwurf,* this applies mainly to legal contexts.

4. See, for example, J. Duncombe and D. Marsden, 'Love and Intimacy: The Division of Emotion and "Emotion Work" ', *Sociology,* 27, 2 (1993), pp. 221–41, and S. Jackson and S. Scott, 'Gut Reactions to Matters of the Heart: Reflections on Rationality, Irrationality and Sexuality', *The Sociological Review,* 45, 4 (1997), p.567.

5. An undated letter, but its content places it in early June.

6. In her letters of 28 May and 30 May.

7. L. Pincus, *Verloren-gewonnen: mein Weg von Berlin nach London* (Stuttgart: Deutsche Verlags-Anstalt, 1980), p.73.

8. V. Klemperer, trans. M. Chalmers, *I Shall Bear Witness: The Diaries of Victor Klemperer 1933–41* (London: Weidenfeld & Nicolson, 1998), p.249.

9. G. B. Ginzel, *Judischer Alltag in Deutschland, 1933–1945* (Dusseldorf: Droste, 1984), p.108.

10. I. Deutschkron, *Ich trug den gelben Stern* (München: Deutscher Taschenbuch Verlag, 1983), p.28. My translation. See M. Roseman, *The Past in Hiding* (London: Penguin Books, 2001), pp.119-120 for further information on Inge Deutschkron.

11. S.Friedländer, *Nazi Germany and the Jews. The Years of Persecution 1933–39* (London: Weidenfeld & Nicolson, 1997), pp.254; Ginzel, *Judischer Alltag,* p.11.

12. Klemperer, *I Shall Bear Witness,* p.253.

13. W. Benz (ed.), *Das Exil der kleinen Leute. Alltagserfahrung deutscher Juden in der Emigration* (München: C.H. Beck, 1991).

14. Ibid. p.62, my translation.

15. See T. Kushner, *The Holocaust and the Liberal Imagination* (Oxford: Blackwell, 1994), pp.93–96, and T. Kushner, *Journeys from the Abyss. The Holocaust and Forced Migration from the 1880s to the Present* (Liverpool: Liverpool University Press, 2017), pp. 118–134.

3

'Brought Recommendation from Bragg'

8/II/37
SARAGA
    Mr Makower:-
    Quite desirable if can get job, but
prospects not good, though not impossible.
He might be let in for a limited period to
go the round of the electrical firms – others with similar qualifications
have found positions, though he has rather less
practical experience. Well trained and good
knowledge.
    Prof Committee would be prepared to keep him for a month but
would undertake no longer liability.

When I found this note, handwritten on a piece of pink paper,[1] in the archive of the Society for the Protection of Science and Learning (SPSL)[2] in the Bodleian Library, I was not aware of its significance. Later I recognized that it marks a decisive moment in Wolja's story. Without this recommendation the Home Office would not have allowed him into the UK at all, and because of it his visa was for only one month.

Wolja's files in the archive contain letters, documents, testimonials, curriculum vitae and many more of these handwritten notes which review or record his situation. The items are not always filed in date order; indeed some are not dated at all, although their content sometimes dates them for me. Many of the papers only made sense because of what I already knew or had learned from my own archive; and conversely, I was now able to understand for the first time some of the items in my collection.

In many memoirs of the Nazi period people attribute their survival, at least partly, to luck, to unexpected acts of kindness, or to sheer serendipity. This is expressed very clearly by Leo Szilard in relation to his own escape from Germany, a few days after the Reichstag fire, on a train to Vienna: 'if you want to succeed in this world, you don't have to be much cleverer than other people; you just have to be one day earlier…[The]'same train on the next day…was stopped at the frontier…everybody was interrogated by the

Nazis.'[3] In Wolja's case it was philanthropy and networking that were crucial – in particular the willingness of establishment, scientific figures in Germany and Britain to use their networks of friends and colleagues to support an unknown but promising Jewish scientist. His PhD had been examined in 1935 by Professor Max von Laue, who won the Nobel Prize for Physics in 1914; Von Laue recommended Wolja to, amongst others, Sir William Bragg, who together with his son Lawrence built on von Laue's work to win the Nobel Prize for Physics in 1915.

The papers in the archive document the never ending series of obstacles Wolja faced from 1933 to 1938 in obtaining his PhD and finding a country to take him. I feel in awe of his persistence, his determination not to be beaten, his sense of his rights, his confidence in his ability as a scientist and his capacity to seek help from a wide range of people. It helped to explain his frustration later in life about the 'wasted years' when he could not further his scientific career.

I read more widely, hoping to understand the nature of the decision making represented by the piece of pink paper, which could have such a profound effect on the life of an individual.

'As a Jew'

Wolja's story in the archive starts on 16 July 1935 when he wrote to the AAC for the first time, in German,[4] on the recommendation of Professor Max v. Laue, shortly after completion of the first stage of his PhD. The second stage, 'Promotion', required him to publish his dissertation within six months. His letter is very polite and respectful, outlining his experience and difficulties and asking directly for help.

> I am a physicist and I completed my doctorate two weeks ago at the University of Berlin. Originally I studied electrical engineering for several semesters at the Berlin Technische Hochschule (with 7 months' practical experience in a factory), I then transferred to the University and entered the Heinrich Hertz Institute; there I carried out several experimental projects that were in part published. One of these I wanted to submit as a dissertation. But in April 1933, as a Jew, I had to leave the Institute and therefore I could not fully complete my work for my doctorate. Instead I was forced to start a new theoretical project, for which I was not dependent on the Institute. Because I was permitted to study further at the University under the 5% limit for Non-Aryans, I was able to submit my new work as a dissertation in May this year, and subsequently to pass the examination. My

dissertation will appear in *Elektrischen Nachrichtentechnik* [Electrical telecommunications].

The phrases 'in April 1933' and 'the 5% limit for Non-Aryans' are references to two Nazi laws that affected him. As a result of the first, the Law for the Restoration of the Professional Civil Service, he was excluded from his work at the Heinrich Hertz Institute, but ironically the second, the Law Against the Overcrowding of German Schools and Institutions of Higher Learning, which was intended to restrict the number of Jewish students at universities, enabled him to continue with his PhD studies at the University of Berlin.[5]

Wolja's letter continues with a description of his very wide ranging, experimental and theoretical education. In addition to his scientific work, he has contributed to the development of patent applications, organized exhibitions, presented lectures, arranged guided tours and acted as the assistant for Professor Leithäuser's lectures on high frequency engineering.

> For the last few years, as a regular contributor to the *Funkstechnischen Monatshefte* [Radio Engineering Monthly] and *Funk* [Wireless] and through my work at the Berlin Radio Exhibition, I was able, before the **Umschwung** in Germany, to earn enough, so that I only needed a small contribution from my parents. Professor Leithäuser had promised me a scientific scholarship at the Heinrich Hertz Institute once I had completed my examination. Today that is of course completely impossible. My father finds himself in dire straits and I therefore need desperately to find some paid work. I would of course much prefer – if it were possible – to work independently in a large scientific-technical development laboratory.
>
> I would be very grateful if you could help me. I believe that the information above, together with the curriculum vitae and testimonials that I have enclosed, will give you a good picture of my qualifications and experience. (My emphasis)

Umschwung seems to be an unexpected word for Wolja to use for the Nazi seizure of power. It translates as 'drastic change', 'reversal', or 'about-turn'. Did he know about the AAC's concern to be 'non-political'?

Esther Simpson, the Assistant Secretary, replied at once,[6] a pattern of communication I was to discover was characteristic of how she and other administrative staff at AAC/SPSL operated. She registered Wolja on their files and sent him a questionnaire to complete. Nothing more happened for nearly a year.

Prussian Replaced by Stateless

A four-page undated typed document[7] sheds light on this. It describes in great detail the difficulties Wolja experienced in completing his Promotion. Its content and style suggest that it was written in 1936 for a lawyer. The journal that would publish his dissertation required Wolja to make some changes. Agreed with his PhD examiners, they would take some time to complete.

> On the day after the examination (which took place on 27 June 1935), I collected my paper from the deanery. The secretary…told me and my co-examinees…that within the prescribed half-year deadline, there was only one Promotion date, in September, so that we would barely have three months to get the dissertation printed. If we could not do it within this time, we must apply for an extension before the 6 month deadline. I therefore had no concerns at all about revising my work calmly and carefully for printing and publication, as I knew that Promotion deadlines were always extended, indeed it happened often. In November I enquired again from Herr Thürling…what steps I should take, and established that it would be completely unproblematic; I must only make the application before the end of the 6 month deadline.

The first difficulty arose when Professor Salinger, who had accepted his dissertation for publication, was removed from his position as an editor of the journal.[8] In this document Wolja says the other editor Herr Dr. Mönch, would no longer accept the article, but in an affidavit for a restitution claim, found amongst our own papers, he writes that the article could not be accepted because he was a Jew. His only alternative was to publish privately, which would take more time and cost a great deal.

The second obstacle was the refusal at the end of December 1935 of his request for an extension. He was advised to resubmit the request with a more detailed justification when he had finished the revisions to the satisfaction of his examiners. His second application in February 1936 was accompanied by letters of support from Professors von Laue and Wehnelt, his examiners, and from Professor Leithäuser, with whom he had worked at the Heinrich Hertz Institut.

At this point in the document, Wolja explains that in March 1935 he was made stateless, when his German citizenship was revoked. After his Easter holiday,

> …I told the University authorities (Registry and Bursary). As a result in place of my previous yellow Jewish-student card, I received on 6

May a blue foreigner student card, and in my record book the nationality 'Prussian' was replaced by 'Stateless'. I then inquired whether my statelessness would affect my admission into the oral examination. The secretary...told me that once I had been admitted as a Jew, my nationality was of no importance. A few days later I registered for my examination, at which point my record book, in which my statelessness was recorded, had, as usual, to accompany my written application.

Herr Thürling asked him to enclose the notification of the removal of his citizenship with his second application for an extension.

In support of his application, Wolja argued that he had made important contributions to promoting German industry and technology as 'a Berlin correspondent and technical contributor to numerous foreign technical journals (in France, Denmark, Romania, Switzerland)'. He had published 'numerous reports and essays on the progress of German technology' making use of 'press and photographic material that was provided for me by press offices of different firms and of the *Reichspostministerium*...I have received letters of thanks from different firms'.

After waiting a long while for a response, he asked Dr. v. Löllhöffel, the Chief Press Officer of Telefunkengesellschaft, who knew his work and his publications, to intervene on his behalf with the University authorities. Dr. Löllhöffel emphasized to the Dean the value of Wolja's publications to the German economy. The Dean, Professor Bieberbach, told him that the Ministry had forbidden the admission of stateless people to PhD examinations. In fact this ruling had been made before Wolja's oral examination, which he should not have been allowed to take. He also expressed his personal regret about the situation and offered to make an application to the Ministry on Wolja's behalf.

But he behaved very differently with Wolja himself:

> He was astonished when I told him that my statelessness had been written in my record book even before my admission to the examination and requested that I submit the record book once more. Likewise he was astonished that I had been resident in Germany since my birth. He told me that I should not have been allowed to take the examination.

The Dean did not make an application to the Ministry. Instead he told the lawyer who Wolja had now involved that he wanted to await the outcome of a similar case being considered by the Ministry. He advised Wolja to submit further written evidence about the circumstances of his statelessness and his involvement in foreign scientific journals. But two days after submitting these additional papers Wolja received a rejection of his second application. At this point the Dean said he could do no more.

Here the main document ends. A final paragraph, written in italics, seems to have been added later:

> *In November 1935 Professor Dr. Forrer of the Technische Hochschüle in Zurich took me on. Through the mediation of the Notgemeinschaft* [Emergency Society of German Scholars Abroad] *I received from the Schweizerischen Hilfswerk für deutsche Gelehrte* [Swiss relief organization for German scholars] *a scholarship of 120 Frs per month for a maximum of 6 months. The Zurich police and the Department of Justice and Police in Bern would not allow me to enter the country and refused a residence permit because of my statelessness.*

I found the end of the story in a curriculum vita written for a restitution claim:

> I was only successful in getting permission for my Promotion after several more months, and after the rejection of various petitions and with the help of a legal advisor on Administrative law and the recommendation of the *Pressechef der Telefunkengesellschaft*, Dr. v. Löllhöffel. As a result I had to pay the costs for the printing of my thesis and lawyers' fees.

Several printed copies of Wolja's dissertation amongst our papers document the date of his Promotion as 29 October 1936.

Learning for the first time about the details of Wolja's experiences in Nazi Germany, I was moved by the extent to which his referees and the press officer, all non-Jewish, were willing to support him both privately and publicly. The use in 1935 of the argument that Wolja, a Jewish scientist, had contributed to the German economy astounded me.

Did the Dean's vacillation stem from fear or from Nazi sympathies? I discovered that Ludwig Bieberbach was a distinguished mathematician, an active Nazi and a founder of 'Deutsche Mathematik?', a Nazi argument that Jews thought differently and therefore could not be instructors of non-Jews. He 'joined the SA (storm troopers) in April 1933 and at this point was promoted dean of Berlin's Philosophy Faculty, which incorporated the natural sciences and mathematics. By November he was seen around the university in a Nazi uniform.'[9]

Yet Wolja writes about him in such a dispassionate way.

A Diligent Young Scientist

A letter, in German dated 3 June 1936,[10] from Professor Max von Laue to 'Sir Wyndham' (from later letters identified as Sir Wyndham Deedes) explains how this document reached the SPSL archive.

> Since it is not certain whether I shall be able to speak to you in person, I should like to hand over to you two documents, which are typical of the difficulties encountered by non-Aryan scientists trying to seek a professional position abroad. The paper from Wolja Saraga (that he did not originally write for this purpose, but drafted for other reasons) shows you moreover how a diligent young scientist through no fault of his own, can get into such extreme difficulties.
>
> However, the worst distress that I know of exists in England itself for one or two dozen young scientists who received 3 year scholarships from the Imperial Chemical Industry in 1933.[11] Already, a year ago, the firm gave them notice for July 1936; most of them have no idea what will then become of them, whereas some of them have obtained secure posts at English universities...
>
> Despite this situation, I want to take the opportunity of expressing the gratitude of the relevant circles and the German scholars who are not in agreement with the race programme of the 'Third Reich' that England has done so much for these displaced persons. We cannot imagine that the attitudes that have been expressed through this gallant assistance will suddenly change and we are convinced that in England there is also the possibility of overcoming the difficulties that stand in the way...But there is one question that is often posed here. Why do the English colonies and dominions take so little part in placing these homeless scientists? They could actually make more use of them than European England.
>
> In the hope that I shall see still you personally, and with the greatest respect.

Laue and Deedes did meet in person. A handwritten letter from Wyndham Deedes in English[12] to the AAC is dated 9 June:

> When I was in Berlin two days ago Professor von Laue (an Aryan) asked to see me and handed me the enclosed cases and this covering letter. The correspondence speaks for itself. It is difficult to see what

can be done in either case. Indeed in one case nothing seems possible. None the less I should like to send him a sympathetic reply and this perhaps you will enable me to do. He is a man of great distinction, who despite the danger is fearlessly standing up for non-Aryans...I need not add that it is essential that his name should be kept secret.

Von Laue's main concern seems to be the continuation of the ICI scholarships, but he did also take the opportunity to further Wolja's case, which, in Deedes' view, was at best not very promising and at worst hopeless. In turn, in his letter to AAC, Deedes' primary concern is to express respect for von Laue, rather than to rescue the scientists. Both men use the Nazi terminology of 'Aryan' and 'non-Aryan' to distinguish between non-Jews and Jews.

Deedes chaired one of the most important Christian organizations supporting refugees. In May 1936 he went to Germany, accompanied by Norman Bentwich, a prominent member of the Anglo-Jewish Community who played a major role in the rescue of Jews,

> ...to consult with the Jewish community leaders about emigration and training plans...he bore a letter from the Archbishop of Canterbury to Hitler's deputy, Rudolf Hess. He had an interview, and was received with soothing words. Yet not even his integrity could prevail over the fanatical hatred of the Nazis. What he could effect was to bring heart and cheer to the much-tried Jewish Community.[13]

It must have been at the end of this visit that Deedes met Max von Laue. Two further handwritten notes in the Bodleian archive one on pink paper and the other on white paper,[14] take the story forward. The first, dated 29 January 1937, states: 'SARAGA Dr Henning said S will make visit to England in February to look for a job.' The second, undated: 'Makower was much impressed by papers; Notgem gave him a grant already in Zurich; candidate for China post'. There is no other reference to a post in China and I have not been able to find one in the SPSL committee papers. Written in much smaller writing on the side of the second note is 'Makower liked him personally'. Perhaps this was added later, after he had arrived, although this was not until May 1938. I have included it because it adds to my sense of the arbitrariness of the decision making. What would have happened if Makower had not liked Wolja? How did Wolja experience the pressure, in an alien culture, to be likeable?

You Must Help Us

Wolja did not pin all his hopes on the UK as his destination. He also tried to obtain a visa for the USA, where his mother had many relatives. Amongst our papers are letters seeking jobs in the USA, an affidavit from one of Eti's cousins, Anna Greenberg, a New York school teacher, dated 14 November 1936, and Wolja's application to emigrate permanently, dated 9 March 1937. In 2016 I was alerted to the existence of papers concerning Wolja in the Einstein archive in Jerusalem.[15] We had always known the story of Einstein's intervention on Wolja's behalf to secure his release from internment – a story that will appear in the next chapter. Now I learned that in September 1936 Einstein had written to the American consulate in Berlin supporting Wolja's application. The letter was solicited by a woman living in New York, Eva Cohnreich, who was, I imagine, a contact or friend of Eti's relatives as I found her name later in Wolja's address book. She sent Einstein a copy of Wolja's CV and two 1934 testimonials from Leithäuser and Lothar Band.

In November 1935 the Swiss had refused him a visa on the grounds of his statelessness; on 15 March 1937 he was turned down by the USA because of his poor eyesight 'and the probability that you will become a burden on the state'. Despite this rejection his mother continued to call on her relatives in New York to help Wolja. She wrote (in English) to 'Minnie' on 6 April 1937:

> Wolja learns that the thing to which objection is made is the fact that he is weak sighted in one eye. We did not realize that attention would be given to such detail, but we have learned that the consul jumps at every chance to obstruct a would-be immigrant.

[She tells Minnie that Wolja's eyesight has never affected his work and the condition is one that does not get worse, as can be confirmed by his oculist.]

> …Wolja has been told that it would be necessary for Mrs Greenberg to send a supplementary affidavit saying she is aware of the Consul's objections…and that she none the less upholds her guarantee that he will not become a public charge. But in addition to this there should be a supporting affidavit from some other of our mutual relatives which would increase the total amount and effectiveness of the guarantee…
>
> Dear Minnie, you must help us and use all your influence with Mrs Greenberg and our other relatives to get these necessary papers. Our own situation is at present very bad, but if Wolja could get his visa and go to the states, it would be a great help for us as well as for him. We are already much indebted to both you and Mrs. Greenberg

for what you have done for us thus far, and we are sure you are willing to do so.

In speaking to the relatives you can point out to them that an affidavit guaranteeing support for immigration, like a labor contract made before immigration, has no legal validity in the United States and cannot be enforced. Aside from this you can be sure that Wolja would never think of trying to make any claims, legal or otherwise, on people who had helped him in this way.

On 19 April 1937 one of Anna Greenberg's brothers, Morris Gottlieb, a 'Counselor at Law', wrote to Wolja, regretting that they were unable to provide any further affidavits. He was sending a copy of his letter to Eva Cohnreich. Nevertheless on 1 March 1938 another brother, Leo Gottlieb, also a lawyer, did provide an additional affidavit. I imagine that Wolja's mother or other relatives had continued to put pressure on them. Whereas Wolja's original rejection had been a single short paragraph, on 28 March the American Consul wrote a long letter to Leo Gottlieb, referring to Wolja throughout as Dr. Sagara.

> Dr. Sagara is only distantly related to you and it appears he has never seen you but, nevertheless, the Consulate General can readily understand your desire to assist him. However this office believes that some additional facts should be presented to you in regard to the condition of Dr. Sagara's eyes before a final decision is made.

[He tells Leo Gottlieb the result of Wolja's eye examination by the United States Public Health Surgeon.]

> I believe that you can readily understand that this is not a case of mere short sightedness...Should you desire to go further into this case it is suggested that you consult your oculist, especially in regard to the possibility of the condition of the left eye becoming more unfavorable. Should this be the case, you can readily understand that Dr. Sagara would then be likely to be wholly dependent upon someone thereafter or become a public charge. If, nevertheless you are willing to assume the responsibility of support for an indefinite period you might so state and include a discussion of the plans you have in mind for the applicant which would include the likelihood of becoming a public charge. The Consulate General will also be glad to receive any additional information which you might wish to send on behalf of the applicant.

May I take this occasion to assure you that Dr.Sagara's case will be given every consideration consistent with immigration laws and regulations.

Leo Gottlieb replied on 26 April:

I appreciate very much both the tone and the content of [your] letter. I am confident that the case is receiving careful and sympathetic consideration. I particularly appreciate your calling to my attention the exact situation with reference to Dr. Saraga's eyes. I find it difficult to obtain, by consultation here, any reliable forecast of the possibility of the condition of the left eye becoming more unfavorable. Accordingly, I am planning to have an independent examination made in Berlin...

Subject to the report on Dr. Saraga's left eye not being unfavorable, I would have no hesitation in assuming the responsibility of his support for an indefinite period, in view of what I know of the demand for qualified physicists.

The following day Leo's brother Morris wrote to Wolja, enclosing the American Consul's letter and Leo's reply: 'The New York section of the National Council of Jewish Women will have a representative of theirs in Berlin examine your eyes and as soon as we get their report, I shall write to you again.'

This additional examination was deemed necessary despite a report from Professor Dr. Oscar Fehr, an eminent ophthalmologist in Berlin, who had treated Wolja for the last four years. Dated 13 January 1938, his report states: 'He is weak-sighted in the right eye. Since his left eye, however is healthy and with a correcting glass has completely normal vision (= 5/4) he is not impeded in his daily life or in his profession. A change in the condition is not to be feared.'

I remember Dr. Fehr. He continued to look after Wolja in London and I also saw him when my eyesight started to deteriorate as a child. Now I have learned that he was the outstanding leader of the ophthalmic department of the largest eye hospital in Berlin for nearly thirty years. He arrived in the UK shortly before the start of the war. 'Some time later he became a student again in order to obtain his Scottish triple qualification, and he passed his finals in 1943 at the age of 71 years. He was then allowed to establish himself as an ophthalmic surgeon in Harley Street. His Continental patients flocked to him...'[16]

Morris Gottlieb's letter of 27 April is the last one that I have from this period. I presume these efforts were ended once Wolja received the British visa which, it appears from our papers, was also assisted by his mother's networking, this time through her sister, Sonja, in Copenhagen. In a letter on headed bank notepaper, dated over a year earlier, 22 January 1937, Fred, Sonja's son in law, tells '*Meine Lieben*' that Storey has written to the Passport Officer in Berlin to support Wolja's visa application and that as soon as it is granted, or beforehand if necessary, Fred will transfer £10 for Wolja to the Midland Bank (£5 from him and £5 from Sonja) to support Wolja when he first arrives in England. In later correspondence with the Home Office, Wolja states that the visa was only granted after the intervention of Mr. Storey, a British Consular official in Copenhagen who was a friend of the family.

L. has Written

Max von Laue was also actively networking on Wolja's behalf. On 15 March 1938 Dr. R. Rüdenberg wrote to Mr. Makower saying that at the request of Prof. Dr. M. von Laue, Berlin, he has looked over the printed dissertation and a number of manuscripts, sent to him by Wolja. He describes Wolja as 'a most capable and serious worker' with 'an open mind for scientific niceties

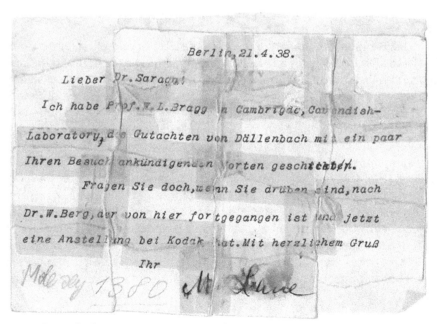

Postcard to Wolja from Max von Laue, 21 April 1938.

as well as for the practical use of the results arrived at'. He concludes: '…his work should be considered very valuable indeed'.[17]

On 17 March 1938 Makower wrote to Wolja[18] telling him that Dr. Rudenberg 'seems well disposed towards' him. But he expressed caution: 'As I already told you, if you decide to come over here to stay for a few weeks to see the various people you know, we shall be able to help you with the means to do so, but I cannot make you any further promise than that.'

Meanwhile amongst our own papers is a postcard from Max von Laue to Wolja. Written on 21 April 1938, sixteen days before Wolja's departure for England, it was once torn into small pieces, later stuck together again with sellotape.

'Dear Dr Saraga, I have sent Prof. W.L. Bragg, Cambridge, Cavendish-Laboratory, the report[19] from Dällenbach, together with a few words to introduce you.' It is one of the items in my own collection that I could now make sense of.

Wolja used the time in which he was waiting for the visa to prepare well – collecting testimonials and names of useful contacts. One of the testimonials in the SPSL archive, addressed to Wolja, begins: 'In response to your request…', suggesting that he had solicited it. Following his exclusion from the Heinrich Hertz Institute, he began systematically to accumulate evidence of his qualifications and experience. In a small black address book in our own collection he collected the names of useful contacts. From the handwriting it is clear that the entries were written not only by Wolja himself but also by Lotte, and by Wolja's father, Ado. Indeed, Wolja's name and address at the beginning of the book are in Ado's handwriting. Some entries are very neat, perhaps written in advance; lots of amendments and additions have been added rather untidily. Sometimes the occupation of the person is included, for example 'journalist' or 'doctor (Psychoanal)', and sometimes the person from whom the contact came or from whom he should give greetings is noted. Prof. W.L. Bragg is included and in brackets '(*L. hat geschr*)' [L has written].

Learning that Wolja was given only a few weeks to build on these contacts to find a job and secure his future in the UK helped to put into context Lotte's attempts in her letters to reassure him and ease his anxiety.

Cheap at the Price

Following Wolja's arrival in the UK on 7 May, things started to happen very quickly. On 12 May Bragg wrote to the AAC[20]:

> I recently had a letter from Professor Laue in Berlin, recommending Dr W. Saraga to me very warmly as an expert in High Frequency and

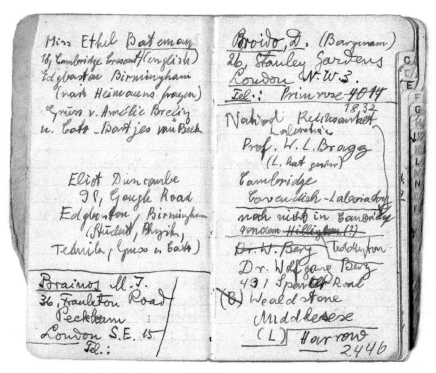

Wolja's address book with contacts in the UK.

Electrical Network theory. I have just talked to him for a few minutes this afternoon, and advised him to contact you about possible posts in this country. Laue's recommendation is reliable and shows he is a good man. I should be very grateful, for Laue's sake, if you can help him in any way.

Once again the request is that Wolja should be helped 'for Laue's sake' and because it is Laue who recommends him, he can be reliably considered a 'good man'. Wolja's visit to SPSL on 16 May is recorded in the file[21]:

SARAGA, W
Brought recommendation from Bragg (London). Has a month's permit, and is allowed to look for a position.
High Frequency & theory of electrical networking? Can we tell him which are the right professors? (Also electronic music).
How can he get introduction to Institution of Electrical Engineering?

Will see Shonberg of H.M.V.

Makower can't help him

Is stateless, Had grant from Zurich Cttee but couldn't use it, as not allowed to live there.

No means. Parents can no longer support him.

Will see Ehrenberg for advice

Has seen Demuth, who will help him if he can find a Professor sufficiently interested in him...

The reference to help from Demuth is clarified in a letter from Esther Simpson to Professor Blackett in Manchester on 19 May. Demuth was one of the co-founders of the *Notgemeinschaft*, referred to in the note as the 'Zurich Cttee'. They had agreed to support Wolja 'financially for a limited period if some professor shows a sufficient interest in him to invite him to work in his laboratory, with prospects of eventual absorption...'.[22] The one month deadline was taken very seriously; letters were written to several professors in English universities. The information that Wolja had been recommended by Professor Max von Laue, that he had permission to look for work – an unusual situation for refugees at this time – and only one month in which to do it, were always emphasized. The replies reveal an active network of academics trying hard to place refugee scientists. Although unable to help personally, they always made suggestions of people who Wolja should contact and these were passed on to Wolja by Esther Simpson on the day she received them. But I was struck by the fact that SPSL did not seem to take any responsibility for having, through Makower, recommended this limited time period.

Wolja was actively making use of these contacts and soliciting more. In an up to date curriculum vitae and a completed questionnaire sent to SPSL on 19 May 1938, he lists eight referees – four in Berlin, one in the USA and three in the UK, including Bragg.[23] In a letter found in our papers, dated 20 May 1939, E.V. Appleton of the Cavendish Laboratory in Cambridge writes: 'In reply to your letter, I have to say that I have no objections to your using my name as a reference in connection with your applications for posts.'

I imagine that these early weeks of visits and talking to people were very frustrating. Wolja was always seen as very desirable, but either not quite right or there were no vacancies. On 24 May Duncan-Jones, the secretary of the Birmingham AAC, wrote to Walter Adams, General Secretary of SPSL:

Cramp [Professor of Electrical Engineering at Birmingham University] was very much impressed...so much so that I had the impression he rather wished he could offer him a post...Saraga's work is not only out of the ordinary but deals with subjects likely to appeal a good deal to such firms as wireless manufacturers or makers of telephones...I rather understated Cramp's opinion in writing to Saraga, as I didn't want to raise fruitless hopes. But I had the impression in conversation with Cramp that Saraga was exactly the sort of man that Cramp would have liked when we actually took on O...

By this time Wolja had been in England for 17 days; his visa was due to expire on 7 June. Without the Home Office file I do not know how it was extended. Writing to him from Berlin on 7 June, Lotte asked: 'Do you still not know anything about your extension?' In 2016 World Jewish Relief digitized their records and I was able to request copies of papers concerning my parents. They include an entry on 14 June 1938: 'H.O. extension until 7/8/38 – To submit future plans'.[24] But there is no information about any further extensions.

The next letter, from my own collection of papers, is a hand written note from Bragg at the Royal Institution, written on 21 June 1938. 'Dear Dr Saraga, Will you lunch with me here on Friday June 23, if you have no other engagement? At one o'clock.'

The industrial research contacts seemed to be most promising. Many of them networked further on Wolja's behalf, using an interesting range of arguments to encourage someone to take him on. Writing to Montgomery at STC on 9 July 1938, Starr of Marconi emphasized not only how good Wolja would be, but also how cheap.

> ...in the matters of salary he is entirely in your hands. Although, naturally, he would like a salary commensurable with his age and qualifications (he is 29), say about £350, he would be quite willing to start at £208 like an ordinary graduate in order to prove his worth...I think that the Home Office and the Ministry of Labour would cause no obstruction, especially in view of his unusual qualifications and the fact that his Jewish origin would not cause him to be connected with any pre-German political movement to the detriment of his work. From the point of view of the S.T.C. this is not an opportunity to miss, as English talent of the same kind would cost very much more to employ. Prof. Mott of Bristol...put the matter very briefly thus: 'He is very cheap at the price.'

This argument was not made behind Wolja's back. This letter, found amongst our own papers, was clearly a letter of introduction that Wolja had solicited.

A Professing Jew

By mid-July Wolja had passed the test – he had found a scientist (Dr. Lowery, principal of the South -West Essex Technical College) who would like to work with him, making him eligible to ask for financial help from the Society. This information was included in a letter of introduction, dated 14 July 1938, from Stanley Levy to Professor Charles S. Gibson FRS, Chair of SPSL's allocations Committee,

> I should be very grateful if you would see Dr. Saraga for a few minutes and indicate to him if there is any possibility that he might obtain a grant. I know how keenly you feel about the present dreadful position of Jewish scientists in Germany, and that is my excuse for troubling you – I am certain that Dr. Saraga would be a very valuable worker in this country if we could find a niche for him.

On this occasion it was Wolja's own qualities and his scientific potential that recommended him and the possible helper was appealed to because of his known concerns for Jewish scientists, not out of respect for a Nobel Prize winner. But I believe that this recommendation came from a friend of a friend, as his name appears in Wolja's address book, next to entries for their friends the Emanuels.

Wolja sent this letter to Professor Gibson on July 20, who forwarded it on 23 July to the new general secretary of SPSL, David Cleghorn Thomson:

> Here is a case for you! It is explained by the letter (enclosed) from Dr S.I. Levy – a barrister and scientist who formerly worked with me and a very good fellow.
>
> If Saraga whom I was telling to come and see you or Miss Simpson or both is, as I suspect, a professing Jew and if he is scientifically worth supporting, a combined grant from the Jewish Professional Committee and the S.P.S.L. might be achieved. I've told Saraga to see Makower before coming to Gordon Square. Levy wouldn't recommend him if he was not good and Saraga has already fulfilled one requirement of having obtained a place to carry on his work.

David Cleghorn Thomson replied the same day saying he already had a 'fair amount of correspondence concerning' Wolja and was awaiting a visit from him.[25]

I was curious about the significance of describing Wolja as 'a professing Jew'. On the SPSL questionnaire Wolja had described himself as *Liberal jüdisch*, translated on the form as 'Jewish reformed'. Wolja was always a secular Jew, but the only other choices on the form were *Orthodox jüdisch*, translated as Jewish Orthodox or *Andere Religionen*, translated as 'Other'.[26]

There are no papers in either collection telling me what happened next, but a letter to Lotte of 9 August 1938 shows that Wolja found it all very difficult: 'I am beginning to get sick and tired of the asking and applying for jobs.' There is also no further mention of Dr. Lowery, or of the South-West Essex Technical College. Wolja was employed to carry out one month's research by the British Electrical & Allied Industries Research Association and by December 1938 he had been offered a job by the radio company, Murphy, at a salary of £4 per week, to be revised after six months. Although he had Home Office permission to look for work, he needed their approval for this particular job. This had to be obtained by SPSL who wrote to the Home Office on 7 December 1938. Before a reply was received, the situation had changed; in January 1939 Wolja was offered a job by the Telephone Manufacturing Company (TMC) who had been advertising 'for some months for a British person'. The salary was nearly double that offered by Murphy. First Makower and then SPSL had to support the change. SPSL applied for Home Office approval on 4 February 1939:

> The Murphy Radio Company have released Dr. Saraga from his engagement and I understand Woburn House is supporting the new application to which I would also like to add the support of this Society.
>
> I understand that the firm has advertised for some months for a British candidate without success, and that it is work for which Dr Saraga is specially qualified by his previous experience. It does appear that there is a real shortage of research workers in this field, and I sincerely hope that it will be possible for the Home Office to grant Dr. Saraga permission to take this work.[27]

The Home Office permission and Wolja's passport were sent on 13 February to the Professional Committee, with a copy to SPSL. He was still only given a temporary visa. An endorsement was added to his passport: 'The grant of leave to land is hereby varied so as to require departure from the United Kingdom not later than 11th **August 1939**'.

I have included the detail of these negotiations because they offer insights into the way in which the individuals and various committees and organizations helping refugees operated in relation to one another and crucially in relation to the Home Office, themes to which I shall return.

I have now reached very familiar, comfortable territory in my reconstruction of Wolja's story. Wolja worked for the Telephone Manufacturing Company (TMC) during the first part of my childhood. It was very much part of our lives. His colleagues all called him 'Doc', either because he was the only one with a PhD and/or because they could not pronounce his first name. We used to go every year to the Christmas party for children. My sense of comfort is combined with other contradictory feelings: frustration that I can't talk to Wolja and fill in the gaps, anger that following all his difficulties in Germany, Wolja had to have the additional stress of a one month deadline and be so dependent upon the goodwill of a range of English establishment figures who must have seemed very alien to him; sadness that comes from identifying with him, imagining his feelings of powerlessness in the dependence upon others and recognising how easily it could have all gone wrong; admiration for his stamina and capacity to make use of the networks; and finally guilt that I did not know any of this, did not ask and was not always sympathetic to him.

Refugee Organizations

These were my emotional responses to the material in the archive. I also recognized that Wolja's personal story adds complexity to the general histories of German-Jewish refugees, many of which assume that those who did not leave until 1938 had not yet recognized the danger.[28] The papers in the archive show that from 1935, if not earlier, Wolja knew that as a Jewish scientist he had no future in Germany. There may have been many other people who, like Wolja, tried for several years to get out but found their way blocked at every turn.

Two aspects of Wolja's experiences aroused my curiosity: how did the refugee organizations in the UK operate at the day to day level both in relation to the refugees they were helping and in their dealings with the British state? And what role did German scientists play in supporting their Jewish colleagues? Was von Laue an exception?

The many different organizations helping Jewish refugees were collectively known as the 'committees', a term used by Lotte in her letter on 13 May 1938 one week after Wolja's departure, when she asked him: 'Are you managing on the money from the committees?'

The story of these committees is a complicated and controversial one; complicated because more and more organizations were formed, they frequently changed their names, developed new subgroups, and grew in size as both the problems for Jews in Germany and the numbers seeking to leave multiplied. The controversies concern the role of these committees in acting as an agency of the British state in its selection and control of those refugees who were allowed in.[29]

The two organizations most important for Wolja's story are the Jewish Refugees Committee (JRC) and the Academic Assistance Council (AAC). The JRC, formed in 1933,[30] helped to rescue and support thousands of men, women and children. In January 1938 it changed its name to the 'German Jewish Aid Committee' to avoid the assumption that German Jews would remain 'refugees' forever, but two years later, during the war, it reverted to its original name in order to avoid the use of 'German'. Money for the work of the JRC and its sub-committees came from The Central British Fund for German Jewry, and from the beginning assurances were offered by Jewish organizations to the Home Office, that no refugees allowed in would be a charge on public funds.[31] This idea, accepted by both the Anglo-Jewish community and by the British State, that the 'Jews should look after their own' is underpinned by a particular notion of ethnic belonging and diasporic identity. Wolja recognized the importance of this when he emphasized in his letters to Lotte in Germany that she must make sure she has a document proving she is Jewish.

By 1939 the many different organizations and committees were co-ordinated through the Central Council for Jewish Refugees and centralized in the Palace Hotel in Bloomsbury Street W1, known as 'Bloomsbury House', a name that was to occur very often in Lotte's letters to Wolja when he was interned.

Alfred Makower, the man who played a crucial role in decisions about Wolja, was the second chairman of the 'Jewish Academic Committee', a sub-committee of the JRC set up to help people of academic and professional distinction. In early 1934 it changed its name to the Professional Committee, because of the confusion and overlap with the Academic Assistance Council. Bentwich describes Makower as 'not an academic, but an applied scientist, who, till his death in 1939, rendered outstanding service by his many contacts with industry'.[32] He worked closely with the AAC often providing maintenance of some refugees in academic posts.

The Academic Assistance Council, which became the Society for the Protection of Science and Learning (SPSL) in 1936, was different from the other committees. Set up in 1933 by William Beveridge, Director of the London School of Economics (LSE), to rescue eminent scholars who had lost their jobs in Nazi Germany, it did not focus specifically on Jewish scholars; many non-Jewish scholars were also expelled from the universities on political grounds, or they resigned in solidarity with their Jewish colleagues.

Beveridge's committee of eminent British scholars decided to remain completely non-political, to make no negative comments about the Nazi regime and not to have any Jewish members on the Council. In part they argued this was to protect their contacts in Germany and we had a glimpse of this concern from William Deedes' letter to the AAC.

Beveridge explains the relationship between the AAC and the Professional Committee: 'We were to limit our activity to helping refugees who desired and were fitted for an academic career. They were to limit themselves to persons fitted to pursue a professional career or studies of a peculiarly Jewish interest...'[33]

All the organizations had to work within the constraints of British policy. In 1938, the year in which Wolja and Lotte managed to leave Germany, only people with good economic prospects or who had permits to do domestic work could get into the UK and they were admitted temporarily on the assumption that they would emigrate further. Only the most eminent scientists were allowed to remain permanently.[34] It is in this context that Wolja's one month visa can be understood.

Both the Jewish Refugees Committee and AAC assisted the Home Office in the selection, co-ordination and control of the refugees and some writers have argued that selection was as important as rescue.[35] Makower's comments on Wolja and his letter to him reflect these processes of selection – a hard headed approach of matching people to criteria.

Wolja clearly existed on the dividing line between the areas of concern of the AAC and the Professional Committee. His non-eminent status and lack of an academic post in Germany put him outside the main focus of AAC/SPSL. In addition his applied interests characterized him as an engineer, more suitable for industry than university, although what was seen as his relative lack of practical experience – a direct result of his expulsion as a Jew from the Heinrich Hertz Institute – was held against him. On the other hand the recommendation from von Laue and the endorsements of his work by other established scientists might have suggested that he fitted into the category of 'refugees who desired and were fitted for an academic career'. And his name is included in a 1937 list of displaced scholars produced for universities by the *Notgemeinschaft*.[36]

Wolja was registered with SPSL, who corresponded with him and did all the day to day networking on his behalf, but it was the Jewish Professional Committee and Makower who made the crucial recommendations about him to the Home Office. When granting permission for Wolja to take the job with TMC, his passport was not returned directly to him, but to the Professional Committee. For a long time, the only evidence of financial assistance to Wolja that I could find was in the records of the Professional

Committee,[37] which made me wonder whether this explains Gibson's reference to Wolja as a 'professing Jew', since the Professional Committee, unlike SPSL, only supported Jewish refugees. Later I discovered that from 9 May 1938, two days after he arrived in London, Wolja received £2 a week from the German Jewish Aid Committee. At the end of May he received free luncheon for a month. In July 1938 his monthly payment was reduced first to 35/- and later to 30/-. Occasionally he also received small sums for travel.[38]

By 1939 the numbers of refugees coming in was so great that the Committees could no longer manage financially. The Government did then provide money, but insisted that this still be administered through the Committees. They wished to encourage re-emigration and did not want charitable giving to decline. It was also important that the committees should remain for the refugees a personal point of both contact and control.[39]

Max von Laue and German Science in the 1930s

The letters from Deedes and Bragg about Wolja to the AAC and the subsequent networking on his behalf show how significant it was for him to have had a recommendation from someone as eminent as von Laue. Was von Laue unusual in his sympathy and activity on behalf of persecuted scientists?

The literature on German Science in the 1930s[40] emphasizes the major contribution of Jewish scientists to innovation and research in the pre-Nazi period. This outraged the Nazis for whom Jews were a source of racial pollution, which affected what became known as 'Jewish science'. Large numbers of non-Jewish scientists, including the Dean who blocked Wolja's doctorate promotion, were willing to go along with not only expelling Jews from the universities but also outlawing so-called Jewish ideas, like those of Einstein. Hitler is quoted as saying 'If the dismissal of Jewish scientists means the annihilation of contemporary German science, we shall do without science for a few years.'[41]

Von Laue is generally seen as an exception. For Fritz Stern: 'In his courage and decency,...[he] stood out in many ways; it was said of him that he never left his home without carrying two brief cases – so as not to have to give the Hitler salute. Apocryphal, perhaps, but telling.'[42] Alan Beyerchen argues that '...there were a few scientists who rejected even a show of cooperation' with the Nazis. 'Foremost among these were...Otto Hahn and Max von Laue...'[43]

Others have been more measured in their assessment of von Laue. Mark Walker suggests that 'even von Laue had to make concessions to

National Socialism...The point here is not to accuse von Laue of being a 'Nazi', rather to illustrate how difficult it was for anyone or any scientist to avoid some sort of submission to or collaboration with National Socialism.'[44] Lisa Meitner, a Jewish physicist, was helped by von Laue and another physicist Otto Hahn, to stay in Nazi Germany until 1938 and then to flee to Sweden. After the war she condemned herself for staying and criticized her friends and colleagues, including von Laue. In a letter to Otto Hahn, she wrote: 'You all worked for Nazi Germany. And you tried to offer only a passive resistance. Certainly, to buy off your conscience you helped here and there a persecuted person, but millions of innocent human beings were allowed to be murdered without any kind of protest being uttered.'[45]

In his memoir Laue describes how, in 1937, he sent his only son to the USA, so that he would not have to fight for Hitler.

> My urgent sense of justice was particularly violated by the lawless capriciousness of National Socialism and my pride as a scholar was hit hard by Nazi interference in the freedom of science and of the universities...As much as I could, I assisted those directly affected, for instance by warning them in time, especially those colleagues who had lost their positions...There were a few rare cases of colleagues who were able, of course not solely because of my assistance, to survive in Germany through that entire unfortunate period. Much more frequently I smoothed the way for those who emigrated by sending advance reports to the foreign aid organizations about their personalities, their domestic circumstances, their particular abilities and desires. Since the postal censor confiscated such reports, we found safer ways of sending them across the border.[46]

Max von Laue certainly 'smoothed the way' for Wolja and his concern to hand the papers to Deedes in person can be understood in this context.

Genteel Paternalism

The correspondence concerning Wolja offers a glimpse behind the scenes of the way in which the networks of eminent people in Germany and in the UK operated – of their system of shared values, codes of behaviour and discourses of communication. Helping was based on mutual personal respect between people of high status. Jeremy Seabrook describes it as 'an idea of *noblesse oblige* [that] had not yet quite faded; much could be achieved by a word in the appropriate ear'.[47]

Those who lent their support to the AAC all knew each other. Many had attended the same schools and universities. A word in the right place, the lifting of a telephone, a friendly note could galvanize like-minded others into action. Their friendships, family relationships and a common experience ensured they would be heard. It was no doubt, patrician and elitist; but it was effective. One can admire their energy and commitment, without necessarily approving of the hierarchies of privilege, to which, in part, they owed their capacity to get things done.[48]

A phrase used by Joe Bord: '(T)he genteel flavour of paternalist behaviour'[49] describes the style and tone of many of the letters concerning Wolja. In his letter to SPSL William Bragg says that he has just spoken to Wolja 'for a few minutes' and Stanley Levy asks Professor Gibson if he would see Wolja 'for a few minutes'. Wolja himself learned this discourse when he wrote to Professor Gibson, also asking if he would be kind enough to allow him to come and see him 'for a few minutes'. It would seem to be a way of not making too many demands. While recommendations are based on this network of relationships, the person being helped must also conform – by being likeable, enthusiastic and worthy of help.

In contrast to the genteel paternalism of the elite, who had the power and influence to make things happen, Wolja's personal file shows the care taken by the individual members of staff with whom he was in day to day contact. The names that appear again and again are all women – Esther (Tess) Simpson, Nancy Searle and Ilse Ursell of SPSL and Ruth Fellner of the Jewish Refugee Committee. They all communicated with the refugees in a very personal way, usually replying to letters on the day they were received.

Esther Simpson is the person most associated with SPSL, 'both the public persona of the Society and the champion of this distinctive group of highly sophisticated refugee scholars'.[50] Seabrook suggests that she became an 'idealized figure' who embodied many of the values of the time – altruism and duty and a devotion to welfare, associated in particular with women shaped by the events of the First World War. Many of her standards were, he suggests 'conventionally those of the upwardly mobile', adding: 'If her admiration for her protégés would now be considered elitist, at the time this would scarcely have been thought worthy of comment.'[51]

In addition to all her official work , advising and supporting refugees in their formal dealings with the Home Office, liaising with other organizations on their behalf and preparing documents for the Executive Committee, she showed a personal interest in and friendship to every single refugee with whom she had contact, networking widely on their behalf.[52] In 1940, following the internment of many refugees, she liaised with them in the camps and also with the Home Office and the Royal Society, who were preparing cases for early release on the grounds of the refugee's potential contribution to science and learning. Examples of all these activities appear in Wolja's file, as does evidence of her expectations of gratitude from refugees and an emphasis on their contribution. To imagine this multiplied by the number of refugees seeking her help is truly amazing. I can see how easy it would be for me too to idealize her.

Esther Simpson retired in 1978 at the age of 75, but remained involved with SPSL as an Honorary Consultant and a regular member of the Council. In an interview with Katharina Scherke in April 1995, when she was nearly 92, she spoke of 'my immigrants' and about the personal satisfaction she obtained from her work and how much it enriched her life. 'You see, you got quite a lot of satisfaction when you dealt with them, when they first came and then find that they found their niche, and were happily settled, and their families doing well, their children at school happy, that's satisfaction.'[53]

After Wolja's death in 1980 Esther Simpson wrote to Lotte in response to a notice we had put into the *Times* newspaper: 'I have such warm recollections of him and was always proud of his achievements and the contribution he made to the intellectual life of this country.' I remember Lotte receiving this letter, but not that Lotte had replied, telling her about Peter and me. In a subsequent letter, Esther Simpson wrote: 'My work for academic refugees gave a meaning to my life and I have been particularly interested in the next generation and their contribution to the cultural life of our society.' She invited Lotte, Peter and me to visit her. She lived near me in North London and I feel a great regret that I did not do this. But I have no memory of this second letter and at that time her significance would not have been apparent to me.

Lotte died on 14 December 1984. I did not remember that I had kept all the condolence letters and the many Christmas cards that Lotte had received that year, nor that I had used these cards to tell a further group of people, who I did not know personally, about Lotte's death. Amongst them I found a Christmas card from Esther Simpson sent on 18 December. On 25 January 1985 she wrote to me.

> I am very sad to have the news in your letter of January 19, which has reached me only today. Your mother wrote to me every Christmas, giving me news of yourself and Peter – she was very proud of you both. I remember your father very well; he was once a grantee of my Society (Society for the Protection of Science and Learning) and we were very proud of the career he made for himself. I esteemed him also as a

person, so friendly, so appreciative. I felt so deeply for you all when he died, and was grateful that your mother had you and Peter. You will miss her, but will be grateful that her suffering came to an end.

I hope that Peter and his David and Rebecca, and his wife, are flourishing. I expect he is still with Philips. In recent months I have thought of you, as conditions in the Northern Poly won't have been easy. My news comes only from the press; it would appear that some temporary solution has been found by the new head. I do hope the Poly will be able to continue its excellent work without further upheavals.

With my best wishes to you all

Esther Simpson

At the time of Lotte's death I was working at the Polytechnic of North London and involved in the events surrounding a student protest about the presence of a student who was a member of the National Front. In her letters to Lotte and to me she emphasizes again Wolja's achievements and contribution and how 'appreciative' he was. At the same time I have direct experience of Esther Simpson's warmth and personal interest in every individual.

***

'The records of the Academic Assistance Council/Society for the Protection of Science and Learning for the years 1933 to 1945 contain the names of 2,541 refugees scholars; in 1946, only 600 were recorded as remaining in Britain.'[54] Many of the more established academic scientists emigrated later to the USA. By contrast, some refugee scientists were able to find jobs in British industry. Esther Simpson confirmed this in her interview with Scherke: 'There were several people who had excellent scientific degrees and knowledge but there simply wasn't room in the universities, but there would be room in industry, and they often did materially far better than those who went into universities because they were better paid.'[55] Based on research in the SPSL files, Paul Hoch names Wolja Saraga (Telephone Manufacturing Company) as one of the refugee physicists hired by industry.[56]

Notes

1. Bodleian archive reference B338/307. The items from the archive to be cited come from two different shelf references: 338/8 and 440.
2. The organization changed its name from the Academic Assistance Council (AAC) to the Society for the Protection of Science and Learning (SPSL) in 1936, although some of the key personnel continued to call it the AAC after the change of name.

3. S. R. Weart and G. Weiss Szilard (eds), *Leo Szilard, His Version of the Facts* (Cambridge, MA: MIT Press, 1978), p.14.

4. B338/300; as in previous chapters, all translations are mine.

5. S. Friedländer, *Nazi Germany and the Jews. The Years of Persecution 1933–39* (London: Weidenfeld & Nicolson, 1997), pp.27, 30-31.

6. B338/302.

7. B338/290-293.

8. In 1936 Hans Salinger was forced to leave the Heinrich Hertz Institute as a 'non-Aryan'. P. Noll, 'Nachrichtentechnik an der TH/ TU Berlin – Geschichte, Stand und Ausblick.'(Version 21.06.2001) http://www.nue.tuberlin.de/fileadmin/fg97/Ueber_uns/ Geschichte/Dokumente/th_nachr.pdf. (Accessed 7 August 2017).

9. J. Cornwell, *Hitler's Scientists: Science, War and the Devil's Pact* (London: Penguin, 2004), p 199.

10. B338/303.

11. D. Zimmerman, 'The Society for the Protection of Science and Learning and the Politicization of British Science in the 1930s', *Minerva* 44 (2006), pp.25–45.

12. B338/319.

13. N. Bentwich, 'Forty Years' Friendship' in E. Elath, N. Bentwich and D. May (eds), *Memories of Sir Wyndham Deedes* (London: Victor Gollancz Ltd, 1958), p. 75.

14. B338/304, B338/306

15. Albert Einstein Archives [AEA] Hebrew University, Jerusalem, Israel. http://www.alberteinstein.info. (Accessed 22 August 2018). My thanks to Tony Davies for alerting me to this archive.

16. See Obituary for Oscar Fehr, *British Medical Journal* (12 September 1959), p. 438.

17. B338/278.

18. A letter in our archive in response to Wolja's letter of 14 March, which does not appear in either archive.

19. B338/279.

20. B338/305. By this time it was called the SPSL, but Bragg calls it the AAC in his letter.

21. B338/309.

22. B338/310.

23. B338/270.

24. Papers received from World Jewish Relief, formerly Central British Fund for German Jewry: http://www.worldjewishrelief.org/archives. (Accessed 22 August 2018).

25. B338/321.

26. B338/271.

27. B440/309.

28. See for example A. Grenville, *Jewish Refugees from Germany and Austria in Britain 1933-1970* (London and Portland, OR: Vallentine Mitchell, 2010), p. 2.

29. For further information, see for example: N. Bentwich, *They Found Refuge* (London: The Cresset Press, 1956); A. Z. Gottlieb, *Men of Vision, Anglo-Jewry's Aid to Victims of the Nazi Regime 1933-1945* (London: Weidenfeld & Nicolson, 1998); L. London, *Whitehall and the Jews 1933-1948* (Cambridge, Cambridge University Press, 2000); Jeremy Seabrook, *The Refuge and the Fortress. Britain and the Persecuted 1933-2013* (London: Palgrave Macmillan, 2013).

30. See Gottlieb, *Men of Vision*, p.7.

31. See Bentwich, *They Found Refuge*, p.16.

32. Ibid., p. 18.

33. Lord Beveridge, *A Defence of Free Learning* (London: Oxford University Press, 1959), p.19.

34. See London, *Whitehall and the* Jews, p.49.
35. See T. Kushner, 'Clubland, cricket tests and alien internment, 1939-40', in D. Cesarani and T. Kushner (eds), *The Internment of Aliens in Twentieth Century Britain* (London: Frank Cass, 1993), p.86; B. Williams, *Jews and other Foreigners, Manchester and the Rescue of the Victims of European Fascism 1933-1940* (Manchester: Manchester University Press, 2011), p.36.
36. Notgemeinschaft Deutscher Wissenschaftler im Ausland, *Supplementary List of Displaced German Scholars*, 1937, p.14.
37. Papers available at the Wiener Library.
38. Papers received from World Jewish Relief.
39. J. Bord, 'Voluntarism and Conservative Pluralism: Reconsidering Jewish Refugee Assistance on the British Home Front (1939-44)', *Contemporary British History*, 16, no.4 (2002) 17-50, p.23; London, *Whitehall and the* Jews, pp.70-71; B. Wasserstein, *Britain and the Jews of Europe, 1939-1945*, second edition (Leicester: Leicester University Press, 1999), pp.74-75.
40. See, for example, M. Walker, *Nazi Science, Myth, Truth, and the German Atomic Bomb* (Cambridge, MA: Perseus Publishing, 1995); Cornwell, *Hitler's Scientists*; A.D. Beyerchen, *Scientists under Hitler. Politics and the Physics Community in the Third Reich* (New Haven, CT and London: Yale University Press, 1977).
41. N. Bentwich, *The Rescue and Achievement of Refugee Scholars* (The Hague: M. Nijhoff, 1953), p.2.
42. F. Stern, *Dreams and Delusions. The Drama of German History* (New Haven, CT: Yale University Press, 1987), p.172.
43. See Beyerchen, *Scientists under Hitler*, p.64.
44. See Walker, *Nazi Science*, pp.75-76.
45. See Cornwell, *Hitler's Scientists*, p.411.
46. M. von Laue, 'My development as a physicist' in P.P. Ewald (ed.), *Fifty Years of X-Ray Diffraction* (Boston MA: Springer,1962), p.298.
47. J. Seabrook, *The Refuge and the Fortress. Britain and the Flight from Tyranny* (Basingstoke: Palgrave Macmillan, 2009), p.23.
48. Ibid., p. 27.
49. See Bord, 'Voluntarism and Conservative Pluralism', p.39.
50. D. Simon, 'Holocaust refugee ethnographies of escape, education, internment and careers', *Contemporary Social Science*, 7, 1, (2002), p. 24.
51. See Seabrook, *The Refuge and the Fortress*, pp. 95-96.
52. K.Scherke, 'Esther Simpson und die Aktivitäten der SPSL', in J. M. Ritchie (ed.), *German Speaking Exiles in Great Britain* (Amsterdam: Rodopi, 2001), pp. 121-130.
53. See Scherke, 'Esther Simpson', p.128.
54. B. Charmian, 'Science in Exile: Imperial College and the Refugees from Nazism - A Case Study', *Leo Baeck Institute Yearbook*, 51, (2006), pp.133-151, p.150.
55. See Scherke, 'Esther Simpson', p.123.
56. P. Hoch, 'The Reception of Central European Refugee Physicists of the 1930s: U.S.S.R., U.K., U.S.A.', *Annals of Science*, 40 (1983), pp. 217-246, p.226.

4

'Send No More Food. Write To Me.'

Onchan I.O.M.
September/ 2nd
1940

Popular University
Academic Seminar
Technical Institute
Jewish Seminar
P.U. Library
Religious Institutions

Our great friend Dr. Saraga
has shown to 1500 Internees on their way
from London via Kempton Park & Bury
to Onchan I.O.M. in a time of great men≈
tal strain / how one man with courage
and initiative can help his fellowman.
By giving his Knowledge he enabled
us to carry our fate in a dignified ~
way and to make internment even a
human inspiration to everyone of us.

Popular University
of
Onchan I.O.M. Internment Camp

This piece of paper, found folded into four at the back of a drawer, contributed to our feelings that we had underestimated what our parents had gone through before we were born. It wasn't that we didn't know about Wolja's internment; on the contrary it was something he did speak about. A story often told to visitors centred on his sense of injustice that he had been categorized by the British as 'German' and an 'enemy alien', despite the fact that the Nazis had revoked his German nationality, making him stateless. At the tribunal that he had to attend after the outbreak of war, Wolja was asked whether he understood how radar worked; when he said 'yes', the judge assumed that he

Onchan I.o.M.
September/2nd
1940

Popular University
Academic Seminar
Technical Institute
Jewish Seminar
P.U. Library
Religions Institutions

Our great friend Dr. Saraga
has shown to 1500 Internees on their way
from London via Kempton Park & Bury
to Onchan I.o.M. in a time of great mental strain, how one man with courage
and initiative can help his fellowman.
By giving his knowledge he enabled
us to carry our fate in a dignified
way and to make internment even a
human inspiration to everyone of us.

Popular University
of
Onchan I.o.M. Internment Camp

Certificate given to Wolja when he was released from Onchan internment camp.

could potentially send messages to the enemy and put him into category B, which led to him being interned seven months later. When Lotte attended a later tribunal and was classified as C, she raised the issue of Wolja's B status; the judge offered to change it if Wolja was present. But he was at work and refused permission to return another day. The punch-line of the story came with Wolja's eventual re-classification as a 'friendly enemy alien' – a term we all laughed at, as something only the British could dream up.

We also knew that Wolja had made some good friends and given lectures at the 'camp university'. But this certificate told us more; it suggested that he had displayed a particular sort of courage. We felt very proud and inspired by it. It was so beautifully presented, that I ironed it flat and had it framed. At various times since then Peter and I have each had it on the wall to support us through difficult times in our personal lives.

Several books, written at different times and in different contexts, helped me to contextualize Wolja's story: a book by Ronald Stent, himself an internee, written in 1980; a Penguin Special by François Lafitte, written in 1940, which I found amongst Wolja's books, and a 1993 edited collection by David Cesarani and Tony Kushner, that puts the 1940s experience of internment into the historical context of the twentieth century and British policy in relation to aliens.[1]

Overnight from 2 to 3 September 1939 an estimated 75,000 men, women and children, considered to be of German nationality, of whom 60,000 were, in Nazi terminology, 'non-Aryans', were classified as enemy aliens.[2] The onus was on the alien to prove that she or he should be exempt from internment. No prejudicial evidence was required.

People were placed into one of three categories – A, B or C – according to criteria of security, reliability and loyalty to the Allied cause. People in A were to be arrested and interned immediately, B was for people whose loyalty and reliability were not absolutely certain, who should therefore be kept under some sort of supervision, and people in C were free from restrictions other than those that also applied to foreigners in peace time. Within the 'C' category a further distinction was made between non-refugees and refugees from Nazi oppression.[3] It was the latter group who constituted the 'friendly enemy aliens' of Wolja's story.[4]

In December 2008 I had a conversation with one of the speakers at the 75th anniversary conference of CARA, the Campaign for At-Risk Academics, the latest incarnation of SPSL.[5] He told me that my family story could not be correct, as radar wasn't known in 1939, or certainly not called radar. I was shocked; I had told this story so often, I felt that it had to be true. If the speaker was right, does it invalidate my memory or did I just get a detail wrong? Did Wolja himself remember his experience inaccurately or in later telling did he use the term 'radar', because this was now the common terminology?

Reluctant to believe him, I checked various sources. Perhaps we were both right: 'In 1940, the U.S. Navy created the acronym *Radar* which comes from "radio detection and ranging"'. However the techniques of radar had been around for many years before the Second World War and it was patented in 1935.[6] A.J.P. Taylor describes a further connection between refugees and radar which fits with Wolja's story:

> The suspicion of refugees had one strange result. When the war started, most British physicists were put on to radar, which was regarded as the most urgent and also the most confidential task. Refugee scientists were excluded from this work and were thus free to continue their research in nuclear physics, which was not expected to have any practical application to the war. They discovered how to control a nuclear explosion – the vital step towards the atomic bomb. When the refugee scientists made this discovery, they were still forbidden to possess bicycles and had to obtain special permission from the local police when they went to London in order to report their discovery to the government's scientific advisers.[7]

This experience raised questions about memory, evidence and truth in relation to my presentation of my parent's story. Stent's book, published in 1980,

> ...is partly based on so many ex-internees' recollections of events which occurred almost forty years ago, not all the details, particularly the impressionistic ones, may be always entirely accurate. I have tried my best to obtain corroboration but it has not always been possible. But I hope that the flavour of the atmosphere in the various camps is right and that the overall picture is accurate.[8]

By contrast, I am not remembering the events themselves, but stories about those events, stories that will have changed as they were repeated many times in different contexts by each of my parents and later by me. The crucial question for me was – 'does it matter whether the details are accurate?' What I have remembered very clearly is the emotional atmosphere of the story, in particular Wolja's sense of injustice which suffuses the correspondence, a sense shared by other internees. The Nobel Prize winner, Max Perutz, interned on the Isle of Man and later deported to Canada, wrote: 'To be arrested, interned and deported as an enemy alien by the English, whom I had regarded as my friends, made me more bitter than to have lost freedom itself. Having first been rejected as a Jew by my native Austria, which I loved, I now found myself rejected as a German by my adopted country.'[9]

An Enemy Alien

The 'internment papers' consist of fifty two letters, four postcards and seventeen telegrams, written in English, between 16 May and 3 September 1940. Both sides of this correspondence have survived.

Lotte and Wolja's understanding of the tribunal decision, expressed in their letters, illustrates the way that category 'B' was premised on the idea that foreigners are unreliable and in need of surveillance. On 15 June Lotte told Dr Starr

> In spite of his very good recommendations he was put in category 'B' because the judge was of the opinion that as the restrictions did not interfere with his work it was not necessary to exempt him...He is extremely unlucky as, in fact, he came over to this country as a stateless person. Unfortunately Bow-Street Police entered in his Certificate of Registration 'German' as nationality saying that they do not use the designation of 'stateless'.

Had Wolja's statelessness been recognized, he would not have been subject to any of the restrictions for aliens, including appearing before a tribunal. On 12 August Wolja explained to Lotte '...at Tribunal judge said he did not give me "C" as I was able to do work of national importance with B, but did not mean to classify me as less reliable.' This fits with Stent's suggestion that 'B' was a compromise category, introduced to allow some discretion to tribunal chairmen, some of whom '...went so far as to create a sort of sub-category of their own devising which, while classing a refugee as a victim of Nazi oppression, also burdened him with the surveillance attaching to those who fell within the "dubious" B category.'[10]

Correspondence in the SPSL archive shows that Wolja attended a tribunal in Acton on 6 October 1939.[11] Lotte attended in Bromley on 13 November. At the outbreak of war, Lotte and Wolja were living in Orpington. Without the Home Office file it is hard to know how Wolja ended up in Acton. Wolja's early appearance at a tribunal may also have contributed to the outcome. Seventy per cent of the B classifications occurred in the first three weeks and the tribunals in Greater London produced 84.1% of the 'B' classifications.[12] As a result of the many protests, a later Home Office circular implemented a change in policy to discourage the use of category B but, in line with Lotte's experience, this was not applied retrospectively to those already classified as 'B'.

On 7 November 1939 Wolja had written to Miss Searle at SPSL. He wanted to appeal against the tribunal decision 'chiefly as a question of principle, since I don't want and don't think I deserve it, still to be considered as a sort of enemy alien...' He was concerned that the restrictions placed on him 'would be a great hindrance in case I lose my present post and have to apply for a new one, and perhaps on other occasions as well.' This letter shows that he understood the importance of expressing loyalty to the allied cause, something he believed could be assessed rationally and tested against evidence.

> In this war between democratic England and Nazi Germany I am wholeheartedly on the English side as a natural consequence of my strong personal and professional conviction that a triumph of Hitler would be disastrous for civilization and progress. Naturally this conviction is strengthened by my personal experience in Nazi Germany which, by being stateless, I was not able to leave before 1938 and I am very grateful to this country which has given me an opportunity to begin a new life...From what I have read in the newspapers I have the impression that other Tribunals did not consider the exemption from the restrictions as a practical question of comfort or hardship but rather a sort of declaration of confidence and so it is considered by many people in this country.

He did not hear from the Home Office. On 30 April 1940 he wrote to Nancy Searle again. The question of his nationality had suddenly become of 'vital importance'.

> I have been told, in the firm where I am working by my chief that the War Office is objecting against the continuation of employment of another German refugee, head of a production department in our Company. I have been told this in strictest confidence but I think I am entitled to mention it to you...At the moment my case is not considered by the War Office and it is a little different since I am not doing production but laboratory work. I am afraid, however, that it may come under consideration at any moment, and in the case of a negative decision I should certainly not be able to find any other opening in my special field for the duration of the war.

Nine days later, on 9 May, his fears materialized. He told Nancy Searle:

...I had to stop working in the Telephone Manufacturing Company this morning by order of the War Office which does not allow any association of the Company with me until and unless I am exempted from all restrictions by the Tribunal. My chief told me that the Company regrets it very much and hopes that the interruption will be only a temporary one.'

Twenty-Four Lines

Internment started on Sunday 12 May 1940 with the rounding-up of all male Germans and Austrians aged between sixteen and sixty, living in the 'coastal belt', with mass internment of male 'B' aliens beginning on 15 and 16 May. This followed the Nazi invasion of Norway and Denmark in April and of France, Belgium, Luxembourg and the Netherlands on 10 May, triggered by fear of an invasion of Britain and widespread newspaper propaganda about 'fifth columns' being responsible for Hitler's success in Scandinavia.[13] Over 30,000 'enemy aliens...eventually found themselves behind barbed wire, incarcerated by their British friends, cheek by Jowl with their Nazi enemies.'[14] Internment of refugees was also justified as being for their own protection. 'The inflamed eye of the man in the street could not be expected to see them as other than German'.[15] Today similar associations are frequently made between refugees and extremism or terrorism.[16]

Wolja was arrested on 16 May 1940. He was able to send Lotte a postcard, written in pencil:

W. Saraga
My dear Lotte
I am very well,
Do not worry, everything
will be all right, I hope,
very soon. Write or go to all
Refugee Committees and to the friends of my parents, Many kisses Wolja

I have no idea whether Wolja expected his arrest, where or at what time it happened and whether he could pack a suitcase. I hoped that Lotte's first letter to him, written the next morning, would provide some clues, but it raised more questions:

Darling,
I am going this morning to the Police station to deliver your meat card. I hope they can forward this letter for me.

I was very pleased that Harrison could see you before you left St. Mary Cray. He and his wife were very nice and optimistic. He said he brought you some nuts but he could not throw them because you were not behind bars. I proceeded then to Mrs Sturge and paid a visit to the refugees in Lynwood Grove on the way. They told me that you certainly would have met Mr Salomon. Mrs Sturge could not say very much. I rang Mrs Peierls and she asked me to come to see her. I met Mrs Hiley there she is very nice. I had got into touch with Mr Flint, your chief, and he came to see me at Mrs Peierls place. He is of no doubt that the Tribunal will prove successful. He has made all possible applications, but he is doubtful about the possibility of speeding things up. He said I should always keep in touch with him also if I should leave Orpington.

This morning your postcard arrived. I was so glad…I am going to London today, see what I can do. I will speak to Rabinovitch too. I have written to the Society. It does not matter when you write too. There was a postcard of your parents yesterday afternoon. They are well but worried because they did not have any news from you for a fortnight. Are you going to write to them, or shall I do it from here? And shall I tell them what has happened?

I am well. It is rather strange to be without you in this house but there we are.

I kiss you, darling

I was very impressed by the quality of Lotte's English. I recognized only the occasional 'Germanism' such as her translation of 'wenn' as 'when' rather than 'if'.

These first two communications contained two themes that I found again and again during this correspondence: reassurance of each other through variations of the phrase 'I am well' and evidence of networking both with refugee organizations and with friends. Mr Harrison was Wolja's immediate boss, and St Mary Cray the place where he had worked until a week earlier. Despite the letter of 9 May, was he still working?

From the addresses and forwarding on Lotte's early letters and postcards I could trace Wolja's movements following his arrest. He was taken first to Chelsea Barracks, but by 23 May he had been moved to the Racecourse at Kempton Park. On 11 June, on the day on which it opened, he arrived at Onchan on the Isle of Man, via Warth Mills Camp and Liverpool Royal Arena Camp. Stent tells us that although Kempton Park 'became the main reception area for Southern England…no preparations had been made for these sudden influxes, nor could they have been made because it was all the result of such a hasty panic decision.' Nevertheless conditions at Kempton Park were 'bearable', by contrast with other camps which were put together at short notice, where conditions 'were at first unpleasant, and at Warth Mill downright scandalous.'[17] Onchan camp was the third camp to open. The men lived in boarding houses quite near the sea, from which the original owners had been turned out. There were between twenty and forty men to a house; they collected rations from the camp store and did their own cooking.[18] Onchan held 1,491 internees, including '121 artists and literary workers. 113 scientists and teachers, 68 lawyers, 67 graduate engineers, 38 physicians, 22 graduate chemical engineers, 19 clergymen and 12 dentists. At the other end of the social scale were 103 agricultural workers…1,230 (82%) were Jewish.'[19]

Communication between Lotte and Wolja was not straightforward. Letters took a long while to arrive and not always in the order in which they were written, especially during the early weeks as a result of all Wolja's moves. Some help for me comes from Wolja. When Lotte did not date her letter, Wolja wrote on it, for example 'post mark 22/7/40, received 4-8-40'. He also referred in his letters to one he had just received. At first I thought this was his usual pedantry, but later I recognized his feelings of powerlessness. These letters were his only link with Lotte and the outside world; perhaps he needed to take some control.

Following the first postcard Lotte did not hear from Wolja again for over three weeks until 6 June when she received a letter dated 27 May with an official postmark 4 June. By this time she had written to him five times. Wolja, arrested on 16 May, did not receive any communications at all from Lotte until 14 June, when two parcels arrived. The camp rules prohibited the inclusion of letters in parcels, so he had to wait another eight days until 22 June, five weeks after his arrest, for his first letter, the fifth one that Lotte had written. By 29 June he had received the previous four items (two postcards and two letters) sent between 17 and 24 May to Chelsea Barracks.

In his first letter, written from Kempton Park on 27 May, Wolja asked Lotte to send him some clothes: '…at once: a small suitcase with mackintosh, old grey jacket, grey trousers new, brown summer shoes, sport shorts and shoes, horn-rimmed and sunglasses with 3 cases.' This letter had an official notification attached to it – strict instructions in English and German on how to send consignments to internees. But on 7 June Lotte had to write to the Commandant at Kempton Park, apologising for forgetting to put her name and address as sender on the label. 'I am very sorry that this mistake happened and should be very grateful to you if the suitcase could be handed over to my husband.' She had remembered to include a list of contents. Only one item was written in German:

    1 jacket,
    1 pair of trousers,
    1 pair of shorts,
    2 pairs of white shorts,
    4 pairs of socks,
    1 pair of shoes,
    2 shirts,
    1 piece of soap,
    1 shaving stick,
    1 dental cream,
    1 pair of glasses,
    1 pair of sunglasses,
    1 box for glasses,
    1 mackintosh,
    1 box with sewing material,
    1 *Schuhanzieher* [shoe-horn]
    2 handkerchiefs.

Letters were also delayed by the process of censorship. Letters going out were censored through the individual camp; those coming in had to be addressed c/o Chief Postal Censor, Liverpool. Wolja's first letter was written on a special form with a label attached showing that it had been opened by the censor. On the front, he wrote: 'Written in English', which I realized was a deliberate strategy, to speed up their letters and to demonstrate their loyalty to Britain. These forms, made from special paper with a concealed layer of chalk that made the use of invisible ink impossible, were used for Prisoners of War. There was soon a shortage of forms, as the owner of the company that made them had himself been interned.[20] Wolja's first two and last nine letters were on forms, but in between he wrote on ordinary sheets of paper. Had they released the manufacturer or found a new one?

At first internees were not allowed to communicate at all with anyone outside the camps, but eventually they were allowed to write two letters per week, each a maximum of twenty-four lines. These restrictions were justified by the sheer number of letters, which was overwhelming the Censorship Office.[21] On 15 June Wolja wrote:

My beloved Lotte. Yesterday I received two parcels with everything mentioned in the lists of contents. Many thanks. Thus I received 1st message from you. I am so glad and ~~looking~~ waiting for a letter. You must do everything in order to be evacuated. It is a terrible thought for me that I am in a safety zone whereas you may be exposed to air-raids. Maybe, we obtain permission to have visitors. Could you afford the rail-way fare? In the small parcel your new address was given, thus this letter will reach you directly. I sent my 2nd letter to my parents, my 3rd one to the chief engineer of my firm, the last one to our friend Ulla Emanuel in Eastcote. By the way you are allowed to send me telegrams; if the answer is prepaid by you, I am allowed to answer by telegram. We are allowed to have our typewriters sent to us. I think, at the moment you need it much more. Please send me sport shorts, old grey trousers, dressing gown, keys of both suitcases, blue training's overall…You should not do domestic work, it would be bad for your health and nerves at present moment…How are my parents, how is your mother? Your sister? My father's birthday is on 30th June. Much love, thousand kisses, Write to Wolja.

Wolja's 'twenty four line' letter to Lotte, 27 June 1940.

It must have been very hard to cover everything in exactly twenty four lines
– hence the very succinct, almost telegraphic style of the letter and the way
in which his writing, initially very small, got bigger as he continued then
smaller again as he reached his twenty four line limit. In a later letter he
explained that he drafted each letter many times.

It is inevitable that such rules are resisted and some of Wolja's later letters
strayed over the twenty four lines. He also made increasing use of the rule
that allowed him to send telegrams or write 'special letters' if the matter was
urgent and he encouraged Lotte to write to him c/o the Commandant in
order to speed things up. Another example of resistance can be found in the
first edition, on 12 August 1940, of the *Mooragh Times*, a camp journal
produced by internees in the Mooragh camp. A *Liebesbrief in 24 Zeilen*
[Love letter in 24 lines], by Harry C. Schnur, is dedicated to the Chief
Censor.[22]

> *Wenn tausend Schreiber schrieben Tag und Nacht,*
>   *sie schreiben meine Liebe nicht zu Ende,*
>   *Nicht meine Sehnsucht, die ich zu dir sende*
> *Und nicht, was ich dir Liebes zugedacht.*
>   *Kein Dichter, der zu sagen es verstände,*
>   *Und füllte er auch tausend Foliobände*
> *Doch ach: die Fülle, die zu dir will eilen*
> *Wird mir gezwängt in vierundzwanzig Zeilen.*
>
> *Wenn Kerkermauren wähnen, uns zu trennen*
>   *So spottet unsre Liebe dieser Schranken*
>   *Leicht zueinander fliegen die Gedanken*
> *Auf Bahnen, die das Zensors Stift nicht kennen.*
>   *Seit wir zuerst uns in die Arme sanken*
>   *An jenem Tage, dem wir heut noch danken*
> *Verbindet uns, auch über tausend Meilen*
> *Mehr als sich zwängt in vierundzwanzig Zeilen*
>
> *War es drum nötig, daß ich ängstlich schrieb*
>   *Um's ja in vorgeschriebenen Raum zu pressen?*
>   *Was tut's, daß man Papier mir zugemessen.*
> *Vier Worte brauch' ich nur: Ich hab' dich lieb!*
>   *Gibt's eine Macht auch Erden, so vermessen,*
>   *Die meinte, jemals könnt' ich dein vergessen?*
> *Mein liebes Herz – dir dieses mitzuteilen*
> *Genügt ein Wort, statt vierundzwanzig Zeilen*

A thousand writers writing day and night
could not finish writing of my love,
Not my longing that I send to you,
and not what I intend for you, my love.
No poet who understands to say it,
who even fills a thousand folio sheets
yet still, the riches I want to speed to you
must be squeezed into 24 lines.

If prison walls imagine they can part us,
our love will scorn these limitations
Our thoughts will fly to one another
on routes the censor's pen knows not.
Since we first fell in one another's arms
on that day, that we still thank,
we have been bound across a thousand miles
more than can be squeezed into 24 lines.

Was it necessary that I anxiously wrote
to squeeze into the prescribed area?
so what if the paper's measured out
I only need four words: I love you so!
Is there a power on earth so presumptuous
it thinks I could ever forget you?
My dearest heart, to tell you this
one word's enough, not 24 lines.

In my translation I have tried to keep the rhythm and style of the original poem, but I was unable to reproduce the rhyme!

Still No Reply From You

The huge delays in postal deliveries were 'the single most important factor in sapping camp morale'[23] and in many letters Wolja expressed his increasing frustration about the difficulties of communicating.

11-6-40
My dear dear Lotte, I have not yet had a letter from you. I hope you are well and there will be a time to begin new, happier life. Most important thing is that you take care of yourself, do everything possible for your safety in case of air raids. You must promise it. I hope

you do not live in Orpington now, I have no idea, where and how you are, what you do. We go to Isle of Man today (but letter-address: c/o. Chief Postal Censor, Liverpool)…

22-6-40
My dear, dear Lotte, Still no reply from you to my first letter, only a short letter from you and L, where none of my questions is answered.

27-6-40
My dear Lotte, I received your 1st and 2nd letter, of 6th and 9th of June. I am happy that at that date you were well and preparing to leave London… Apart from these two good news, I was bitterly disappointed by your letters, which are ridiculously short unconcentrated and consist chiefly of stories about the various babies of our various friends. Your letters are only link between me and outer world! But there was only 1 line about my parents! You ask whether I need money, write twice I should buy everything I want. But you don't inform me about our financial position. How much did you pay for rent, income tax, removal, storing of our things? Where are our various things? Send me the addresses! How much has my firm paid to you? For how many weeks? Where are the curve sheets for the Patent Application? Has the firm made the Patent Application? Is my name mentioned? You write, you have written and wired to my cousin in U.S.A. I should like to know details, Lotte. I know that everything was and is very difficult for you after my internment. You had a lot of work and responsibility. I am sure that you have done everything very well, but it is very sad for me, that you seem to feel so tired so much that you send me such letters…

Worried about his parents, following the establishment of a fascist government in Romania, he asked the Camp Commandant for permission to send Lotte a telegram asking her to cable his parents and wire him their reply. On 3 July he wrote to Lotte:

My beloved Lotte. Your wire just arrived, thanks. I am glad my parents are well. I understand your wire that you received wire from my parents, it was not clear. In future please wire two words more, to make everything clear…

The following day he complained again about the lack of letters from her and the complaints continued for the next month.

My beloved Lotte. Two wires excepted, no news from you since your letter of 13th. Other people receive letters every day from wives and friends and firms.

8-7-40

...Lotte, you could help me a bit by writing every day (then the chances are that not all letters are delayed). I have only permission to write 24 lines, twice a week. There are no limitations for you! Don't submit to them voluntarily... Other people here receive letters daily, long letters (2 sheets, typewritten in single lines). Give me more details; not only half a line about my parents.

18-7-40

It is so discouraging to be limited to 2x24 lines per week, to have to draft letters many times in order to produce a concentrated 24 line letter and to obtain in so many cases no answer at all or something more confusing than nothing. May be you had no time to do it, you did not know how to do it, but why don't you reply? Thus I have to waste more than half of the valuable space of my letters for repeating questions, for urging answers. Even this is in vain. Please do read my old letters when you write to me...

19-7-40

Reply to all questions

2-8-40

In my wire I asked you about your and my parent's' health. For 2d you could have added 6 words, I hope you do it in future. Please write me text of my parent's wire...why don't you send me photo of you, the one you sent me two years ago...Put name on it, to prevent loss. Put my address inside your letters, to prevent confusion. Number your letters. Address them and parcels directly to Dr. W. Saraga...Do not drop 'Dr.' as internees who deliver letters to houses are definitely more careful if addressee has degree...do read my letters! Read Hansard reports!...PS send list of contents with food parcels too!

During this time he must have received Lotte's letter of 3 July responding to some of his complaints: '...don't be angry with me dearest. It is not easy to get accustomed to correspond with internees and now since I know your final address everything will be easier'. On Sunday 4 August she replied to his letters of 18 and 19 July:

I am very sorry that you feel confused and think I do not answer your questions properly. You must not forget, however, that I receive your letters with a fortnight's delay sometimes and not always in the order you wrote them. Your letter telegrams reached me as letters after two days. Well, darling, you will have a lot of answers today. You will have received a lot of answers in the meantime…

But by 16 August Wolja had given up on getting Lotte to communicate in the way that he wanted.

Dear Lotte. 3 months interned. I can't stand another 3. But no hope of release because of 'B' case…In addition to this your strange attitude towards me. 'Writing regularly' means that gaps between your letters are not more than 6 days, compared with 17 days before. It's a progress of course, and your letters are longer. I shall never again ask you to write daily. You are evidently unable to do it. But if you have no time to do this for me, please do not waste your time in posting parcels for me; they are utterly unimportant compared with letters…

As in the 1938 correspondence, Lotte comes across as defensive and apologetic, while trying to conciliate and carry the optimism for both of them. Wolja's anxiety and powerlessness are expressed through instructions and criticism. But I was moved that he asked for the photograph that had been so significant two years earlier. He was worried about Lotte being in London during the air raids; although interned, he was safe. From the end of June Lotte lived with Austrian friends, officially working for them on a domestic permit, looking after their child. They were evacuated from London. She tried to reassure Wolja that she was OK.

We have gone now to a lovely place in the country near Dorking. It is very beautiful and we are enjoying it… (30 June)

…It is marvellous to be in the country. I am looking very well as there is very little work. I eat a lot and I am looking very well… (26 July)

…there is one thing you need not worry about that is myself. I am well, fit healthy, living in beautiful surroundings, well fed and there is only one thing missing, that is you…Wolja, darling, please do not worry too much about all of us. You cannot help it, I know, but it does not alter anything and you must not get nervy. We do not know yet what else we may have to suffer in the future and we must remain strong. I am with you all the time and I kiss you, darling…(31 July)

Send No More Food

In addition to sending Wolja the books and clothes that he requested, Lotte also sent him lots of food parcels. Although he was pleased to receive them, food was not as important as letters. On 6 July he wrote: 'Thanks for food parcel. Send no more food. Write to me at once and immediately.' By the time Lotte received this letter at the end of July, more food parcels had arrived, which Wolja seems to have appreciated. On 19 July he wrote: 'My dear Lotte, thanks for the chocolate, it did not last more than 1 hour.' And on 24 July:

> Yesterday I also received food parcel with marvellous real brown bread, liver, cheese, chocolate macaroons (I don't really like the other biscuits) and two fruit tins. I had a delicious supper of my own, really enjoyed eating. Cheese and liver so essential, because I am completely unable to eat white bread with margarine. On the other hand I can't afford not to eat it at all. It must be question of education and habit. You may send me Kraft cheese in one big piece the next time. I am getting now some milk on medical certificate, thus you need not worry about my health.

On 8 August he wrote: 'You ask what I want? The keys of my two suitcases, urgently, very much nut-milk chocolate and macaroons and brown bread.' And four days later (12 August) he regretted his earlier statement: 'I hope you don't stop sending food parcels because of letter of 6th of July.'

I imagine that for Lotte sending parcels was a form of material support for Wolja. In my family, as in many others, food was clearly associated with love. After I had left home, when I visited my mother, she would often buy several of my 'favourite foods' for me, even though it was impossible for me to eat them all in one visit. And my 'favourites' could never change, for fear of disappointing her.

On 24 August Wolja wrote: 'I get an orange or apple per day on medical certificate, and sometimes we can buy oranges in the canteen.' But apart from these references to food, his letters rarely included information about how he was living; perhaps this would be a waste of his limited words. But on 31 August, in his very last letter, he wrote: 'For some weeks we were able to buy butter…I'm living in a house with 100 persons, mostly nice ones…I am sleeping in room for 2, with decent Viennese man. Last 6 weeks I have single bed. Sea view…Once a week everybody has to help in the house or kitchen for some hours.'

The Popular University

Maxine Schwartz Seller suggests that 'education was a major survival strategy' for internees and this is in line with Wolja's experience of the importance for him of his scientific reading, discussions with other scientists and the lectures for the 'Popular University'.[24]

> 3-7-40
> I have met interesting scientists here, we are discussing Logical Empiricism. They will help me to try to find university post in U.S.A.

> 4-7-40
> Make arrangements that things can be despatched if you are interned too. Take my scientific books with you, and typewriter, perhaps we meet in a camp. Send me slide rule, scarf. from Foyle's: 4-figure logarithmic and trigonometric etc tables (cheap ones) and sectional pad (millimeter paper), Penguin book 155, Pelikan books, A44, A3, S23, and others if you like.

> 24-7-40
> Dear Lotteli. You are trying to make internment comfortable for me aren't you? 4 parcels in 4 days! I received warm underwear and glasses for swimming (it has been too cold for swimming until now), books on Television and Operational Calculus, two Penguin books, logarithmic tables, pullover, scarf, tie, 2 p.o. socks, slide rule, square. I am really happy with these books. I am very busy studying them and the book on Radio-Engineering I had with me. I am reading a book on Correlation Theory (Statistics) together with a lecturer in economics of Oxford University, 2 hours daily. Three times a week I attend a colloquium on Logical Empiricism by a professor of Vienna. This morning I gave my second lecture (three times per week) on Differential Equations for Students of London University who are preparing for Finals. B.Sc. (Engineering) Exam. I am preparing a short publication on 'Quasi – Stationary Physical and Biological Systems'… I hope you will also send me the graph paper pad I asked you for. This will enable me to write the publication on 'Equalizer Design'. Did Mr Flint ever receive my report on 'Variable equalizers'?

Dear Eva

In 1938, when Lotte was trapped in Germany, Wolja's letters were important to her as physical objects that he had touched. She could hear his voice in them as they conveyed his emotions. Two years later when it was Wolja who was trapped, living with fear and uncertainty, Lotte's letters were crucial for his personal survival.

I wondered whether I could find other examples of such communication and came across the letters from an Irish Republican prisoner to his wife. Peadar Kearney was interned by the British from 25 November 1920 for one year in Dublin. Only Peadar's letters, published later by his nephew under the title 'My Dear Eva', have survived.[25] They show remarkable similarities in their style and concerns with Wolja's letters to Lotte as the following extracts will illustrate.

My dear Eva

Received letter Wednesday & parcel on Thursday...I had been without butter for some time...Send as much butter as you possibly can...Your letters are getting shorter every time & as I never hear from anyone but you might make them a little longer. There is never anything to write about from this end...You may reduce the quantity of tea until further notice. In fact you might cut it out for the present. (23 April 1921)

I was certainly disappointed last week. I got butter & milk on Thursday and no letter till Saturday. As usual you did not date it, but the post mark was Tuesday. At the end of another 6 months, I suppose I won't get a letter at all...you did not make the slightest reference to my letter...I don't know whether you got it all or not...(23 May)

Got letter on Tuesday Parcel (Wednesday) contained only ¼ lb tea & ½ lb butter first since Tuesday week. Do you think its worth a shilling postage? Do you know the parcels I get are a joke? I call them parcels because they're not letters....I have asked time after time for better packing & list of contents to be written in every possible space. Whats the use?...Do you read my letters? Have you...tried to realize how hard it is for me to say what I want to say in letters like these & Im quite sure Im no fool at writing a letter...Don't stop writing anyhow as its the only link I have with home. (21 July)

...my heart is broke asking for a list to be written...I dont know whether anything is missing or not. Even your letter tells me you are sending me "everything I asked for" but does not mention the articles why? (28 August)

...Another thing it is very evident you write your letters in a hurry; now sit down and write me a long newsy letter. I'm worth one half-hour... (14 September)

... another 10 months here is appalling to think of, but the regular letter & parcel keeps up the link with home if that ceased life would not be worth living. (5 October)

...its a good job to growl now and again it makes you write long letters. (9 October)

Peadar's letters to Eva, like Wolja's correspondence with Lotte, demonstrate the crucial importance of communication for people who are trapped or imprisoned, especially in times of great uncertainty. Today, if communication is possible, then it may also be instant and allow us to see the person we are talking to. But you cannot hold these communications in your hand; they don't bear the physical mark of the person who sent them

This Permanent Fear in my Heart

Lotte and Wolja also had to use their correspondence to develop strategies for Wolja's release. This involved three interrelated struggles. Their primary concern was to rectify Wolja's nationality status. To be considered German and an 'enemy alien' was not only the cause of his internment, but also a gross injustice. He was afraid that if he was reclassified in terms of the nationality of his birth – Romanian – he might be expected to 'return' to Romania. Their second strategy was to enlist the support of TMC for an application for Wolja's release on the grounds that he could contribute to the war effort as a telecommunications expert. Not having much faith that either of these would be successful, Lotte also applied again for visas for the USA; the only other way of securing release from internment was to agree to emigrate.

Although they sought help from the Refugee Committees and from SPSL, they predominantly made use of friendship networks, which included contacts from Berlin as well as friends and colleagues (old and newly established) in England. Maxine Schwartz Seller describes such networking or 'social capital' as one of the internees' major survival strategies, together with 'cultural capital (knowledge and skills accumulated through past education...and personal strength'.[26]

Many of Lotte and Wolja's contacts came from Wolja's parents. Their networking started with Wolja's very first letter, written on 27 May:

My dear Lotte, How are you and my parents? Send me their letters. Write to them. Tell them about internment, maybe they can help.

Ask Dr Starr, Dr S. Whitehead, Mr. Pritchard for help. I hope Telephone Manufacturing Co. will help me and you. But do not rely on it. Prepare everything for an early emigration. I trust you have written urgently to my cousin in U.S.A. about internment and necessary new affidavit…to emphasize urgency, write once more, by air mail, or send cable. Ask also for affidavits from friends in U.S.A., my weak-sightedness has to be mentioned in affidavit, also the first refusal. Go to U.S.A. Consulate at once, enquire about all steps to speed up granting of visa. Register at Consulate yourself! My parents should register too. Could we go to your uncle in Uruguay in the meantime?

All three strategies are apparent in his letter of 22 June:

I am still waiting for news from my firm and Society for Protection of Science and Learning. I realize that personal fate appears unimportant at present moment. Still 'B' decision by Tribunal was completely unjustified and undeserved discrimination. Moreover I have strong legal claim to be considered as non-German. Therefore I am strongly in favour of having solicitor, particularly in order to clear question of nationality which is purely personal question, not connected with internment only, but may become of essential importance. Since my firm does not do anything for me and I am wasting time instead of doing useful work for this country as an engineer and scientist, prepare earliest emigration to U.S.A. Prospective emigrants are registering here. I have not done so as I do not know whether new affidavit has arrived. Enquire at US Consulate now what you will have to do when affidavits arrive, as our passports have expired and mine is with the British authorities. Prepare everything possible beforehand. Even with good affidavit, visa chances are not good because of my bad eyesight. Therefore you must try to find friends who secure for us banking account in U.S.A. This is very essential! …

On 3 July Lotte sent Wolja lots of specific information about what she was doing, none of it very hopeful:

1) Your firm: I saw Flint the day you were interned. He was kind but had the same attitude that he was helpless. I have the impression that he does not want to make any further applications for you. The firm paid me the salary they promised to you, no more. I wrote to Flint again because I heard that some firms could do something for

internees and asked him if he could make an application. He never answered this letter…

2) I tried to get Pritchard's helping the question of your nationality. He told us he wrote to the Home Office but did not receive any reply. He does not want to urge now.

3) Society did not get any reply regarding your nationality. I send you two of their letters.

4) I am sending you as well correspondence with Starr and Research Association. Negative.

5) I wire you tomorrow morning that you shall register as would be emigrant. I do not understand about registering with Jewish Committee.

6) Not yet any reply from U.S.A. Wired for the second time on Friday. Hope to receive answer this week. Wrote to Hans and Valja about additional affidavits. Registered with Bloomsbury House regarding the question for your release for medical examination at American consulate. Travelling papers can only be applied for when you have a certificate that you can have the visas.

The urgency of their struggles increased towards the end of June, when internees started to be deported to Canada or Australia. The official justification for the deportations was the fear that anyone who remained could render help to invading German forces. They were very frightened that Wolja would be deported without Lotte. The married internees at Onchan sent an 'anguished telegram' to Anthony Eden, Secretary of State for War, seeking assurance that if they were deported, their wives would be able to join them.[27] In a letter dated 12 July Nancy Searle of SPSL told Lotte: 'The Home Office also assured us that married men would not be sent'.[28] Events moved so fast that between 3 and 15 July, when the danger had passed, eight telegrams and nine letters were sent between Lotte and Wolja.

On 3 July Wolja wrote: 'I am also sure you are doing everything possible to avoid that we become completely separated. I hope my fear is without foundation, I do not know. Is there still a chance for me to continue my work with my firm, or is Canada or U.S.A. our only hope?'

The following day he sent Lotte a further list of people to contact.

Ask Mr Flint, Dr Whitehead, Dr Starr, Mr Pritchard, Mr Brewer, Mr Emanuel, Mr Makower, Miss Searle, Dr Demuth for new reference letters, in case I am heard by tribunal here or I am brought to Canada and have to prove my loyalty, reliability, usefulness there. In Makower's letter, recommendation by Rabbi Cohn and Mr. Stahl should be mentioned. You need reference letters too! Demuth should mention my research scholarship in Switzerland. In Canada internment for duration - or even after - and special difficulties for immigration to U.S.A. may result from 'B' classification if protest against this undeserved discrimination is not continued by me and you. Explain this to all people concerned. I think especially, in light of Canada plans it is of utmost importance that question of my nationality is finally settled with Home Office. Do take solicitor to speed up matters! Our whole future may depend on it. Apart from reference letters, ask Mr Flint for ordinary testimonials, and Mrs Brewer for testimonial for you (baby-nursing should be emphasized). Send me originals of reference letters and testimonials (keep copies) and ca. 5 copies or translations in English of my former testimonials (under separate cover, not in your ordinary letter). Sorry to cause you so much trouble, it's necessary. Send me, and keep yourself, addresses of U.S.A. relatives and friends (also Dr Begum, Dr Gemant, Miss Trolle) and U.S.A. registration No's. With regard to our belongings: Send most important things directly to U.S.A., even if it is not sure we go there. Ask for money for transport from Committees, but don't wait for decision, borrow it from friends. Make arrangements that things can be dispatched if you are interned too...

Wolja clearly did not know that Makower had died in 1939. On 5 July Lotte sent another telegram: 'firm hopeless usa yet no reply register usa any case love Lotte'. The following day Wolja replied by telegram: 'Departure imminent solicitor should interview Home Office immediately establishing non-German nationality to secure release pending it postponement departure. Telephone Manufacturing Company and Research Associations should repeat release application.'

He repeated this request in a letter the same day, adding SPSL as an organization that should apply for his release:

It is really a pity that I should waste my time in internment camps although I could do extremely useful work for this country. As the Authorities sometimes object to my having applied for naturalization in Germany, I want you to explain in reply: my parents came to

Germany because of antisemitic persecution in their home countries, Rumania and Poland. Thus, in comparison, Germany before the national socialism appeared to me to be a refuge. Then I was persecuted in Germany as a Jew. That is the whole story. Thus there should be no reason not to allow me to continue my work, or some work, for this country. I hope you will succeed. We have been told to-day that there is a new antisemitic government in Rumania. I am so much worried about my parents. Lotte, it is almost too much for me, the separation from you, the threat that the separation will become still more complete with my departure. The news from my parents. The fear for your safety. I know we are helpless. But maybe, you find a way out. Please send me heavy overcoat, scarf, gloves, a pair of black shoes, some (not much) underwear.

On 8 July Lotte sent another telegram: 'seen flint applications home office running prospects doubtful wired commandant visiting application love'. The same day she wrote that he would not harm his case by registering for emigration to the USA: 'The risk to employ foreigners now seems to be too great and if that attitude should change before your departure and you should be released you could always stay and work here…' Wolja replied by letter on the same day:

Just received your wire about Home Office Application. Thank you very much. Main point is: I cannot bear a separation from you, I cannot be in safety if you remain here. I won't stand it. If I have to leave, you simply must make it possible to come with me or at least to follow me within a few days. We are living here at a beautiful place, but this doesn't help the general strain and excitement. On Saturday it seemed I would have to leave very soon. I have registered on a list of experts with Home Office permits. It may be that I have to leave later or not at all. I do not know. Nobody knows. Today we had to give the names of wives whom we wish to leave, in case we are leaving. This was an official list. Thus we have some hope. I am extremely grateful to you that you applied for permission to see me. I doubt whether you will obtain it. I am afraid to see you if this would mean parting from you for a long time. Lotte, it must not happen! In case I am asked to leave I shall apply for postponement for 3 reasons. 1) Home Office application running in order to establish non-German nationality. 2) Firm's application running. 3) Hope of early U.S.A. emigration…Don't write me it is better that at least I am leaving this country. I cannot do it without you.

Three days later he thanked her for sending £5 by wire.

> It is very good of you, but you shouldn't do it, having nothing yourself.
> Who lent it to you? I was rather sad when the money arrived, it
> seemed to me that you had no more hope that my departure without
> you could be prevented. I tell you one thing. I have not resigned and
> shall never resign, I shall fight against any separation from you. Please
> don't say, it is safer for me to be away. I don't care for my personal
> safety if you are not with me. My parents are already in danger in
> Bucharest. That is enough for me. It is utterly impossible for me to
> leave you here. I couldn't do anything for you or my parents with this
> permanent fear in my heart...(11 July)

On 15 July Wolja told Lotte 'I do not think at the moment that I shall be sent
overseas'.

Stent's description of the organization of the Onchan camp provides a
context for the enormous level of despair and powerlessness conveyed in
Wolja's letters. Internal self-government, with a 'camp supervisor' from
among the internees, was encouraged, so long as it was compatible with good
order, discipline and security. The camp supervisor was also expected to
select internees for overseas deportation.

> Early in July the supervisor was told that three hundred internees had
> to be readied for overseas shipment within forty-eight hours, no
> destination being mentioned. How the quota was to be filled was up
> to the supervisor and his staff. If he could not get enough volunteers
> it would be up to him to pick up the rest by whatever criteria he
> considered fairest. This caused an uproar in the camp and for the next
> two days was the sole topic of excited conversation.[29]

In the absence of enough volunteers, they put all unmarried men on the list.
'...the Commandant agreed that it would be cruel to send family men
overseas.'[30] The first boat of internees being deported had sailed on 21 June.
On 2 July, on its way to Canada, the *Arandora Star* was torpedoed by the
Germans. Many people drowned. Some of those who survived were sent on
the last boat, the *Dunera*, on 10 July to Australia. A tremendous scandal
about the conditions in which the prisoners were held on this boat, led to
an end of the deportation policy and 'crystallized opposition to
internment...'[31]

By the end of July Wolja was very pessimistic about being released unless
he agreed to leave Britain. His sense of injustice continues to pervade the

letters. On 25 July he wrote that permission to visit him had not been granted. 'Just now internees who have wives interned in Isle of Man have obtained permit to visit them. I always belong to a group with minor rights. Unfortunately the group of interned 'B'-men with non-interned 'C' wives is so small that there is small hope that there will be any provision for us.' I learned later that it was unusual for Lotte and Wolja, as a married couple, to be in different categories.[32]

And on 31 July: 'I have been photographed here and hope to obtain photos very soon. Then I think I'll send application [for US visa] with photos to Bloomsbury House. Their Liaison Officer has been here, but had, of course, no time to see ordinary people like me. He was so tired after seeing only a few prominent ones. Did you expect anything else?'

Wolja's temporary visa was due to run out on 11 August 1940. Lotte applied for its renewal and on this date, having received a further US affidavit for Wolja, told him:

> I am going now to Bloomsbury House on Monday because I do not know if I should not keep the affidavit until I get a reply from the American Consulate as all replys and answering of letters takes now so much time. I know Bloomsbury House too and am fully aware that they are very unhelpful. On the other hand, the appointments at the American Consulate and documents for internees can be handled only through them...I know now two people there who make a good impression and I think they will try to make things correctly for us... In case we should get an appointment you would be brought to a special camp and then escorted to the Consulate and to Bloomsbury House to get your papers in order and I think, in the end, brought to the ship.

Their experience with the refugee committees is in line with historical accounts which stress both the elitism of the Committees, as well as the huge numbers they were helping.[33]

Is Saraga of National Importance?

Meanwhile the possibility of being released as a scientist had increased. On 19 July the Home Secretary confirmed that he would sympathetically consider the cases of internees recommended to him by 'bodies of recognized standing in the sphere of science and learning'. A. V. Hill persuaded the Home Office to extend this to humanist scholars, to be considered by a tribunal set up by the British Academy.[34] The application by TMC for Wolja's release had been taken over by SPSL, whose role once again included not only supporting individual refugees, but also selecting suitable people, recommending them to the tribunal set up by the Royal Society. SPSL carried out a very careful process of collecting and presenting evidence, careful never to be 'sentimental' about individuals.[35]

On 10 July Lotte had written to Nancy Searle of SPSL 'I have read in the paper on Saturday about the new category of "useful aliens". Do you think there is any chance for him?' Across the top of this letter in the Bodleian file is written: 'Is Saraga of national importance?'[36] The answer must have been 'yes' as Wolja's name was included on the list of internees recommended for early release. As well as the information supplied by TMC, his case was supported by a letter from Einstein solicited by his parents, networking from Romania. This letter was sent initially to Lotte. On 23 August she told Wolja:

> ...Hurrah! I am convinced now that I will have you back one day but afraid that it will not happen in time for a birthday party together...I send you copy of a letter from Professor Einstein for you. I sent the original to Miss Searle asking her to make best use of this letter. If she should send it on to the Home Office or if you should perhaps have the original for the tribunal. I rather prefer that she should send it to the Home Office. I could not do it without her because the Society for the Protection of Science and Learning is making the application for you and I cannot do anything without them. I wrote you already that your parents wrote Valja if he could do anything for you with Professor Einstein. You must be a nice fellow, Wolja, because you have marvellous friends...

Several copies of Einstein's letter to the Home Office, dated 8 August 1940, are amongst the papers. Sadly the original letter, signed by Einstein, must have perished with Wolja's file at the Home Office.

> I have learned through News Dispatches that the British Home Office is now willing to release such foreign internees about whom reliable and favourable information is available. This gives me occasion to give such information in behalf of Dr. W. Saraga, Electro-Engineer, who has been employed in the British Radio-Industry. He is a close friend of my absolutely reliable assistant Dr. V. Bargmann of the Institute of Advanced Study in Princeton N.J., who knows Dr Saraga since the days of early youth. On the basis of my information I am able to take any responsibility for the personal and political reliability of Dr. Saraga.

'It was officially stated in the House of Commons that personal intervention by influential people on behalf of individual internees would hinder rather than help the consideration of the appeal'. SPSL's experience belied this. Indeed A.V.Hill went so far as to suggest: 'The fact that they took the trouble in Parliament to say that it did not, suggests that there was a widespread opinion, probably based on fact, that it did...'[37] Once released, Wolja helped to get Einstein to write a letter on behalf of a fellow internee, Otto Neurath, an Austrian sociologist and philosopher of science, with whom Wolja had become very friendly in Onchan camp.

On 30 August Wolja received a telegram from Lotte: 'letter Einstein for you forwarded by science society to prof hill royal society in charge of your application Simpson confident don't be depressed both affidavits likely sufficient have wait reply consulate love kisses = Lotte.'

On 1 September she told Wolja:

> You will appreciate that, after the Society for Protection of Science and Learning, the firm, and the Royal Society have taken your case in hand, it is for my feeling, impossible, to do anything apart. These two Societies are a better representation towards the Home Office than any other lawyer or person. I did not think, the application would take so much time but nevertheless, I am afraid to spoil everything by muddling in between. The Society is very touchy in these points.

But before receiving this letter, on 2 September, Wolja had sent a telegram to Lotte: 'Am released leaving here Tuesday morning arriving Euston evening love Wolja.' Their birthdays were 3 and 4 September; he arrived home on 3 September in time for the joint birthday party. In the end he was very lucky, interned for less than four months. In 1946 his name appeared under the heading of 'Telecommunications' in a list compiled by SPSL of refugee scholars who had been engaged in war service.[38]

Gratitude or Injustice?

Working on this correspondence made me aware of the general silence about internment during both World Wars. In 2004 I attended a talk by David Baddiel at the time of the publication of his novel, *The Secret Purposes*,[39] based on his grandfather's experience of internment. He asked how many people in the audience knew that Jewish refugees had been interned. When many of us put up our hands, he wondered whether it was because we were all Jewish. It was not. During the discussion, I tried to point out that internment had not only happened in the two world wars, it had happened several times since, and indeed if one counted as internment all indefinite imprisonment without charge, it was happening right now. I was very quickly cut off by the chair. The term 'internment' was known primarily through its use in Northern Ireland since 1971. At the time of the first Gulf War in 1991, several Iraqi nationals in the UK were detained without trial, though the term 'internment' was rarely used, and discussions of such policies did not refer back to the use of internment in the two World Wars. Since that time the use of indefinite detention, again without calling it 'internment', has been a continuous feature of UK policy in relation to both asylum and anti-terrorism.[40]

The title of Stent's book: *A Bespattered Page?* comes from a comment in the House of Commons by a Conservative MP, Major Victor Cazalet.[41] Stent uses it to emphasize the widespread protest against the policy that accompanied the xenophobic calls to 'intern the lot'. 'There was much contemporaneous public criticism of the internment process. In the late summer of 1940 particularly, the issue was widely discussed in liberal circles…as well as debates and questions in parliament and criticism in the press.' This was followed by 'the almost complete absence of debate' by the end of the war.[42] It is widely assumed this is mainly because it was indeed a 'bespattered page' in British history, one which challenged the dominant mythologies of the Second World War.

David Cesarani and Tony Kushner suggest a very different, and in their view much more significant, reason why these events were invisible – the dominant view of the Jewish refugee community that the experience of internment was as nothing compared to the experiences of millions of people, Jews and non-Jews, both as a result of the war and also of what has become known as the Holocaust. The refugees wanted instead to emphasize their gratitude to Britain, rather than to focus on any unfairness or injustice resulting from internment.[43] In 1960, when *AJR Information*, the Journal of the Association of Jewish Refugees wanted to publish material to mark the twentieth anniversary of internment, they were very clear that they wanted material of 'personal interest' not 'from the political angle'.[44] At the end of his book, Stent suggests:

> The blots which Victor Cazalet castigated have long since faded and been forgotten; the page of history was soon wiped clean by the protests of so many enlightened politicians, journalists, academics and artists, by the humane response of so many civil servants and soldiers (once they knew with what sort of people they were dealing); by the way the British people allowed the refugees to integrate themselves into war-time Britain once they had regained their freedom.

Referring to his reflections in 1944 on his own experience he adds

> Those five months of internment had been a strange experience,
> harsh, testing, stimulating, not a bad preparation for what came
> afterwards. The memory of the unpleasant aspects and experiences
> had already faded; what remained was the awareness that it had also
> meant a stretching of stamina and intellect and memories of the
> people and the challenges that had been met. It had, after all, not been
> a wasted period, not a bad time. That was the perspective in 1944. It
> is still the same in 1980.[45]

Should these ideas influence my use of these letters? If I focus on the injustice
and suffering associated with internment, am I 'breaking ranks' with the
community of German-Jewish refugees? My decision to continue was
influenced not only by the power of Wolja's feelings in his letters and the
memories I have of him continuing to talk about it, but also by a book by
Francois Lafitte, written in 1940 as a Penguin Special, which criticized
government policy. Wolja owned a copy of this book. In an Introduction
written for a re-issue of his book in 1988, he wrote:

> The only blessing for which we can thank Britain's rounding up of its
> "enemy aliens" in 1940 is that it unintentionally accomplished the
> genesis of the Amadeus Quartet...Little else can be pleaded in
> defence of the way in which Britain had then treated its refugees from
> Nazi persecution. Yet, given what we *now* know about the world war,
> it might seem that this book is concerned with a trifling and short-
> lived episode – hardly worth writing about at the time, certainly not
> worth reissuing nearly half a century later...Catastrophe and
> holocaust...seem to dwarf into insignificance the subject matter of
> my book...But this is not at all how we saw matters in the summer of
> 1940.[46]

Acknowledging that 'Forty-eight years later...A very substantial literature
has explored almost every aspect of the events', nevertheless in 1988 he found
'astonishingly little that I would wish to rewrite.'[47]

∗∗∗

On 10 July 2002, while reading papers on internment held in the archive of
the Imperial War Museum, I came across the papers of Captain H. Salzbach,
also interned in Onchan camp. Amongst them is a certificate, dated 22

October 1940, identical to the one with which I started this chapter apart from a reference to 'his literary events' rather than 'his knowledge'.

Notes

1. R. Stent, *A Bespattered Page? The Internment of His Majesty's 'Most Loyal Enemy Aliens'* (London: Andre Deutsch, 1980); F. Lafitte, *The Internment of Aliens* (London: Penguin Books, 1940); D. Cesarani and T. Kushner (eds), *The Internment of Aliens in Twentieth-Century Britain* (London and Portland, OR: Frank Cass, 1993).
2. See Stent, *A Bespattered Page?*, p.11.
3. Ibid., pp. 35- 36; Lafitte, *The Internment of Aliens*, p. 62. For the way the tribunals were set up and operated see also B. Wasserstein, *Britain and the Jews of Europe, 1939-1945*, second edition, (Leicester: Leicester University Press, 1999), pp.76-78.
4. T. Kushner, *Remembering Refugees* (Manchester: Manchester University Press, 2006), p.6.
5. In 1999 the SPSL changed its name to the *Council for Assisting Refugee Academics (CARA)*. This was modified again in 2014 to become the *Council for At-Risk Academics*. http://www.cara.ngo/
6. M. Guarnieri, 'The Early History of Radar', *IEEE Industrial Electronics Magazine*, 4, 3 (October 2010), pp.36 – 42, p.38.
7. A.J.P. Taylor, *English History 1914-1945* (Harmondsworth: Penguin, 1970), footnote 2, p.598.
8. See Stent, *A Bespattered Page?*, p.10.
9. G. Ferry, *Max Perutz and the Secret of Life* (London: Chatto & Windus, 2007), p.68.
10. See Stent, *A Bespattered Page?*, p.37.
11. B338/327.
12. Imperial War Museum Archive, *Onchan Internment Camp Papers*, Misc 175, Item 2659.
13. See Lafitte, *The Internment of Aliens*, p.70.
14. See Stent, *A Bespattered Page?*, p.14.
15. Ibid., p. 24. Statement by an anonymous Home Office official.
16. https://rli.blogs.sas.ac.uk/2018/01/25/terrorism-and-asylum-unravelling-the-myths (Accessed 11 July 2018).
17. See Stent, *A Bespattered Page?*, p. 142.
18. Y. Cresswell, *Living with the Wire: Civilian Internment in the Isle of Man During Two World Wars* (Douglas, Isle of Man: Manx National Heritage Library, 1994), p.50.
19. P. and L. Gillman, *'Collar the Lot!' How Britain Interned and Expelled its Wartime Refugees'.* (London: Quartet Books, 1980), p. 176.
20. See Stent, *A Bespattered Page?*, p. 149.
21. See P. and L. Gillman, *'Collar the Lot!*, p.227.
22. Mooragh Internment Camp (RAMSEY, Isle of Man), *Mooragh Times*. Issued by enemy aliens interned in the camp, No. 1 (12 August, 1940), p.15. My translation.
23. See Stent, *A Bespattered Page?*, p.146.
24. M. Schwartz Seller, *We Built Up our Lives. Education and Community among Jewish Refugees Interned by Britain in World War II* (London: Greenwood Press, 2001), pp. 8 and 156; P. and L. Gillman, *'Collar the Lot!*, p.226.
25. Kearney, Peader (1976) *My Dear Eva. Letters from Ballykinlar Internment Camp 1921*, Dublin, Seamus de Burca Dublin P. J. Bourke. Page nos. of extracts: 7,10,18,21,23, 25 & 27.

26. See M. Schwartz Seller, *We Built Up our Lives*, pp.8 and 242-3.
27. See P. and L. Gillman, *'Collar the Lot!*, p.211.
28. B338/342.
29. See Stent, *A Bespattered Page?*, p.181.
30. Ibid., p.182.
31. See, for example, A. Grenville, *Jewish Refugees from Germany and Austria in Britain 1933-1970* (London: Vallentine Mitchell, 2010), p. 32.
32. Email to author, Roger Kershaw of the National Archives, 10 September 2003.
33. See, for example, T. Kushner, 'Finding Refugee Voices', in A. Grenville and A. Reiter (eds), *Political Exile and Exile Politics in Britain after 1933* (Amsterdam: Rodopi, 2011), p.128.
34. R.M. Cooper (ed.), *Refugee Scholars. Conversations with Tess Simpson* (Leeds: Morland Books, 1992), p.141.
35. Ibid., pp.138 and 152.
36. B341.
37. See Cooper, *Refugee Scholars*, p.161.
38. Ibid., p.195.
39. D. Baddiel, *The Secret Purposes* (London: Little, Brown, 2004).
40. See, for example, https://www.theguardian.com/uk-news/2018/oct/10/revealed-sick-tortured-immigrants-locked-up-for-months-in-britain. (Accessed 5 November 2018).
41. V. Cazelet in *Hansard*, Vol 364, col. 1538, 22 August 1940.
42. See Cesarani and Kushner, *The Internment of Aliens*, p.4. See also the debate in the House of Commons on 'Refugees', *Hansard*, Vol 362, cc 1208-306, 10 July 1940.
43. See Cesarani and Kushner, *The Internment of Aliens*, p.4.
44. *AJR Information* (July 1960), p.14.
45. See Stent, *A Bespattered Page?*, p.263.
46. F. Lafitte, *The Internment of Aliens* (London: Libris, 1988), pp. vii-viii. Originally published by Penguin Books in 1940.
47. Ibid., p.ix.

5

'I Am Definitely Not German'

31 March 2010. My new biometric passport arrived yesterday. It cost a lot of money, and I really don't like the photograph, but getting it was very straightforward. The first time I went abroad I was fourteen, and on my own, travelling with the son of friends of my parents to Munich to stay with a family. I remember being nervous in advance about going through passport control and customs. A letter to my parents written on the train reminds me of these anxieties:

> Getting from the boat to the train was easy, there weren't any customs! The girl opposite me was very nice. Her name was Helen Carr, she was Dutch but has married an Englishman. It was the first time she had ever travelled on a British passport and she kept going the wrong way…When the customs officer saw our British passports he didn't say anything, but just gave us a yellow ticket each which enabled us to get to the trains.

So my fears were allayed and I learned the value of a British passport; and indeed I have never had any difficulties at Passport Control. Travelling to Spain in 1998 with a friend, also British but black, I was waved through without my passport being looked at, while she had hers examined. Today passports are scrutinized, not only by the Borders Agency at frontiers, but also by a range of other organizations who do the Home Office's business for them, checking people's eligibility to travel, to work, for services or for benefits. In the early twenty-first century, working for the London Region of the Open University, I had to look at the passport of everyone we interviewed for a part time position as a tutor. I tried to object, saying that I didn't work for the Home Office. In practice my task was to confirm that the copy the OU had made for its records, matched the candidate's actual passport. I could comfort myself that I was not the person making the decision about the candidate's eligibility to work.

The notes that accompany my new passport tell me that it is 'biometric', 'also known as an ePassport'…introduced to help fight identity fraud and forgery'…the government is 'considering including finger prints in biometric passports in the future'; but my passport will not be affected and is valid as it is for 10 years. I am pleased about this, despite the terrible photograph.[1]

I doubt whether the arrival of my new passport would have provoked such thoughts if I had not at that time been thinking about Wolja's statelessness, recognising for the first time the enormous impact it had had on his life.

At about the same time I came across, by chance, a book on the history of the passport[2] in a second hand bookshop in Edinburgh – the kind of serendipity I was getting used to while working on these papers. I learned that passports developed in the form with which we are familiar during the nineteenth century, as documents that both identify people as citizens, allowing the state to know who belongs and who is an outsider or alien, and also as a means to control the movement of both groups of people – aliens and citizens – in and out of the nation's territory.[3] They operated originally more like letters of introduction or guarantees of safe passage when travelling. Only in the early twentieth century did they become the kind of document with which we are familiar – linking individual identity with national identity.[4] Nevertheless Wolja's experience in 1938 shows how important personal recommendations continued to be. The decision to grant him a UK visa rested on expert opinions of him as a scientist as well as the recommendation of a family contact who worked in the British legation in Copenhagen.

Caplan and Torpey argue that the history of the passport has to be understood in the context of the development of nation states. 'The international passport system that was consolidated in the aftermath of the First World War bore witness to a system of controls over international movement that took as its baseline assumption "one country to a person".'[5] Statelessness both challenges the system of passports and national belonging, and also illustrates the importance of such means to document identity. 'Perhaps only those who experienced the limbo of statelessness can appreciate the value of that kind of belonging.'[6]

Statelessness continues to be a hidden but enormous problem. The UNHCR estimates that 'at least 10 million people around the world are denied a nationality.'[7] In a world premised on the idea that everyone belongs to one country, not to belong anywhere has a very significant personal impact. Stateless people have used terms such as 'Kafkaesque', a 'nightmare', or a 'grim world' to describe their situation. They are seen as the 'excluded', 'living in the shadows' and as 'non-persons', who have no legitimate legal or political status.[8] Stefan Zweig, an Austrian author made stateless in 1938 following the Nazi annexation of Austria '…ceased to feel as if I quite belonged to myself. A part of the natural identity with my original and essential ego was destroyed forever.'[9] For Hannah Arendt, 'to be stripped of citizenship is to be stripped of worldliness; it is like returning to a wilderness as cavemen or savages ...they could live and die without leaving any trace.'[10] In February 2019, controversy surrounding the case of Shamima Begum, who was stripped of her British citizenship because she joined the Islamic State group in Syria aged 15, highlighted once again the issue of statelessness.[11]

Being stateless, not having a document to show who you are and where you belong, also creates material and practical problems, as for Wolja when he was refused permission by the Swiss authorities to take up a scholarship in Zurich. Without papers it is impossible to claim any rights. Writing in1937, Joseph Roth asked: 'And what is a man without papers? Rather less, let me tell you, than papers without a man!'[12] And these ideas are as relevant today for the members of the Windrush generation who suddenly found themselves denied services, detained or even deported, because they could not produce an 'acceptable' document – one they had never been told that they needed.[13]

But papers are also used for surveillance and control: 'The words "papers please" have terrible echoes of Europe's most repressive history. The rounding up of Jews, the oppression of migrant workers, and the removal of political undesirables have all been made easier by efficient identity controls.'[14] And I have become aware that I am using the term 'papers' in two senses in this chapter – both as the collective term for the many different kinds of bits of paper we found, and also in the sense in which 'papers' refers to identity documents.

Returning to my own papers (in both senses of the word), I recognized that although Wolja was originally persecuted as a Jew in Nazi Germany – he was unable to study or work and denaturalized – it was his statelessness rather than his Jewishness that caused most of his later difficulties. The British insistence that he was German, because he was born in Germany, must have felt like the ultimate irony. No wonder he protested.

Over a fifteen year period (1932 to 1947), he was formally identified in many different ways by state authorities: born in Berlin in 1908 of a Romanian father and a Russian Polish mother, he was deemed under German law to be **Romanian**; in 1932 he was naturalized as a **German citizen** and renounced his Romanian nationality; three years later in 1935 he was de-naturalized by the Nazis, rendering him **stateless** and an **alien** in Germany, so that he required a resident's permit; in 1938 the British recognized him as a **refugee** from Nazi persecution, treated as far as visa requirements go as a **non-German**, rather than a non-person; nevertheless in 1940 they interned him as a **German 'enemy alien'**. In 1942 the British recognized him as **stateless** and a further seven years later (1947) he was naturalized as a **British citizen**.

These eight different identifications were often overlapping and contradictory. Wolja had different relationships to them – they were variously claimed, refused, imposed, resisted and denied. Yet each of them had such significant consequences that he had to try to manage and negotiate the changes and contradictions in order to influence the outcome. Wolja often writes as if for him statelessness was just another status (or even national identity) like Romanian or German and he travelled on what he called his 'stateless passport'. His relationship to statelessness was further complicated by the fact that, in the UK, it became for him a desired status in comparison with the alternatives – German or Romanian.

Documenting Identity

My meanderings had taken me from my own passport, via Wolja's statelessness, to a discussion of the shifting ways in which he was formally identified by state authorities. Could my collection of papers help me to explore the way in which Wolja negotiated his way through these changes?

In order to do this, I am taking a pause in my telling of the story. Instead of focusing on a particular set of letters written under specific circumstances, as I have done in previous chapters, I am looking across the whole collection of papers, at letters and documents dating from different times and circumstances. I did not find them all in one place, and treated them at first as separate items, often surprised or confused about their significance. Now I recognized that they told their own story. Several of them opened up areas of historical research, which not only helped me to contextualize them, but which in turn raised further questions about their significance for Wolja.

Dated mostly between 1932 and 1939, a series of official letters, membership cards and documents suggest ways in which Wolja tried to document himself and was documented by the Nazi state, in terms of his national and ethnic/racial identity. They help us to imagine Wolja's sense of who he was and who he had to try to be in Nazi Germany as he lost rights, and tried to find a way to study, work and emigrate. Unless indicated all the papers in this section were written in German and translated by me.

1. Wolja's certificate of naturalization, issued by the Prussian Chief of Police, dated 23 February 1932 and its revocation dated 25 February 1935

The student and specialist writer Wolja Saraga in Berlin, born on 3 September 1908 in Deutsch-Wilmersdorf has acquired Prussian

Nationality through naturalization from the moment at which this certificate was delivered, and has therefore acquired German nationality. This naturalization does not extend to family members.

Under Paragraph 1 of The Law Regarding Revocation of Naturalization and the Revocation of German Citizenship of 14. July 1933...I hereby revoke your naturalization. From the moment of delivery of this order, you have lost Prussian nationality and with this ceased to be a citizen of the German Reich...There is no legal appeal against this revocation.

An official Romanian document and a copy of a German translation, both dated 8 June 1932, show that, following his naturalization, Wolja had formally renounced his Romanian citizenship. An English translation, dated 8 June 1939, perhaps reflects his fear, described in the previous chapter, of being considered Romanian by the British.

The 'Denaturalization Law' of July 14, 1933, 'called for the cancellation of naturalizations that had taken place between November 9, 1918, and January 30, 1933...' and it was one of the 'measures taken against the so-called Eastern Jews'.[15]

2. A letter dated 4 March 1935 from the President of the *Reichsschriftumskammer* [Reich Writing Chamber, RSK]
One week after his denaturalization, Wolja received the following letter:

Wolja Saraga
With regret I must inform you that I have to decline your admission into the *Reichsverband Deutscher Schriftsteller* [Reich Association of German Writers, RDS] and thus into the *Reichsschrifttumskammer*. It is the wish of the Führer and the Chancellor that the administration of German cultural possessions be reserved for suitable and reliable national comrades, as defined in § 10 of the first order for the implementation of the *Reichskulturkammergesetz* [Reich Chamber of Culture Law]. Because of the great significance of intellectual and culturally creative work for the life and future development of the German people, there can be no doubt that the only persons who are suitable to carry out such an activity in Germany are those who belong to the German people, not only as citizens, but also through the deep attachment of nature and blood. Only one who, through his racial community, feels himself connected and committed to his people may undertake to exercise an influence on the inner life of the nation by

**Der Präsident der
Reichsschrifttumskammer**

Berlin W 8, den 4. März 1935.
Leipziger Str. 19
N j Jäger 3043/44

Herrn
Wolja Saraga,
Berlin-Zehlendorf
Sven Hedin Str. 68

Zu meinem Bedauern muss ich Ihnen mitteilen, dass ich Ihre
Aufnahme in den Reichsverband Deutscher Schriftsteller und
damit in die Reichsschrifttumskammer ablehnen muss. Nach
dem Willen des Führers und Reichskanzlers soll die Verwal-
tung des deutschen Kulturgutes nur geeigneten und zuverläs-
sigen Volksgenossen im Sinne des § 10 der ersten Verordnung
zur Durchführung des Reichskulturkammergesetzes vorbehalten
sein. Bei der hohen Bedeutung geistiger und kulturschöpfe-
rischer Arbeit für Leben und Zukunftsentwicklung des deutschen Volkes sind zweifellos nur d i e Persönlichkeiten
geeignet eine solche Tätigkeit in Deutschland auszuüben, die
dem deutschen Volke nicht nur als Staatsbürger, sondern auch
durch die tiefe Verbundenheit der Art und des Blutes angehö-
ren. Nur wer sich aus der rassischen Gemeinschaft heraus
seinem Volke verbunden und verpflichtet fühlt darf es unter-
nehmen, mit einer so tiefgreifenden und folgenschweren Arbeit,
wie sie das geistige und kulturelle Schaffen darstellt, einen
Einfluss auf das innere Leben der Nation auszuüben. Durch
ihre Eigenschaft als Nichtarier sind Sie ausserstande, eine
solche Verpflichtung zu empfinden und anzuerkennen. Ich muss
Ihnen daher die Zuverlässigkeit und Eignung, die die Voraus-
setzung für eine Mitgliedschaft bei der Reichsschrifttumskammer geben, absprechen und auf Grund des § 10 der genannten
Verordnung eine Aufnahme in den RDS, den für Sie zuständigen
Fachverband der Reichsschrifttumskammer, ablehnen. Die Ver-
öffentlichung schriftstellerischer Arbeiten innerhalb des
Zuständigkeitsbereichs der RSK ist Ihnen damit untersagt.

Im Auftrage

Für die
Richtigkeit: gez. Suchenwirth.

A letter excluding Wolja from membership of the Reichsschrifttumskammer, 4 March 1935.

means of such a profound and momentous activity as intellectual and cultural creativity. Because of your characteristic as a non-Aryan you are not in a position to feel and accept such a commitment. Therefore I must find that you do not have the reliability and suitability which form the prerequisite for membership of the Reich Writers' Chamber and in accordance with §10 of the above mentioned order turn down your application to join the appropriate professional association of the RDS. The publication of literary work within the area of responsibility of the RSK is hereby forbidden to you.

When I first came across this letter, I found it very hard to read because of the formal German – or at least I thought that this was the reason. On reflection I decided it was because it was emotionally hard; it was the first time I had encountered an explicitly Nazi characterization of one of my parents. I became aware of my emotional reaction after I had rather aggressively asked a German friend to tell me what it said, behaving as if somehow she was personally responsible for it. It was also one of the few papers for which I paid for a translation.

The letter shows very clearly that national identity is as much about inner life, moral obligations, belonging, home and acceptance as about legal status. A clear distinction is made between citizenship and the idea of a people or nation based on blood and nature. Wolja cannot feel the necessary commitment and attachment required to belong to the nation because of his non-German nature and blood and therefore he is not able to contribute to the nation's inner life. We saw in the last chapter that this characterization of him as unsuitable and unreliable would be repeated five years later, as an alien in Britain, attributed by the British to the very same Germanness that the Nazis denied he was capable of experiencing. This illustrates what Kay Saunders describes as the 'easy slippage of the distinction between racial origins, nationality and disloyalty'.[16] And at the time of first reflecting on these issues, the same thing was happening in the UK and USA in relation to Moslems, terrorism and internment in Guantanamo.

The *Reichsschriftumskammer* was one of the associations of the *Reichskulturkammer* (RKK) [Reich Chamber of Culture], an organization set up by the Nazis in 1933 to control all cultural life in Germany. In order to participate in any cultural activity, including publishing, it was necessary to be a member of one of the Chamber's subordinate associations. For Friedländer the RKK was significant as part of the '"de-Judaization" of cultural life'.

As peripheral as it may seem in hindsight, the cultural domain was the first from which Jews (and 'leftists') were massively expelled...Thus, even before launching their first systematic anti-Jewish measures of exclusion, the new rulers of Germany had turned against the most visible representation of the 'Jewish spirit' that henceforth was to be eradicated. In general the major anti-Jewish measures the Nazis would take from then on in the various domains were not only acts of terror but also symbolic statements.[17]

In 1935 Wolja was completing his PhD. He had been earning money by writing articles for scientific journals, an activity that he could not continue unless he was accepted by the RSK. I tried to imagine how he felt when he received this letter. Two years after its formation, he must have known the likely outcome of his request to join. Perhaps it was a formality, a process he felt he had to go through? He may have seen such a letter before, if friends of his had already received one. All of this is speculation on my part. What I do know is that Wolja was in good company; in the same year, 1935, the last prominent Jewish writers like Martin Buber were expelled from the RSK.[18] The only writers who could be members were those whose work was either explicitly pro-Nazi or at least approved of by the Nazis as 'non-degenerate'.

These three official letters document Wolja's exclusion from being German. A series of membership cards and certificates, dated between 1934 and 1936, perhaps represent Wolja's own attempts to document himself as Jewish.

3. A membership card for BZV - *Berliner Zionistischer Vereinigung* [Berlin Zionist Association] with subscriptions paid from February 1934 to September 1936.

This card seriously challenged my image and memories of my father. He had described his family as secular and non-observant and his mother as an active member of the Bund, a left-wing secular anti-Zionist organization. How should I interpret his membership?

Research on this period in Germany describes a split within the Jewish community in Germany, between the Zionist organizations and the much larger group of so-called 'assimilationists', organized by the '*Centralverein deutscher Staatsbürger jüdischen Glaubens*' (CV) [Central Association of German Citizens of Jewish Faith].

Luise Stein grew up in an assimilated German Jewish family. Her membership of the Zionist movement was 'too much' for her father:

Wolja's membership card for BZV, *Berliner Zionistischer Vereinigung* (Berlin Zionist Association), with subscriptions paid from February 1934 to September 1936.

We didn't talk to each other for weeks. He would become outraged
when anyone would ask him if he felt the Palestinian blood in
his veins. He would then pull out the family Bible to prove in "black
and white" that our ancestors had been living in Germany since before
the Thirty Years War, around 1600. The mere fact that Hitler said he
was not a German did not by a long shot mean that he wasn't one.[19]

Ruth Gay suggests that Zionism was not very popular in Germany before
the First World War, but nevertheless

> ...the Zionists were a source of concern for the Centralverein (CV)
> because they undermined its attempt to show primary Jewish loyalty
> to Germany. The Zionist view that there was a separate Jewish
> nationality, with its own history and culture, only confirmed the long
> standing anti-semitic accusations that the Jews were not and could not
> become part of the German people.[20]

The CV accused the Zionists 'of advocating an isolationist policy and a
"return to the ghetto".[21] Others went much further in their criticism. In his
diary entry for 13 June 1934, Victor Klemperer describes the Zionists as 'just
as offensive as the Nazis'.[22] It has been pointed out to me that his views may
not be representative. 'Even though he was the son of a rabbi, Klemperer
converted to Protestantism in 1912, married a non-Jew, and was rather
nationalist and elitist in his political views.'[23]

On the other hand, Benz argues, 'The more radical the Nazi state became,
and the more threatening the situation for the Jews in Germany, the greater
the persuasive power of the Zionists became.'[24] Gay also argues that the 'shock
of the Nazi takeover strengthened the Zionist movement', although 'whether
Jews had changed their minds about their place in Germany or whether this
was an expedient measure in the attempt to migrate to Palestine is not
certain, but membership jumped from 7,500 in 1931-32 to 43,000 in 1933-
34 and rose again to 57,000 in the following year'.[25]

Wolja joined the BZV at a time when membership generally was rising. I
imagine for him it was 'an expedient measure', but once again I am speculating.

4. A membership card for the RJK - *Reichsverband der Jüdische Kulturbünde in Deutschland* [Reich Association of Jewish Cultural Organizations in Germany], for the period October 1935 to September 1936.

The *Kulturbünde* were cultural organizations founded initially in Berlin in
1933, partly as a response to their expulsion from German cultural life. They

provided a place for Jewish artists and somewhere for Jews to go. On 19 June 1938 Lotte told Wolja she had been to see a film at the *Kulturbund*.

Like Zionism, the *Kulturbünde* were controversial within the Jewish community. For some Jews they were 'morale-building institutions',[26] even though what they were allowed to perform was controlled by the Nazis. Kurt Baumann, one of the founders of the Kulturbund acknowledged this contradiction: 'We really did enter the ghetto, but we brought the Jewish

Wolja's membership card for the RJK, *Reichsverband der Jüdische Kulturbünde in Deutschland* (Reich Association of Jewish Cultural Organizations in Germany), for the period October 1935 to September 1936.

public – at least for a time – a cultural forum with the kinds of offerings to which they were accustomed, and in surroundings that protected them from all sorts of unpleasantness.'[27]

Other Jews were more openly critical, arguing that they were doing the Nazis' work for them by establishing cultural ghettos. The leader of the Berlin Kulturbund was Kurt Singer, former deputy director of Berlin City Opera. Friedländer argues that 'Singer's Kulturbund fitted Nazi needs. When Singer's project of autonomous cultural activities by Jews and for Jews (only) was submitted to the new Prussian authorities, it received Göring's approval.'[28] As with the Zionist organization, Klemperer was scathing in his view of the Kulturbünd. On 9 September 1936 he wrote: 'The Jewish cultural leagues (they should be hanged) have issued a statement, saying they had nothing to do with sensational foreign news reports about the situation of German Jews. Next they will certify that *Der Stürmer* published nothing but the truth in fondest fashion. Bolshevism rages in Spain, while here there is peace, order, justice, true democracy.'[29]

And Joseph Roth, writing in 1937 described the Kulturbund as

> ...the officially sanctioned centrepiece of the new ghetto...This Kulturbund, however high-minded its inception, is nothing more or less than unwarranted concession on the part of the Jews to the barbarous theories of National Socialism. Its basis is not the assumption – accepted by so many Jews today – that they are a separated race, but the implicit admission that they are an *inferior* one...yet the Kulturbund Jews have simply accepted this discrimination as a given.[30]

Wolja's membership card, on which he has signed a statement that that he is a Jew or of Jewish origin, is for an organization formed in 1935, when all the different Jewish *Kulturbünde* were amalgamated under the control of the Reich. Once again I have no knowledge of why Wolja joined, but the dates of his membership do relate to other events in Germany and in his own life. He joined one month after the 'Nuremberg Laws' were passed, laws through which a legal definition of a Jew in terms of blood and inheritance was established by the Nazi state,[31] and like his Zionist one, his membership ended in September 1936. Both memberships spanned the time at which he was actively trying to emigrate.

5. A copy of Wolja's birth certificate dated 19 February 1936 in Berlin.

Wolja's birth certificate, reissued in February 1936, was another document that confirmed his Jewishness, as his parents are described as being of the

'Mosaic religion'. Amongst our papers is a translation of the birth certificate into English dated 19 September 1938.

6. A paper dated 1 April 1936, confirming that Wolja's father and Wolja are members of the Sephardic Jewish community in Ploesti, Rumania.

With this document, found together with a translation into French dated 7 April 1936, Wolja's Jewishness was confirmed by a non-state community organization.

Taken together, these last four documents illustrate the way the need to identify publicly as a Jew developed in parallel with being excluded from being German. Being a Jew offered no status in the world, but Wolja was also now stateless. He needed documentary evidence of his Jewishness in order to claim refugee status and obtain a visa for emigration. In Chapter 3 we saw how his Jewishness continued to be significant for him in England in 1938 in order to claim support from a variety of refugee organizations.

The next three documents show Wolja's capacity to network and his willingness to make use of his Romanian origins, and perhaps his father's contacts, to gain professional credentials.

7. Three press cards, for the years 1935, 1936 and 1937, which identify Wolja as the representative of particular organizations:

These documents variously identify Wolja as: a correspondent and technical contributor to *Radio Si Radiofonia* – Rumania's only radio journal'; a 'Correspondent' for *Cinema*, based in Bucharest; and a member of the Federation of Foreign Journalists, representing *Radio Bukarest, Der Radio-Hörer Basel* and *Cinema Bukarest*. In the first two cards there is a statement requesting 'authorities' to assist and support the person named in the card – very similar to the statement found in passports.

At first sight these cards might not seem relevant for this discussion of formal identification; but further consideration suggests they may also have served, in professional contexts at least, as identity documents for Wolja.

8. Olympics press badge

The last of my finds is another press accreditation. It does not really fit into my story here, but it aroused my curiosity. It is a brooch and ribbon for the 1936 Berlin Olympics. How did this come into Wolja's possession? I know that he was involved in the development of electronic music with colleagues at the Heinrich Hertz Institut and that one of these instruments was played for Hitler at the Games. Did Wolja himself go the Olympics or did a colleague give it to him? Sadly I shall never know.

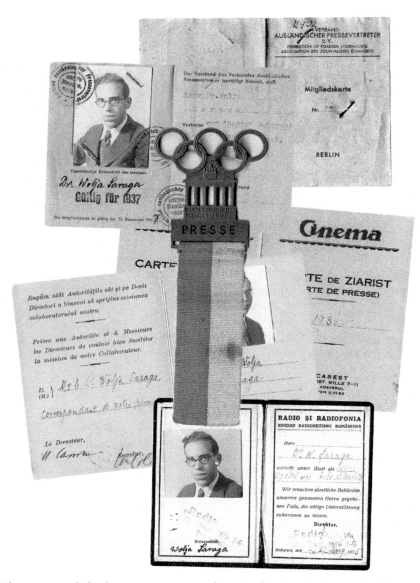

Three press cards for the years 1935, 1936 and 1937, and a 1936 Olympics press badge.

German Jews, Jewish Germans and Jews Living in Germany

By exploring the historical context of each document, what seemed to be a random collection of papers has helped me to understand the ways in which, in the early years of the Nazi regime, persecution was symbolic as well as material, as much about loss of identity, in particular the right of Jews to be German, as about material discrimination or persecution. 'German Jew' was not only a description of a person, but also a very particular identity, with a long history related to the history of Jewish emancipation and assimilation in Germany.[32]

From 1935 Jews were formally no longer allowed to describe themselves as 'German' and the names of Jewish organizations had to change from being associations of 'German Jews' to associations of 'Jews in Germany'. This is entirely in line with the letter from the *Reichsschrifttumskammer*, showing again that the process of exclusion of Jews operated not only through the big picture of for example legal rights to citizenship, but also through everyday knowledge and activities and social interactions with others.

I was aware that I kept coming across these distinctions between German Jews, Jewish Germans and Jews living in Germany. Three incidents in particular came to mind:

1. In March 2004 Esther Dischereit, a novelist born in Germany after the Second World War to a Jewish mother and non-Jewish father, was 'in conversation' with a British journalist at the Goethe Institute in London. Twice during the conversation she was asked whether she was German or Jewish. She didn't answer directly (hence the question being repeated) but she did say that within the literary world she was described as a Jewish rather than as a German writer. In the discussion afterwards, I asked why the question had been posed as: 'German **or** Jewish?' Couldn't she be both? I enquired further whether it would make a difference to see oneself as a German Jew or as a Jewish German. My question produced no answer, only laughter.

2. In her book *Long Shadows*, Erna Paris explores the sense of identity of Jews living in Germany today. Many people born in East Germany after the war described their reluctance to see themselves as German, preferring to describe themselves as 'Jews living in Germany'.[33] I was shocked; did they know this was the way Jews were described by the Nazis after 1935?

3. When I meet Germans who express amazement that as an English person I can speak some German, I often say *'meine Eltern kamen aus Deutschland – vor dem Krieg'* [My parents came from Germany – before the war.] The pause between the two halves of my statement is important. The response I get can tell me a great deal about the person I am speaking to. I am aware that I can be wary of Germans, especially older ones, and use this as a kind of 'test'. The best response for me is

one that recognizes that my parents were probably Jewish. The 'came from Germany' is important too in conversation with English people. I was amazed to hear Liz tell the German owner of a restaurant in Yorkshire that my parents were 'German'. But of course she was right and they did not choose voluntarily to become not German. Long before I learned of the possibility of claiming German citizenship, I wondered whether my parents, or I, had a right to reclaim this Germanness.

This brings me back to the question of how my parents might have felt in Germany as they grew up. My mother used to speak about her non-religious family, whilst at the same time telling me that she was one of three Jewish girls in her class, and that they tended not to be invited to the birthday parties of non-Jewish girls. But I know that she also had non-Jewish friends. She told me a moving story of the night before she left Germany, when a friend called her and said 'I think it so terrible that you have to leave – please remember that not all Germans support the Nazis.' In contrast to Lotte, Wolja grew up with parents who were immigrants. But I had never thought about this parallel with Peter's and my experience until I was standing in the street in Berlin in which he was born and in which he lived for the first few years of his life. The impact of the physical surroundings, imagining him there with his parents, made me realize that he too had 'foreign' parents. The differences between us occurred at a formal, legal level. Born in the UK in 1942 and 1945, Peter and I became British citizens automatically as a result of our birth, even though at that time our parents were still officially 'stateless'. Not something that would happen today. By contrast Wolja was ascribed his father's nationality of Romanian. In some of the letters he refers to living under the regulations for 'Foreigners' in Germany, but I have no knowledge – neither from memory nor from the papers – of what this would have meant for him.

In 1995 on a visit to an exhibition in the Martin Gropius Bau Museum in Berlin I came across an extraordinary book – a 1994 reprint of the second edition of the *Jüdisches Adressbuch für Gross-Berlin* [Jewish Address book for Greater Berlin]. I flicked through it and found some additional addresses for both my parents. I did not buy it – it cost £40 and I could not imagine using it further. Once I had started on this project I deeply regretted this, but discovered it was out of print. Luckily it is available in several libraries and most recently as a digital download.[34]

In addition to the addresses, this extraordinary document offers further insight into how German Jews saw themselves, at least in Berlin. It includes long articles about all aspects of Jewish life, culture and business. Entries were constructed from membership of Jewish congregations and organizations. People were not consulted about being included and the authors acknowledge that some people whose addresses are given no longer considered themselves Jewish, or might even wish to hide the fact. Nevertheless they believed the book would strengthen Jewish and non-Jewish relations, by creating for Jews and non-Jews a simple way of knowing who is a Jew, as well as providing an education about Jewish life and culture and its importance for the fatherland. This second edition was produced in 1931 at a time of increasing anti-Semitism and a strong Nazi party. For my purposes here, what is of particular interest is a section of the Foreword which reviews the position of the Jewish community in 1930:

> German Jewry has a very difficult time ahead. Political and economic worries cloud the horizon. Anti-Semitism is increasingly being wielded as an indiscriminate weapon…Should we in times such as these shrink back like cowards and deny our nature? Doing this would achieve nothing, since the enemy would still point the finger at us. This is out of the question if we are to do justice to the magnificence of our tradition, which goes back thousands of years, and to the sense of our history. We know that we are Jews and we wish to declare ourselves members of the Community, in keeping with a natural sense of loyalty to our roots. On the other hand, being good Jews, we are also equally good Germans, and the Jewish community in particular, which through its life and activities displays the virtues of a great tradition can also come to appreciate and love those virtues, which are based on the traditional links between German Jews and the German nation past and present. We Jews do not just live in Germany; we are German as our forefathers were before us. We were born on German soil and are firmly rooted, body and soul, in the German community. However much anti-Semites would like to deny our Germanness, it is nonetheless a fact which we live out every day, and no power in the world will be able to sever our innate bond with the German people, to make us question our sense of belonging in Germany.[35]

It is harder to imagine a stronger statement of how German Jews felt about being and wanting to remain German. At the same time, with hindsight, I was appalled to think about how wrong they were and to feel that they were doing Hitler's work for him in identifying all the Jews in Berlin. It is striking to see that they describe the attachment of Jews to Germany in language similar to that used by the Nazis to exclude them.

In contrast to Lotte, Wolja did not have the same connection across generations. I wondered whether he had a more precarious sense of who he was, with a greater need to document his commitments and loyalties. By bringing these papers with him, Wolja showed that he understood their importance and I am reminded of the earlier argument about stateless people knowing the value of documents.

It is Only Here that I am at Home

The letters, documents and membership cards I have discussed so far do not tell me how Wolja juggled and negotiated these different identities, knowing their consequences. I turned to a second very different set of papers which offer Wolja's own words – statements from him about who he is, and his claims for rights and for justice. They are all concerned with the consequences of his statelessness, the place from which I started this chapter. In each case, Wolja is writing for a particular purpose, desirable of a particular outcome; he attempts to persuade, to convince or at least to argue his case. I was aware how important it was to keep this context in mind.

Following the revocation of his naturalization, Wolja had once again become an 'alien' in Germany. On 3 April 1935 he wrote to the police in Berlin to apply for a residence permit.

> I am respectfully applying for a residence permit. I was born on 3.9.1908 in Berlin, went to school here, and studied at the University of Berlin. I enclose proof of my attendance from the University. I live with my parents and am supported by them. I was originally a Romanian national, naturalized in Prussia on 23.2.1932 and de-naturalized on 25.2.1935. (I received notification of this on 6.3). I shall therefore today also make an application for an alien's passport.
>
> Since I was born and grew up here, and have lived continuously in Berlin, and since German is my mother tongue, it is only here that I am at home. I am therefore respectfully requesting a *dauernde* resident's permit.

'Dauernde' can be translated as 'permanent', 'lasting' or 'continuous'. Just one month after receiving the letter from the *Reichsschrifttumskammer* that denied the very possibility of his being German in any essential way, Wolja was asserting an aspect of that same Germanness. Whether or not he was allowed to stay in Germany was a bureaucratic process, unaffected by how he felt about being German or about Germany. Nevertheless he demonstrates his understanding of the relationship between national identity, belonging and loyalty, which we have seen was so much a part of the German-Jewish identity. He did not claim that he was German, emphasizing instead that he was 'at home' in Germany, thus invoking 'home' as the site of everyday lived experience and rootedness rather than in terms of belonging to the 'nation'. To what extent was he writing what the authorities required, or what he thought they wanted to hear? Or should we see this as a polite expression of his sense of injustice?

I discovered later that he had to apply for such a permit on a regular basis. Without it he could not get a visa for travel. The two earliest letters between Wolja and Lotte date from 1937. Lotte was clearly on holiday in Italy. Both letters are handwritten and difficult to read; their relationship seems established but still relatively new. On 10 June 1937 Wolja tells her that his main activity for the last 10 days '…has been to go every morning to the Alien's Department. I have had difficulties with my residence permit. … Therefore I could not travel. Today at last I got my visa. I shall perhaps travel tomorrow morning, perhaps not until early on Monday. In any case, when you come back I shall not be here…'

In the four page document written for a lawyer, discussed in Chapter 3, Wolja explains why he applied for naturalization in the first place. He uses nearly identical phrases to those in his letter to the police applying for a residence permit, but expands them.

> Since I was born in Berlin, lived continuously in Berlin, went to school, Hochschule and University in Berlin and because German is my mother tongue and absolutely the only language in which I can express myself fluently, and because I have worked scientifically, technically and journalistically (I have also given lectures at the Radio exhibition) in Germany and only in Germany, it was natural for me to make an application for naturalization in Germany. My application was approved at the beginning of 1932, because of the relaxed regulations for those applicants who have lived in Germany since birth and who apply between their 21st and 23rd birthdays.[36]

To emphasize his Germanness, he argues that German is the only language in which he is fluent. By contrast, in his CV in the SPSL archive, also written in 1935, he claims he speaks German, French and English well and has some knowledge of Russian and Dutch.[37] This offers another example of the way in which he has to juggle and present information for different purposes.

Four years after his attempt to persuade the German police of his Germanness, Wolja was still an alien, but now in the UK. This time he wanted to persuade the authorities, the Metropolitan Police Aliens Registration Department, that he was not German. He wrote in English.

In my…Certificate of Registration my nationality is stated as "German". I am a Jewish refugee from Germany. I was, however, a Rumanian by birth until the age of 23 when I acquired the German nationality. When still in Germany, my naturalisation was cancelled in 1935, according to the new laws, so that I possessed the German nationality only for about three years. By this cancellation I became Stateless and was subject not only to the restrictions for Jews in Germany but also to the regulations concerning foreigners in Germany. Likewise I was considered as "Stateless" by foreign Consulates in Germany and thus my efforts to emigrate from Germany were rendered considerably more difficult. When I obtained a grant for research work in Switzerland, I was not, as a Stateless, given the necessary Swiss visa which I would have easily obtained as a Jew of German nationality. Also when I tried to get permission to come to this country the British Passport Officer in Berlin considered me as Stateless, not as a German Jew, so that in 1937, at a time when German Jews could still enter this country without any visa, in my case an application for a visa had to be sent to the Home Office and was only granted because of my profession of research engineer.

I should be very grateful if you were kind enough, in view of the above mentioned circumstances which I should be glad to prove by documents if desired, to cancel the entry 'German' under "Nationality" and to replace it by "Stateless" in my Certificate of Registration. When my Certificate of Registration was issued to me, I pointed out that I am stateless but was informed that, since my stateless passport (Fremdenpass) was issued by the German authorities, the entry "German" would be as good.

But in view of the present newspaper reports that German Jewish refugees, in case of an emergency, will be considered as German subjects, the entry "German" in my Certificate of Registration would be likely to lead to serious consequences for me which would be obviously be quite unwarranted by the actual legal and technical facts.

I hope that you will agree that, after my having experienced so many additional difficulties by losing my German nationality when still in Germany and becoming stateless and having obtained the permission to enter this country under the regulations for Stateless persons which, at that time, were much more severe than the regulations for Jewish refugees of German nationality, I ought not to be considered as of German nationality (28 August 1939).

In this letter Wolja makes a range of different statements about identity and identification: he describes himself as 'a Jewish refugee from Germany'; he uses the term 'nationality', not making a distinction between citizenship and national identity, and shows how nationality can be both linked to birth and acquisition (by naturalization), an acquisition that can also be cancelled. Although documents were important as evidence for his statements, how you are viewed by state authorities - foreign consulates, Swiss visa officials, or a British Passport Officer may sometimes be more important than official documents, for example when applying for visas. His final argument moves away from formal processes and logical arguments, appealing instead to natural justice.

It is perhaps not surprising that Wolja did not receive a reply to this letter; the Second World War started six days later. In a later letter to Nancy Searle (April 1940) Wolja explains:

In August 1939, however, my wife (after consulting you) went to Bow Street and asked for an alteration in the Certificate of Registration. The official said that the entry stateless was made very seldom and that it was now too late. Thereupon I made an application in writing, copy of which I am enclosing. I did not receive any answer. At the Tribunal the judge had this letter but did not give me an opportunity to discuss this question.

If I had had the correct entry in my Certificate of Registration at the outbreak of war I should not have had to register as an enemy alien at all or to appear before a tribunal. Also my employers, in view of all the facts, did not consider me as German at first, but slowly they are changing their attitude seeing that I am now considered German by the police.

I hope you will understand that I am not trying to obtain any preferential treatment with regard to other German refugees. But I lived in Germany as an alien and under the restrictions for aliens for more than 23 years and after a break of three years of German nationality again for three years. I really cannot feel as a German quite apart from being a refugee…

From this letter, we see the power of the document, the importance of the attitudes of the authorities, and the context of the war. Although his employers know all the 'facts', they have become increasingly apprehensive about Wolja's position – if the police see him as German, should they do so too? In total contrast to the way he wrote to the German authorities, here he asserts his lack of Germanness, but in both letters he recognizes that this operates not only at the legal level, but also in terms of how he feels. The arbitrariness of bureaucracy, and the consequences of such arbitrariness, is revealed in the phrase: 'the entry stateless was made very seldom and that it was now too late'

Wolja's complex negotiations around his identities are illustrated most clearly in an exercise book found amongst the letters from internment. He has copied out a form, on which he is applying for release from internment. The form is dated 15 July 1940, his first wedding anniversary. According to Stent release was the main preoccupation of internees, and in some camps they were invited to apply to keep them occupied and less restive, even though there was no chance of it being granted.[38] On this form Wolja gives his nationality as stateless, and his wife's nationality before marriage as 'German, Jewish'. I was particularly fascinated by his response to question 24:

> 24. Have you any special reason to urge why you should (a) be kept in internment in this country rather than in a British Dominion or Colony, (b) be released from internment?
> (a) (1) I and my firm are applying for my release from internment. My firm has also applied that I should not be sent overseas
>   (2) I object to be separated from my wife who is without any relatives in this country and wholly depending upon me.
>   (3) If however my services as a physicist and engineer are no longer acceptable, which I should deeply regret, I would have a chance of emigrating to the U.S A in a few months time (I registered at the American Consulate in Berlin in March 1937, a year before I came to this country). I should like to stress that I lost all interest in emigration, after I came to work in this country

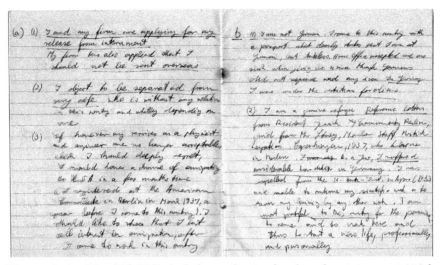

The exercise book in which Wolja drafted an application for release from internment, 15 July 1940.

(b) (1) <u>I am not German</u>, I came to this country with a passport which clearly states that I am not German, but stateless. Home Office accepted me as such when giving me visa though Germans did not need any visa. In Germany I was under the restrictions for aliens.

(2) <u>I am a genuine refugee</u>. <u>Reference letters</u> from President Jewish Community Berlin, and from Mr Storey , Member Staff British Legation Copenhagen, 1937, who knew me in Berlin. As a Jew, <u>I suffered considerable hardship in Germany</u>. I was expelled from the H.-Herz-Inst.in April 1933 and unable to continue my scientific work or to earn my living by any other work. <u>I am most grateful to this country</u> for the permission to come and personally.

(3) <u>I am most anxious to help</u>, my <u>sympathies</u>, wishes and hopes on this war are <u>wholeheartedly on the British side</u>. It is my strong personal and professional conviction that a victory of Hitler would be disastrous for civilisation.

Signature   W. Saraga, Dr Phil

Date   15-7-40

(4) I think I was able to some <u>work useful to this country</u> with Electrical Research Association and Telephone Manuf. Co. <u>I hope to be allowed to continue this work</u> Telephone Manuf. Co has made <u>application for my release</u>.

Wolja always impressed upon us the importance of keeping copies of forms you have filled in, and I could imagine the care he had taken with this form. He seems to be trying to negotiate a very careful route through a series of oppositional identifications. He understands that these designations are not only about legal rights, but also about personal attachments. Thus in his struggle not to be deported, he makes reference to his responsibilities as a husband to support his wife, even though in fact at this particular time, and previously in Germany, Lotte was the main breadwinner; he emphasizes Lotte's isolation, and also his own potential contribution to Britain as a physicist. He needs to present himself as loyal to Britain, to reject his identification as German and to emphasize his status as a 'genuine refugee'. He has to try to get it right simultaneously for both possible outcomes, i.e. staying in the UK, or emigrating to the USA. Once again he presents the case about his nationality in a very logical way, pointing out the lack of logic in the Home Office position, but also being respectful.

Writing to Wolja in internment on 24 August 1940, Lotte explained the Home Office view:

> With regard to nationality, I received reply from Home Office. As long as you have not acquired any new nationality they must continue to regard you as German...the English standpoint is that you have the nationality of the country where you are from. I do not think they mind that you applied for naturalisation but they do not recognize statelessness. It is futile to argue.

For the British, Wolja's nationality derived from his place of birth (Germany), reinforced by the fact that it was German authorities who issued the stateless document that allowed him to travel. This is further illustrated in a letter from the Home Office to Mr Flint, Wolja's boss at TMC, which he forwarded to SPSL on 31 July 1940. 'In the absence of documentary evidence that Dr. Saraga is now recognised as the national of some other State, he must continue to be regarded as possessing German nationality.'[39] This justified his continuing internment. In the context of war the primary concern was questions of loyalty; what was seen as Wolja's 'national identity' was more important than his legal status or the fact that he was also Jewish and a refugee – and hence likely to be anti-Nazi.

After his release from internment, this view of Wolja as German continued to have a considerable impact on his capacity to work. He was still officially German and still potentially unreliable and disloyal. To re-employ him, his firm had to give an undertaking that as a 'German national' he would have no access to any secret or confidential work. Perhaps for this reason and also for fear of what might happen to his rights to remain in Britain, Wolja continued his struggle with the Home Office. On 1 October 1941 his German refugee solicitor, Mr. Cromwell, told him about a precedent in which the Home Office had recognized a 'Mr. S' as stateless. He advised Wolja to instruct 'Mr Binford Hole, Solicitor, and consider the question of bringing an action in case of refusal'. On 1 January 1942 Elwell & Binford Hole Solicitors invited Wolja to visit them:

> ...kindly bring with you any documents that bear upon the question, and in particular, your passport issued in May 1938 which, we understand states that you are not of German nationality and which was visaed by the British Passport Control Officer in Berlin, and also any notice you may have informing you that your German citizenship had been revoked pursuant to the law of 1933, and any correspondence with the Home Office.

On 23 June 1942 Mr. Cromwell wrote to him: 'To my satisfaction I have heard from Mr. Hole that the third application was successful and you are now registered as stateless...I think in all the circumstances, particularly the danger of a Rumanian alternative, our efforts have not been wasted.'

What a good thing Wolja had been so conscientious in keeping all his documents. His experiences illustrate what Jane Caplan and John Torpey describe as 'the relationship between the emancipatory and the repressive aspects of identity documentation.'[40] I wonder whether Lotte and Wolja later found it hard to throw anything away, just in case they needed it. I think again about the Windrush scandal and all the asylum seekers who are refused entry today because they can't prove their nationality, date of birth or family membership. Many of them probably had to flee much more quickly than Lotte and Wolja did.

Wolja's difficulties did not end with this success. Officially he was stateless, but we have seen that attributions of national identity do not depend only on legal categories of citizenship. In many ways he was still seen as German. In May 1944 he was denied membership of the Institution of Electrical Engineers under Bye-Law 23.

> Any member of any class who is the subject of a country or state at war with His Majesty or his successors shall ipso facto cease to be a member of the Institution and shall not be eligible for re-election to membership of the Institution so long as the aforesaid state of war shall continue and for such further period thereafter as the Council may determine.

In response, the Chief Engineer of TMC wrote to the Institution:

> …As you quote Bye-law 23, I should be grateful if you would be good enough to explain how this applies to Dr…the candidate in question, as he is not "a subject of a Country or State at war with His Majesty"; he ceased to be such a subject in February 1935, i.e. more than four years before the outbreak of war, and entered this country after he had ceased to be of German nationality, as recognized by the Home Office.

Sadly, I have no idea of the outcome of this letter, but I do have papers concerned with Wolja's application for naturalization, which provide me with an ending to this particular story. With support from the Telephone Manufacturing Company and from the Society for the Protection of Science and Learning, in July 1946 Wolja was able to make a claim for priority in relation to an application for naturalization as someone who had 'made a substantial contribution in some civilian capacity to the war effort, or is by his business or profession making a substantial contribution to the economic welfare of the nation…'[41] This was the third time within eight years that Wolja's status as a scientist had been crucial – for getting him the UK visa, for an early release from internment and now for priority in relation to naturalization.

Wolja's name appears in the London Gazette of 24 June 1947, in a 'LIST of ALIENS to whom Certificates of Naturalization have been granted by the Secretary of State and whose oaths of Allegiance have been registered in the Home Office during the month of May, 1947.'[42]

> Saraga, Wolja: Of no nationality; Physicist and Research Engineer; 43 Kingsway, Petts Wood, Orpington, Kent. 26 April 1947.[43]

Lotte had to apply within twelve months if she wished to become a British citizen too. She applied immediately; her naturalization is dated 9 May 1947. Their status in the UK was now secure.

Notes

1. The coalition government of 2010 dropped the fingerprint idea.
2. J. Torpey, *The Invention of the Passport. Surveillance, Citizenship and the State* (Cambridge: Cambridge University Press, 2000).
3. See also J. Caplan and J. Torpey (eds), *Documenting Individual Identity. The Development of State Practices in the Modern World* (Princeton, NJ and Oxford: Princeton University Press, 2001).

4. D. Cannadine, 'A Point of View', *BBC Radio 4*, 18 June 2010.

5. Caplan and Torpey, *Documenting Individual Identity*, p.10.

6. Ibid.

7. http://www.unhcr.org/uk/stateless-people (Accessed 11 July 2018).

8. All these terms are used in UNHCR, 'Special Report. The strange, hidden world of the stateless', *Refugees*, 147, 3, 2007. Downloaded as pdf from www.unhcr.org (Accessed 5 December 2018).

9. UNHCR, 'Special Report', p. 19.

10. Ibid., p.5.

11. See, for example, https://www.parliament.uk/business/news/2019/march/shamima-begum-subject-of-urgent-question-following-the-death-of-her-baby/. https://www.amnesty.org.uk/press-releases/uk-revoking-shamima-begums-british-citizenship-legally-and-morally-questionable (Accessed 18 March 2019).

12. J. Roth, *The Wandering Jews,* trans. Michael Hofmann (London: Granta Books, 2001), p.126. Originally published in German as *Juden auf Wanderschaft.* This quote appears in the Preface to the New Edition 1937.

13. https://www.amnesty.org.uk/britains-shame-70-years-after-windrush. 29 May 2018 (Accessed 11 July 2018).

14. A. Gentleman, 'ID cards may cut queues but learn lessons of history, warn Europeans', *The Guardian*, Saturday 15 November 2003.

15. S. Friedländer, *Nazi Germany and the Jews. The Years of Persecution 1933–39* (London: Weidenfeld & Nicolson, 1997), p.27.

16. K. Saunders, 'The Stranger in our Gates': Internment Policies in the United Kingdom and Australia during the Two World Wars, *Immigrants & Minorities*, 22, 1 (March 2003), pp. 22-43, p.29.

17. See Friedländer, *Nazi Germany and the Jews,* p.10.

18. https://en.wikipedia.org/wiki/Martin_Buber (Accessed 27 July 2018).

19. M.Limberg and H. Rübsaat (eds), trans. A. Nothnagle, *Germans No More. Accounts of Jewish Everyday Life, 1933-1938* (New York and Oxford: Berghahn Books, 2006), p. 145.

20. R. Gay, *The Jews of Germany. A Historical Portrait* (New Haven, NJ and London: Yale University Press, 1992), p.209.

21. W. Benz, trans. J. Sydenham-Kwiet, *The Holocaust. A Short History* (London: Profile Books, 2000), p.18.

22. V. Klemperer, trans. M. Chalmers, *I Shall Bear Witness. The Diaries of Victor Klemperer* (London: Weidenfeld & Nicolson, 1998), p. 64.

23. Email to author, Jane Caplan, 18 August 2014.

24. See Benz, *The Holocaust*, p.18.

25. See Gay, *The Jews of Germany,* p. 260.

26. Ibid., p.264.

27. See Limberg and Rübsaat, *Germans No More,* p.120.

28. See Friedländer, *The Jews of Germany,* p.65.

29. See Klemperer, *I Shall Bear Witness,* p.181.

30. See Roth, *The Wandering Jews,* p.130.

31. There were two laws – *Gesetz zum Schutze des deutschen Blutes und der deutschen Ehre* [The Law for the Protection of German Blood and German Honour] and the *Reichsbürgergesetz* [Reich Citizenship Law].

32. G.L. Mosse, *German Jews Beyond Judaism* (Bloomington, IL: Indiana University Press, 1985), p 2.

33. E. Paris, *Long Shadows, Truth, Lies and History* (London: Bloomsbury, 2000), p. 22.
34. *Jüdisches Adressbuch für Gross-Berlin* (Berlin: Goedega Verlags-Gesellschaft m.b.H. Berlin, 1931). Reprinted by the Arani Verlag, 1994. Available to download at: http://nbn-resolving.de/urn:nbn:de:kobv:109-1-2414417. There were only 2 editions; the first one was in 1929.
35. Translation by H. Simon. Available at the Wiener Library.
36. B338/290. I have been unable to find any historical references to this naturalization regulation.
37. B338/274.
38. R. Stent, *A Bespattered Page? The Internment of His Majesty's 'Most Loyal Enemy Aliens'* (London: Andre Deutsch, 1980), pp. 142-3.
39. B338/354.
40. See Caplan and Torpey, *Documenting Individual Identity*, p.5.
41. *AJR Information* (January 1946), p.6.
42. *The London Gazette*, Tuesday 24 June, 1947, p. 2858.
43. Ibid., p.2881. The date indicates when the Oath of Allegiance was taken.

6

'Oh, This Separation of Parents and Children is So Terrible'

As a child, I envied my friends who had grandparents – it seemed to be a very special relationship – one that I am very conscious of now as I observe my friends with their grandchildren. At the time I thought it was just another way in which we were different from our English friends. I didn't really worry about what had happened to them, reassuring myself that they were 'old'.

Working on these papers made me aware of how little I knew about my grandparents – only a few stories. Every year, on his parents' birth or death days or on their wedding anniversary, Wolja would show us photographs and cry – something that was both painful and embarrassing to me as child – very unEnglish and unmanly! I knew that Wolja's mother Esther (known as Eti), after whom I was named, was originally Russian and a qualified doctor. She was very small, with lots of sisters; his father, Avram (known as Ado) was Romanian with many brothers and sisters. Wolja himself was an only child. His parents met in Berlin, where they had both come to study. Wolja's parents spent the war in Romania, where his mother died. After the war Ado came to live with us, but he died just before I was two. I have no conscious memories of him, only photographs of myself with him and stories of how much he loved us. Peter does remember him.

By contrast Lotte rarely talked about her parents. We knew that her father, Hermann, a secular assimilated Jew, had died before the war and her mother, Erna, went to Palestine to join Lotte's older sister. Lotte told me that as a child she was allowed to kiss her father once a week. Peter has a further memory – that he was a furrier and took care of his workers, at great cost to himself, during the inflation in the early 1920s. Lotte spoke about his death for the first time after Wolja died, while we were reading the condolence letters. Turning to me, she said: 'I know this is your loss too; I remember what it is like to lose a father'. I now know that she was 21 when he died. A telegram was sent to her on 24 May 1935, while she was living in Milan: 'Father seriously ill. Come'.

The only story I remember about Lotte's mother, Erna, is the one I described in Chapter 1, when Lotte said goodbye to her in Berlin. I have a

My grandparents: Hermann and Erna Isenburg, Eti and Ado Saraga.

sense of her being a very loving mother, a feeling strengthened by hearing Lotte's last words before she died – 'Mutti, Mutti'.

On 29 March 2005 I wrote in my notebook:

Today I noticed for the first time a reference (20 June 1938) to Lotte getting a *Nachweis* [certificate] for her grandmother – I hadn't

Telegram to Lotte in Milan, telling her to come home, 24 May 1935.

registered this before, though I had copied the German into my notes. I know what happened to her mother and sister, but I have no idea, have never asked, never wondered before about any of her other relatives, including her grandparents.

In their letters in 1938 Lotte and Wolja discussed what Wolja's parents should do. As Romanian citizens, they did not qualify as refugees and on 16 June Lotte was told by the *Hilfsverein* [Aid Association of German Jews] that, despite their experience and qualifications, they were too old (in their early 50s) to obtain visas for the UK. It was always Lotte and Wolja's intention that Eti and Ado should join them in London once their own position was secure. Why did this not happen? Perhaps it was time to find out some more.

Over 500 letters and telegrams cover the period of time between May 1938, when Wolja left Berlin, and January 1947 when Ado arrived in England. The majority (about 450 items) are from or about Wolja's parents. Many are several pages long and handwritten in German, French or English. Before the war broke out they communicated in German, subsequently, whenever possible, in French or English. What remains of Wolja's side of the correspondence with his parents consists of carbon copies of letters, drafts in which he seems to be practising his French and draft telegrams. From early 1941, following the advent of the fascist dictatorship, no letters could be sent directly to Romania. At first they communicated through friends in the USA and later through Ado's sister Amelie and her son Mondy in Zurich or occasionally also through Eti's sister, Sonja, in Sweden. Many letters are stamped by the censor, which presumably added further delays. Whenever there was urgent information to convey or when the anxiety about not having heard from the other party became too great, they sent telegrams. These difficulties made it very hard to conduct a dialogue; by the time an answer to a question arrived, several more letters had been sent and many more questions asked. It was even harder for me to reconstruct their dialogue as some letters are not dated and I do not always know when the letters arrived. Most confusing were two letters which I eventually realized from the content had been dated in the wrong year.

The correspondence between Lotte and her mother and sister is not nearly so extensive. She did not need to draft her letters as she was writing in German and she did not always keep copies. Only six of her letters to her mother have survived. Some of the letters from Palestine are difficult to read as they are not only handwritten, but sent as 'airgraphs' (copies of reduced microfilms).

I decided to start with correspondence between Wolja and his parents and to organize my reading around the themes of separation and loss, inevitable experiences for any refugees. The letters also offer a story of extensive networking and negotiations with the Home Office in order to obtain permission for Ado to join Wolja in the UK. I shall return to this in the next chapter.

Please Come Now

From their letters to Wolja I can trace Eti and Ado's movements. On 25 September 1938 they were visiting Eti's sister Sonja in Copenhagen, but by December 1938 they were in Bucharest, living with Ado's brother, Achille. Ado had not lived in Romania for over thirty years. In his letters he complains about his family's bourgeois lifestyle which is anathema to him. Although he established some business contacts in Romania, he could not find a job. One of his contacts, Oscar Otineanu, would later introduce Wolja to some influential people in England.

Contact between Wolja and his parents was quite frequent, but Wolja was concerned that some letters had gone missing. In January 1939 he learned that his grandfather, Elias, was very ill. On 8 February 1939 Wolja told his parents that he was going to number his letters and keep a copy, 'otherwise it is impossible to remember three weeks later what I have written in a particular letter'. He enclosed a letter for his grandfather and reacted to his parents' frequent complaint that he did not write often enough and to their question about whether Lotte could help him with his job applications.

> Lotte and I wrote a joint very lovely letter to you all. We do not have a copy and have no time to write again. I feel very harassed by the amount I have to prepare for the new job and at the same time I have to work for the Research Association...Apart from that there are daily so many arrangements and letters. By the way, why do you presume that Lotte has lots of time? It is true that she has more free time than housemaids usually do. But she washes and darns all my things and also her own laundry and irons it, and then her free time is over. It is really not the case that she can do things for me as well as her paid work.

For Wolja, Lotte doing his laundry clearly did not count as doing things for him! Sadly for me, only one more letter is numbered, and some of his letters (referred to by Ado) are missing from my collection.

The Telephone Manufacturing Company had just received a temporary permit to employ Wolja. Although he was able to start work, he was still on a temporary visa and Oscar Otineanu advised him to wait until his position was more secure before trying to get his parents to the UK. Nevertheless on 18 March 1939 he sent them a formal letter of invitation in English, so that they could apply for a visa and be ready to travel at short notice should the situation become serious. Eti and Ado continued to complain about their relatives, who at first did not want them to leave Romania and later seemed to find them a burden. Wolja's letters are written in the rather polemical style he used with Lotte in 1938. He expresses considerable exasperation with them, while at the same time apologising for writing so prescriptively. His letter of 12 April is a good example, which also offers insights into how he felt himself as a refugee:

> ...I know that it is psychologically very difficult in your situation there, but don't forget that the majority of refugees not only have such concerns, but also immediate worries about getting enough food, suffer from hunger and have to live in terrible conditions, and don't always have relatives who are when it comes down to it good and well-intentioned, but have to deal with Committee officials, who

deliberately humiliate refugees as much as possible to make them go away.

We see and hear here a great deal about so much misery and I am so pleased that you are no longer in Germany and that I am in a position to be able to help you in an emergency. Dear Papa, I know myself how difficult it is always writing applications rather than being able to do productive work, but that is the fate of hundreds of thousands of people at the moment and not personal at all. In the meantime you should simply be pleased that you are able to live and that everything is looking very hopeful for me, so that we shall definitely be able to see one another soon. I long to see you and would be very happy if we could see one another. But from a sheer economic standpoint it is definitely better to wait a while.

By 23 June Wolja's parents had obtained their passports but not the English visa or transit visas, as they were only valid for a month. In case of emergency it was difficult to know what would happen. In his letter on that date, Ado refers to their Babylein, asking how far it is. I know that Lotte became pregnant before the war and had a termination. Given the probability of war and the possibility of a Nazi invasion, it did not feel like the right time to have a child. Through friends a doctor helped her and refused to charge her as a refugee. Two years later, when she miscarried, she felt very guilty about it. Lotte spoke to me about this in the last years of her life and she wrote a moving letter to a friend of mine, who had a similar experience in the 1970s.

On 23 August Wolja sent a telegram, which simply stated in English: 'Please come now'. Three days later, Ado replied, also in English: 'OBTAINED VISAS READY TRAVEL .The following day, his sister, Lorica sent a postcard in German: 'Ado and Eta left today at 7pm, full of joy about seeing you again soon...' But before it arrived, Wolja received another telegram, dated 29 August, this time in French: 'MUST RETURN SERBE FRONTIER ITALIANS REFUSE TRANSIT OTHER FRONTIERS ALSO CLOSED VERY SAD MANY KISSES HOPE WRITE SOON.'

A long letter in German, dated 29 and 30 August and sent express, explains why his parents were unable to leave Bucharest earlier. By the time Wolja received it on 7 September, they had written six more times – five postcards and one letter, presumably reflecting their level of distress. Wolja's reply in English tries to reassure them that even if they had left a day earlier, the frontier would have been closed. Once again he apologises for writing prescriptively, but says they will need all their strength for the time ahead, not knowing when they will be able to see one another again. He advises them to try to get on better with their relatives in Bucharest.

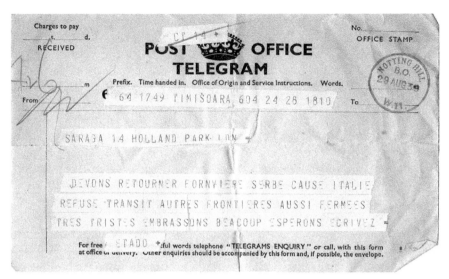

Telegram to Wolja from his parents telling him they were turned back at the Serbian border, 29 August 1939.

...You must not forget that human beings can have many feelings simultaneously and you should never forget their helpfulness because they sometimes show a lack of understanding...

Please write as often as possible. We shall do the same. Please write in French or English, then we shall get your letters quicker. It would also be useful if you could write on the typewriter...You must promise us that you will be reasonable and do all to remain strong and in good health. Do not loose courage, even if we have to wait now, we will do all we can so that we can see you as soon as possible.

If the war should spread to Rumania too, please buy gas masks and do all other necessary precautions and try to leave Bucarest. Please write if you need more money.

'£6 for Lotte from Roumania'

Despite the start of the war on 3 September, Lotte and Wolja continued to try to get Ado and Eti to London. A letter dated 18 March 1940 from Neil Pritchard at the Dominions Office to 'Dear Lotte', informs them that his second application on their behalf has been turned down as it is not 'sufficiently exceptional.' I imagine Neil Pritchard was a contact of Aaron, a

British civil servant in the Colonial Office who had married their German friend Ulla.

With visas and travel now impossible and written communication increasingly difficult, their letters are testimony to the high levels of anxiety they were all experiencing, anxiety intensified by Wolja's internment on 16 May 1940. He was frustrated by his powerlessness to help his parents, while they were actively networking from Romania on his behalf. After his release Lotte and Wolja decided that the UK offered them no security and applied again for visas for the USA. A folder amongst their papers contains all the relevant correspondence and documentation – visas, finger prints, statements of 'good conduct' from the police in Nazi Germany and details of all the financial assets of their guarantors, Morris and Leo Gottlieb, distant cousins in New York. Attached to Wolja's papers is a 'Medical Notification' with the results of his eye examination on 10 October 1940, 'WHICH MAY AFFECT ABILITY TO EARN A LIVING.' The visas were only granted following an additional affidavit from one of the guarantors who, despite never having met Wolja, was nevertheless still willing to provide for them financially for an indefinite period if necessary.

Lotte and Wolja sold the furniture they had acquired and planned to stay with their friends the Bikermanns in Glasgow to wait for a passage on a boat. Between November 1940 and February 1941 they repeatedly gave their parents and friends the Glasgow address, but it is not clear from the correspondence whether they did ever go there. In February 1941 they gave up and returned to Orpington. TMC, for whom Wolja had worked prior to his internment, had a vacancy and invited him back.

On 16 February 1941 Eti and Ado wrote in English to the Glasgow address:

> We are very sad, that we haven't now the possibility neither to correspond nor to wire you directly, But we have the possibility of telegraphic communication via Zürich, Therefore we ask you to wire every four weeks to Amelie Bollag ...with how you are. We shall do the same. Amelie will inform us of the content of your telegrams and vice versa. This is the only way to hear about each other...

From later letters I learned that in January 1941 Ado and Eti were imprisoned and in danger of being shot during the Legionnaires' rebellion.[1] They did not tell Wolja. Instead they continued to try every possible way to be in touch and to support Wolja and Lotte using an extensive network of contacts, beyond the extended family.

In February a woman called Florence Embury wrote from Istanbul to Dr. Bikermann in Glasgow: 'I am a good friend of Emily's and before I left Bucarest, she begged me to write to you from here as there may be more chance of this reaching you!...Emily has arranged for her bank to pay £6 for Lottie and hopes she will receive it safely...' On 9 June Dr. Bikerman told Wolja:

> I have received from Mr. W. Elmer, 54 Victoria Street, London...£6 for 'Lotte from Roumania'...As I know of no other 'Lotte' having any connection with Roumania, and as your parents are the only Roumanian residents knowing my address, I do not doubt that the money is intended for you. Your parents addressed it to 'Lotte' instead of to 'Wolja' since they believed that you were still interned. That is the best hypothesis I can invent so far. Please agree with it, and then I shall send you a cheque for six pounds.

One Must Accept One's Fate

Back in Orpington, Wolja too started networking again, making use of every possible contact to try to help his parents. On 31 May 1941 he asked Morris Gottlieb in New York if he knew of any organizations to help Jews in Romania. By the time the reply arrived on 6 July, the war situation had changed dramatically. Lotte replied the same day, thanking him for his kindness.

> ...we are extremely worried about my parents because they have to live in Rumania, where the Jewish persecution is now especially severe and cruel. Since the outbreak of the German – Russian war[2] this situation is still more precarious. We think, however, that as Rumania is now in a state of war and the U.S.A. virtually in the opposite camp, it may be dangerous for them to be connected with this country, and for their own safety should not receive letters or anything from America. But events change so quickly that there may be a situation when they will need help from abroad, if there should be, for instance a deportation of Jews, or some other now unforeseen event. In this case we should be extremely grateful to you if you could do everything for them in your power.

It was in this context of difficult communication and a fast changing political situation that, on 12 August 1941, Ado wrote to Wolja in French to tell him that his mother had been very ill for several months.

The worst is that there is no appropriate treatment for this illness, only a dietary regime that progressively weakens the patient. Your mother is permanently in the hands of these doctors who assure us it is a benign case and nothing serious. As you see, there is no reason to worry, but since the illness is a long one and because your mother is very weak and because our relationship has always been very close and open and because we have never had secrets from one another I think it is better that you know the truth.

I shall keep you well informed of how your mother is doing. She does not know, and she must not know, that I have written to you about her health; that is why I am sending you another letter as well, signed also by her and you must reply in the same way,

Do not worry, my dear son; I hope that it will all go well. I know that you have a lot of sorrows, but I think it is my duty to tell you the truth.

Ado's letter, sent via Amelie in Switzerland and passed by the censor, took a month to arrive. On 11 September Wolja wrote three letters in French. To his father:

It was a very sad letter that I received from you. Poor little maman, being ill again. To be separated from you is particularly sad, knowing that our darling Eti is ill. I know that you will do everything possible to help her and make her better. I hope with all my heart that it will be possible and that I will see you both again.

Although your letter gave me a terrible shock, you had to let me know. I hope it makes it easier for you to know that I am with you and Eti with all my thoughts and my hope.

You write that I have a lot of sorrows. It is not so. We are very well. Our only sorrow is that you are not with us. All my life, you and Eti, you have given me so much love. You have always been my best and my most loyal and genuine friends. It is terrible to think that now that I am capable of doing something for you, to take care of you, to give you some joy and happiness with Loti and me, that at this time we are separated and Eti is ill.

You write that Eti must not know that I know that she is ill. Perhaps you are right, but I think that perhaps it will be a joy and consolation to her to know and to read that our thoughts are with her. Be brave, my dear Papa, do not forget you have a son who loves you with all his heart and is with you in all his thoughts.

The second letter was to 'my dear, my beloved parents':

> It is now more than three years that we have been separated. It is so
> sad. You know that you have promised me many times that you will
> not lose hope of a happy future, a future in which we are all reunited.
> You have only one obligation – to remain healthy.
>
> We are very well, we are working. I am having some success in my
> scientific work. We had some holiday time which we spent with
> friends.
>
> In seven months' time Lotte is having a baby. We are very happy.
> We hope that by then we shall be reunited and you will help us to look
> after the new baby. We send you our love and embrace you
> affectionately.

This pregnancy of Lotte's was to miscarry.

The third letter was to his aunt Amelie:

> I am trying hard to be brave. I hope with all my heart that it is possible
> to save my mother…in general we live quite a solitary life. We would
> be very happy if we did not have these serious worries about my
> mother's health. Alas the last years have been very hard for us all, and
> it looks as though the future will bring a lot more sadness.

Four days later, on 15 September, Wolja received a telegram from Amelie in
English: Eti and Ado are well many heartiest wishes from them and us for
your birthdays…' But on 18 September another telegram arrived. Timed and
dated 16.45 on 16 September 1941, also in English, it came from Amelie's
son Mondy: 'Our dears we are so sorry to inform you that our dear and loved
Esther has left us she died yesterday in the afternoon heartfelt condolences'.

Lotte told me a painful story about receiving this telegram. She took it
upstairs to Wolja and smiled as she gave it to him, fearing its content. He
shouted at her: 'how can you smile when my mother has died!' I imagine
Lotte was trying inadequately to express some love for him as he read this
terrible news. And it will presumably have reminded her of the telegram she
had received in 1935 about her father.

The difficulties of communication must have added to Wolja's grief.
Telegrams in English were exchanged with Amelie in Switzerland, who told
him on 9 October: '…from ado nothing heard in meantime letters go 20 days
patience much love.' Ado had written to Wolja on 1 October in French with
more information about his mother's illness and death, but the letter did not
reach Amelie until 22 October and Wolja even later. He wrote in detail about

Eti's illness, the operation and treatment she underwent and finally her death. They tried to keep the truth from her:

> ...but as the illness progressed this became harder and harder for me, because as she was herself a doctor, she began to understand the cruel truth, but only out of consideration for me, she pretended to believe the lie, and she continued this game right to the end. But her farewell letter shows that she knew the truth. What dignity, nobility of soul!

Ado's reference to Eti's farewell letter suggests that it was included it with this letter. I had found it on its own, when I had first started sorting the papers. It is the most painful and poignant letter in the collection. Reading it for the first time was very distressing. I put it aside and out of my mind for several years. Reading it now can still make me cry, not because it is sad but because it very loving and lacking in self-pity. It is handwritten in German, but together with it we found a typed version, with its carbon copy. I have no idea who typed it. I am presenting it here in full. I hope that my translation does justice to it.

> My dearest beloved Wolja
> When you read this letter I shall no longer be here. You can imagine how hard it is for me to write this to you. But one day it has to happen, there's nothing one can do. One must accept one's fate. I have a big request for you and you must promise me to carry it out. I know what this will mean for you, but you must not take it too hard. You must think of your own life and I hope that dearest beloved Lotte will support you in this. You are both young and have already been through so much, hopefully you will soon be able to control your lives. I would die more easily if I knew that you were out of danger and that you at last have the possibility to live your own lives. In any case you should know that all my thoughts until my last breath belong to you and to darling Ado. Please be brave and do everything in your power to be with Ado, because it will be hardest for him, to be alone without me here with all these people who think only of themselves and of others only if they are rich. We have been through a lot here, but we were together, so it was easier to bear, but now he will be alone and my heart bleeds when I think about it, and the parting is even harder. It is terribly sad that I was not granted the chance to see you once more, but I would die happy if I knew that this sacrifice was necessary to keep you alive. I'm not making a sacrifice, that's what fate wants. If

anything like it is possible, my soul will hang over you to protect you. Think well of me, forgive me everything bad that I have consciously or unconsciously done. I kiss you both with all my heart and soul Your Eti-mother.

The typed version of the letter has an extra paragraph at the end.

My one and only Ado
The separation from you is very very hard for me. We two belong in life together, in happiness and sadness we have always been true to each other; only death will part us, but only physically, I know I will always be in your thoughts in the same way that, if anything like this is possible, I shall watch over you and Wolja. Be brave, one day it has to happen, one must bow to the inevitable.

Wolja's pain and grief is expressed in a letter (in English) to his aunt Rosa in America.

It is so difficult to write about it. My dear dear mother, my little Eti, your sister has died, 6 weeks ago. I feel I have to let you know. I still cannot understand it that I shall never see her again. Only a week before we received this news I heard that she is ill and we know now that she has been ill for some months. As terrible as it is for me, it must be a thousand times worse for my poor father who is now quite alone, and under such terrible conditions. But I cannot do anything for him at the present. I must wait and hope that after the war I shall at least him see again. You know probably how hard I tried to get my parents over to this country before war broke out but they hesitated until it was too late and they had to return.

Lotte's miscarriage must have occurred at about the same time. Although it is not mentioned explicitly, in a letter of 1 November 1941 Lotte's friend Ulla expresses her condolences to Wolja and describes Lotte as 'ein Ambulance Hospital case', adding 'no sooner do you put your heads above the parapet then something else hits you.' Lotte was pregnant again very soon as Peter was born on 22 September 1942.

Further evidence of the impact on Wolja of Eti's death comes from his letter dated 15 November 1942, to his old school friend Valja in Princeton:

I am very worried that I had no news of you for such a long time. Your last letter arrived here more than a year ago, informing me of your marriage. Just then I received the news that my mother had died. You can imagine what a terrible shock that was. It is more than a year ago, and just as ununderstandable as it was at the beginning. I wrote to you about it, I think last November or December. I never had any reply. I do hope that you are well. What about your parents, have you any news? Oh, this separation of parents and children is so terrible. Please write to me!

Unlimited Patience

In 1942 communication became even harder. Ado's letters, written usually in English or French and sent via Zurich, were further delayed by the censor. Several of the envelopes contain copies of a formal notice: 'Persons wishing to communicate with enemy or enemy occupied territory are informed that at the present time no letters of this nature can be forwarded except through an authorized intermediary'. Thomas Cook was appointed to act as intermediary. In addition: 'Personal messages of not more than ~~20~~ 25 words between relatives, and written on a prescribed reply form, may also be sent through the British Red Cross Society…The messages can only be sent from a Citizen's Advice Bureau or other agency mentioned on the Post Office List.' An updated version of this notice states: 'The prohibition covers messages intended to be transmitted by a third party as well as the transmission of actual letters or written documents'. In their communications via Amelie in Zurich, they seem to have ignored these regulations.

On 2 August 1942 Ado had just received Wolja's letter of 7 June. Every letter starts with a list of the letters and telegrams that have been received. Some letters did not arrive at all – they were either returned to Amelie or simply lost. There were long periods of time with no news, certainly no direct news, so they sent many telegrams, but no meaningful dialogue was possible.

In the first year after Eti's death Ado was very sad and he apologised for his expressions of grief. He carried out a small ceremony putting Eti's ashes in a 'niche' with her photograph.

On 15 July he described how he spent his wedding anniversary. Speaking with Eti all day, it was a day of happiness as well as terrible sadness. He reassured them that he had not become a mystic.

From these letters we gain a glimpse of his life in Romania. He was less isolated, living near a brother and a sister, and by 2 August 1942 he had found employment in a technical bureau. The work was not interesting, but he earned enough to cover essential expenses and to save a little, so that he would have the means to join them.

The 'niche' in which Ado placed Eti's ashes. Photo in the possession of the author.

Ado's letters arrived in envelopes which had been 'OPENED BY EXAMINER'. I wonder what the censor would have made of the content of this letter, written in French on 2 August 1942:

> I have not yet found the strength to concentrate in order to do anything positive. I live a very solitary life. I don't go to the theatre, the cinema I don't even read a book, I'm ashamed to say. My only distraction is boating…I live in a bachelor flat…very near a park and a splendid lake. Every Sunday and every free afternoon I spend several hours in the boat on the lake. As well as giving me a great deal of pleasure it is also a great comfort for my soul and it is the main medicine for my shattered nerves…every Sunday too, I visit Eta at the crematorium…My food regime is 98% vegetable – almost exclusively fruit and vegetables and I feel very well on this regime…What I lack most here is a small intimate group of intellectuals. I don't have any friends, many acquaintances, but not a single friend. Although I have three married brothers and two sisters, and even though I live close to my oldest brother, I am nearly always alone. They live for themselves and they have a completely different mentality from me…most people here are petit bourgeois with a very limited outlook and the souls of shopkeepers, whose interests, apart from affairs, are exclusively gastronomic, Bacchic and sexual pleasures, these last in a purely animal sense, with no soul. They have very strange habits. They detest exercise and shun the air and the sun, and live summer and winter with closed windows, in summer out of fear that the sun will enter their homes and in winter to get away from the polluted air and throughout the year they devour enormous quantities of meat and all sorts of unnatural food. It is because of this that almost everyone I know here, male and female, young and old is obese and arthritic, whereas I have kept my figure and my weight of 60 kilos, and I don't know what it is to have rheumatism or sciatica, because I sleep summer and winter with the windows open, I do a quarter of an hour's gymnastics every morning, after which I take a cold shower, because every Sunday I walk for several hours in the park and row on the lake and because I nourish myself only with raw vegetables and fruit…in vain I have tried to find a companion from amongst my acquaintance for my walks on Sundays, but without exception they have refused. They prefer their usual pleasures, restaurants, card games, bars and brothels; of the kind of I have given up completely, so I organize my life alone in my own way, without them. Pure air, fresh water, blue sky a strong sun and a calm moon are enough for me. They not only

strengthen my muscles and my lungs, but they also refresh my soul and my spirit. For me they completely replace people who alas, bore me, and who I can do without. Please do not think, my dears, that I have become arrogant, that I am judging people too severely, that I demand too much of them; I have become very modest since I have lived here, I demand nothing from them, neither to share my opinions nor my way of life...on the contrary it is I who tries to accommodate to them, to their way of living...I try to understand them...but because I have my own particular lifestyle they tell me, in fun, that I am mad. It amuses me...At the beginning of the next month I shall start a new more serious life. I shall improve myself, learn your language, so that we can understand one another when we meet again.

Wolja also loved fresh air and had a cold shower every morning, saying that a hot one would make him sleepy.

In September 1942 Peter was born. At the beginning of 1943 they learned that if they could get Ado into a neutral country there was a slight chance of getting him into the UK. Between 15 February and 10 March 1943 they wrote to Esther Simpson of SPSL, Leo Rabinovitch, a Romanian business man introduced to Wolja by Oscar Olitineau, Mr. Storey, the British Consular official who had helped Wolja with his British visa, Wolja's cousin Mondy in Zurich and Mr. Sarna of Messrs. Spitz Ltd. the Bristle works at which Lotte worked before her pregnancy. Several of the letters start with an apology for not having been in touch for a long time and expressing long overdue thanks for earlier help. Although not very hopeful of success, they felt they had to try everything. 'I know how terrible difficult these things are, but sometimes the most unexpected things happen.'[3] But no-one could offer any hope.

In the letter to Mr.Sarna Lotte added information about Ado:

[He] is 58 years old, and very healthy. He studied economics at Berlin University and had a great variety of commercial and economic jobs with several great firms. He has special experience in the oil and wheat trade and in transport and insurance matters. He knows Rumanian, French, German, Russian and some English.

By the way, his father was a well known publisher and bookseller in Rumania. When he died in 1939, there was an obituary notice in the Jewish Chronicle. Do you think that would help in any way? Perhaps it may interest people in him.

In his reply, Mr Sarna wrote 'For the time being nothing we may wish to do can help us in any other way but to have unlimited patience...'

In March 1943 Amelie forwarded a letter from Ado, written in eight short instalments between 15 December 1942 and 26 January 1943. In each instalment he writes how long it is since Eti died, how old Peter is today and how sad he is that he has not been sent a photograph of Peter. Sending photographs was strictly forbidden without special permission and Wolja did not apply for such permission for six months. This may have been because another momentous loss hit them on 26 June 1943 - a telegram from Lotte's sister in Palestine telling them that Lotte's mother had died. Lotte had never spoken to me about her own mother's death and I had never asked her. I would have to tackle yet another set of correspondence, all in German, between Lotte and her mother and sister in Palestine.

One Does Not Die From Grief

Lotte and her mother had parted in Berlin on 16 August 1938. Their letters similarly illustrate the impact of separation and the difficulties of communication, as well as the joy that letters as material objects could bring. When Erna received a long letter from Lotte for her birthday in May 1939, she wrote: 'your lovely birthday wishes arrived so punctually, that my maternal heart leapt for joy. In addition the letter was so long and detailed and written on the typewriter, in a word, a birthday present.'

In the first year of their separation Erna wrote approximately every two weeks, complaining that Lotte did not write often enough, but later in September 1939 she acknowledged that she too had not written for a long time; she had been told that no post was being sent. On 28 January 1940 she complained: 'My darling Lotte, what is wrong with you? Why do we always have to wait 3-4 weeks before you can bring yourself to write a few lines?'

In the first letter of Lotte's that I have, dated 18 March 1940, she describes in great detail how they are living:

> Anyway, we have rented a Bungalow on a monthly contract. Bungalows are houses that have all the rooms on the ground floor and no second storey. Wolja was absolutely right...flats are the most expensive in England. The rents outside London are significantly cheaper than in London, and minor officials live in houses like these... Mostly English people live in 'houses' that is houses with another floor above. The bedrooms are upstairs, the living-room, dining room and kitchen below. Everything is standardized here, including the building of these houses. Well, we live in a bungalow (it is a solid house without wheels), with a garden, which for the moment is a wild wasteland and

which we must now quickly work on. The rent is 25s. per week, which in England is incredibly cheap. The house is about 20 minutes away from Orpington High Street where the shops are. The landscape is hilly here and our house is high up, which is a very good thing, given the English weather and dampness. But we are not God knows the only people who are out on a limb. The house is in a street with lots more similar houses. It is much more rural here than below in the town, and therefore much prettier. The milkman and baker call, that means that their vans come every day and bring what and how much one wants. The milk in England is an ode to fat and beauty. I kill myself dragging home vegetables and fruit. Larger quantities are delivered. We also have a branch of Woolworths here. Woolworths is the most practical and cheapest shop that you could ever imagine. There isn't a household without goods from Woolworths. They also have incredibly practical things for hanging curtains, so even this is not a problem. We have furnished one room for the time being: a wide double couch, two comfortable chairs, not lounge chairs, but with arms, a nest of three small wooden tables, very sweet and practical, a desk with its chair, a carpet and curtains. We are completely un-English, as we sleep in the living room and don't go into an ice cold bedroom. It is nice and warm here and now spring is breaking out, outside (not in our garden) the crocuses, daffodils and narcissi are flowering and there are little cats. Apart from that we have a wonderful radio with shortwave, with which we can even listen to American stations. Then we have a wonderful worklamp, made out of hinged arms, which can be turned in all heaven and wind directions. And we have two electric fires. Apart from that there is a fireplace with a coal fire in our room. We have a plywood table, a trolley (a serving trolley out of the same wood), two old kitchen stools, bought for one shilling each, we have a chest of drawers, but not yet a wardrobe. We shall have try to get one from somewhere on credit, which hopefully will happen one day. We are, as you can see from our list of purchases, broke. Meanwhile some of our possessions are in trunks, some are hanging neatly on hangers on the picture rail, which is very useful for this purpose. I have not nearly finished. We also have a second couch, so that, if one of us is ill (which touch wood has not happened for a year) they don't infect the other one. This couch even has a storage box! We have sweet blue crockery that was ridiculously cheap. I had luckily brought some bed linen with me, quilts and woollen blankets that Wolja's parents had given us. We haven't stocked up with more bed linen, pillows and woollen blankets yet, as these things wear out very quickly here. As you can see, we were once well off and now we are poor and happy.

I was delighted to see that Lotte had finally acquired the couch with drawers about which she had fantasized in 1938.

On 1 June Erna wrote that she did not know whether Lotte was receiving her letters.

> There is no news here. I don't want to use up my energy with stories that are not important, nor take up the time of the censors with unnecessary matters. We sit with a sword over our heads that then turns into a bomb. ...otherwise we are well, we shall see how it goes in future...my beloved child, I haven't given up hope that well and happy we shall see one another again and when a pessimist like me can hope this, it will come true.

On 18 July she responded to the news that Wolja had been interned.

> Darling, I am of course intelligent and I understand how you are suffering and how worried you are. But I am not a novice in suffering from grief, and I know that one does not die from grief, otherwise the majority of people, particularly women, would already be dead and die daily in their millions. Perhaps Wolja is already with you again. I don't dare to hope. Believe me the happiness of seeing one another again, which will come, is so great that it is almost worth the personal heartache. At least it was like that for us.

I presume that Erna was referring to her experience during the First World War when Lotte's father was a soldier in the German army, as well as to his premature death in 1935.

> I am not going to be a Jeremiah about your short time of happiness in your bungalow. Hopefully in the not too distant future, we shall hold one another in our arms and for now I don't want to know anything else. My biggest worry is whether we shall have money for the journey...I hope that if you have heard about the terrible things happening in Germany, you didn't believe a word of it.

Was Erna trying to protect Lotte or reluctant to believe the news herself? This was before the formulation of the 'Final Solution' in 1942, but in February 1941 Ben Gurion, returning to Palestine from the USA, 'expressed astonishment at the apparent complacency in Palestine toward the war in Europe and the destruction of the Jews there', although the information was certainly available.[4] I wonder whether Lotte's family were an exception to this.

Letters continued to take a long time to reach their destination. Mara's husband Georg suggested that they send telegrams to him at the Bank and the suggestion was repeated every few months when they had not heard from Lotte. On 14 February an air letter, dated 10 December, arrived from Lotte. Erna had sent four or five letters without getting a response and given up writing: 'I couldn't simply write into this uncertainty, as every letter costs me so many drops of heart blood.'

Dated 3 March 1941 is the second letter in my collection written by Lotte, addressed to 'my beloved sweet cuddlemummy'.

> I have no idea any more how long it is since I last wrote. I shall send you a telegram tomorrow, which tells you that we are well, even very well. It makes me very sad and sentimental to write to you – the worse the behaviour, the better the excuse, as I know how much you worry and how hard it is for you. We speak about you a great deal and we think about you all the time, so very much. But there is no point in being sentimental and we are not the only people who are separated and who long to see one another. Perhaps one day the world will return to its senses. Whether dear God will play a part in this or not is all the same to me...We are now in London...in the last few months it has become much quieter. I no longer know what it was like to be without blackout and sirens and when planes flew in peace. It is much less bad when you live through it yourself.

The next letter of Lotte's is dated June 1942. This means that I have no correspondence that even mentions either Eti's death or Lotte's miscarriage. I have to presume that correspondence is missing. The huge delays in receiving letters must have made it very hard for Lotte to feel loved and supported by her mother during these very difficult experiences.

From June 1942 letters from Palestine were sent as airgraphs, a system, introduced originally for the Armed Forces, of writing on forms, which were then photographed and sent on rolls of microfilm.[5] As a result letters began to arrive much more quickly, but there was a limit to the amount that could be written and they are much harder to read.

In early 1943, when Lotte and Wolja started to try to get Ado out of Romania, they also sought help from Lotte's family. On 1 January 1943 Lotte wrote: 'Our biggest joy is Peter and our biggest worry Wolja's father. If you should hear anything there about being able to help to get Jews out, then write or better wire us. We will reimburse the costs of course. Unfortunately when I am alone all day, I have too much time to think about all the atrocities.' Later I would discover how much this affected Lotte's mental health later in her life. She wrote again on 7 February 1943, having heard that the immigration quota for Palestine had been lifted. 'I have great confidence in Georg's abilities and he did it so well for Mutti, perhaps there are ways and possibilities, and perhaps it will even succeed. We have no illusions, but it cannot remain untried. We cannot help from here unfortunately.'

Erna was very sad that they could not help. On 28 March 1943 she wrote: 'Our efforts here for your father have sadly all failed.' Mara had heard that adults who accompany a transport of young people out of Romania or who are accompanied by children will be provided with a certificate. She recognized how hard it was, but suggested he must 'put all his energy himself into trying to get out. (Russia, Turkey). From there, there must be some kind of help.'

On 15 April 1943 Lotte sent birthday greetings to her mother, telling her about Peter and adding at the end: 'I'll write separately about Wolja's father'. Erna received the letter on 11 May and replied immediately by airgraph, apologising for not writing often enough and telling Lotte she enjoyed the descriptions of Peter. This was her last letter before her death. On 24 June

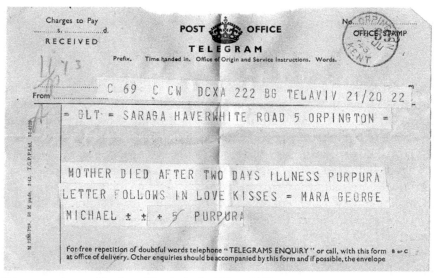

Telegram to Lotte telling her of Erna's death, 24 June 1943.

the telegram (in English) arrived: 'MOTHER DIED AFTER TWO DAYS ILLNESS PURPURA LETTER FOLLOWS IN LOVE KISSES'.

Mara's letter was written on 8 July:

> She must have had a cerebral embolism. For her it was a wonderful death, I think she had it easier than father did. Mima [Mara's son, Michael] reacted wonderfully quietly and seriously. He thought that if he or I had had this illness we would have recovered, but she had to die as she was already old. Her longing to see you once again is sadly not fulfilled and also your beautiful photos did not come on time, but nevertheless we must be grateful that the end was so easy for her.

Lotte never spoke to me about receiving this telegram, but the impact of this devastating news on Lotte is revealed in a letter from Wolja to his father two years later on 7 September 1945, the first time he could write to him directly:

> Lotte's mother died two years ago. Quite suddenly, after an illness which lasted two days only, probably caused by her rheumatic condition. The shock of the news was probably one of the causes of Lotte's pneumonia. This was two years ago. Last year Lotte again had a difficult time when she was in Cambridge. This year she is well and looking forward to the new baby which is expected in November.

'Keep Smiling, Chin Up and Hope for the Best'

It was perhaps because of these events – Erna's death and Lotte's illness – that it was not until 24 December 1943 that Wolja wrote to 'The Controller General, Trading with the Enemy Department' to ask for permission to send Ado some photographs of Peter.

> My father is a Jew. He is a widower and very lonely since my mother's death two years ago. He is according to reports very depressed and has made bitter remarks about not having had a picture of his only grandson who is now 15 months old. I hope that the enclosed photos will do much to help him sustain the hardships of racial persecution and separation from me...I would ask you for the great privilege to pass the letter and photos...

Under the 1939 Trading with the Enemy Act,[6] a person was deemed to have traded with the enemy if they 'supplied any goods to or for the benefit of an enemy, or obtained any goods from an enemy, or traded in, or carried, any goods consigned to or from an enemy or destined for or coming from enemy territory...' Romania was 'enemy territory', and once again I am impressed with Wolja's capacity to negotiate the political landscape. A printed card dated 3 January 1944 told him: 'the enclosure has been approved and forwarded on 31 December.'

During 1944 Wolja had no direct communication with Ado at all. The only news they received came from eleven telegrams and two postcards from Switzerland, two letters from his aunt Rosa in New York, and a postcard and two letters from his aunt Sonja in Sweden. Switzerland was the most reliable route and this way, about once a month, he heard indirectly that his father was well.

But in early 1945 the possibilities of communication suddenly changed. An army air letter arrived, written by 2613084 Sgt T.E. Rowell, C.M. Police, British Mission, Bucharest, C.M.F. The letter is not dated and only '45' is legible on the post mark, but Tom Rowell writes 'spring has come'. On the outside is written: PASSED BY CENSOR No 7391 and. the following statement is signed: 'I verify on my honour that the contents of this envelope refer to nothing but private and family matters.'

> Dear Sir
> I expect you will be rather surprised to receive this letter and wonder from whom it has come, but you will see by the address and will understand. I have been here for some considerable time now and like the country and place very much indeed.
> The other day I had the privilege of meeting a friend whom knows your Father and he has sent you the following message. He is keeping very well indeed and sincerely hopes you and all his parents are well. About three and a half years ago he lost his very best friend, perhaps you will know whom this friend maybe. He would also like news of you if at all possible so if you drop me a line that will be very well.
> I expect the old country is looking very fine these days, especially now spring has come. Still one of these days we shall be able to return home again, and see all these things for ourselves. I have not been at home for nearly four years, but we are very contented with being here as everything is very much the same as being at home. Still never mind, one of these days it will all come to an end we hope. Keep smiling, chin up and hope for the best. I shall be very pleased to hear from you in the near future.

I imagine that the odd expressions in the letter arise from Ado's English, which was not fluent; 'you and all his parents' probably means family or relations and I presume he referred to Eti as his best friend as well as his wife. I discovered from subsequent letters that Sergeant Rowell had a girlfriend who was Ado's next door neighbour.

Now that direct contact was possible, albeit mediated through a third party, Wolja and Ado started to exchange a bit more news, rather than just saying 'we well'. On 11 April Wolja thanked Sergeant Rowell, saying how happy he was to hear from his father. He enclosed a letter for Ado.

> We escaped the bombs and the flying bombs and the rockets and now we are looking forward to the final collapse of the Nazis…Our second Embi is two months old, and if Lotte remains well, Peter will have a sister or a brother in November. Lotte is tired, as Peter is not an easy child and probably I am not an easy husband. When you are with us you will help us to bath the new baby. I wish so much that you can be here very soon, I think very much of you, and of our Eti. Have you heard from Eti's sisters? Could they escape from the Nazis? Sonja could escape to Sweden.

Rowell wrote again on 20 May 1945, telling Wolja 'It gave me very much pleasure when I saw the results of my letter.' The war in Europe was over.

> Well the great day has passed now. I suppose you all celebrated very much at home after waiting six long years for the day to come. The boys and myself had a real time here as you can well imagine as you know it better than I do and I know it during the war. The town is getting very normal again and the town is looking simply lovely. I like being here very much and I am considering as to whether I should like to come here when I have finished being a soldier. I have a very nice girl friend whom knows your dad very well and asked me to write. She would like me to return here when I have finished, whether I shall or not I do not know.

Rowell clearly assumed that Wolja had lived in Romania. Over the next six months, he wrote to Wolja three more times – in June, August and at the end of November. His letters took about six weeks to arrive, but Wolja did not always wait to receive a letter before writing again. On 28 June Rowell told Wolja:

> He also says that he had a very exciting time during the bombing of Bucharest. He was very pleased to hear that you will have an increase in the family in November this year…He wants so much to see you

and states that after 8 years of bitter separation it cannot come quick enough for him. He says he has nothing to retain him here and now the war is over he wants to know if it is possible to get the permission for him to come and see you.

I imagine the term 'exciting' has been translated from the German word *aufregend* which can mean 'exciting', 'shocking' or 'upsetting'.
   He was enjoying life in Bucharest and thought he could settle down there.

Your Dad is always asking my lady friend if have a letter for him, and she tells me he gets really excited when she gives him the letter, and cannot thank her enough for it. I hope you are still keeping well also your wife and Son. I don't know you but I feel as if I do that's all what matters...

On 9 July, replying to Rowell's second letter of 20 May, Wolja says he received it 'a few days ago'.

I was very happy to hear from you and from my Father. I have not seen my Father for more than seven years, and I am very glad that due to your kind help, I am at least getting some more news from him...I wonder how long it will be necessary to wait until travelling will be possible again in Europe. Since I wrote to you last we have all seen the end of the war in Europe and the collapse of this evil thing: Nazism. The world seems a better place after the death of these arch-devils Hitler and Himmler and Goebbels. I can imagine how you celebrated V-E day. We went to Trafalgar Square, with Peter, listened to Churchill's speech and then walked through St. James Park. Then Peter got hungry and thirsty and we had to go home.
   The end of the European war was particularly noticeable in Kent as it brought us the end of the bombs, flying bombs and rockets. Lotte (my wife) and Peter were evacuated during the main flying bomb period last summer, but they were here at Orpington during the rocket attacks. We have been very lucky; apart from some plaster coming down we have come through it unscathed.

On 12 July 1945 Wolja's aunt Sonja wrote to tell him she was now back in Copenhagen. She tried to trace her sisters, but presumes they did not survive.
   In his letter of 9 August Rowell switches from writing about Ado in the third person, to writing as if he is Ado, and finally as himself; the meaning is slightly confused in places.

Thanks very much indeed for your letter of congratulation for your Dad's birthday. He was very pleased indeed to think you had not forgotten him. He is always keen to have a letter from you and to know more about you and your family. Nothing ever happens here, and all he is longing for is to be with you. Don't you take any steps to obtain permission to come to you, before November, when you await for the birth of your new baby. I think I would be very useful in those circumstances. Please let me know as soon as possible so I can make the necessary arrangements. Nothing retain me here and everything makes me want to come to you...I am very well and wish you all the very best of luck, and hope to hear from you in the near future. I'm well, and still enjoying myself, it's certainly a grand place. Wishing you all the best of luck.

In early September 1945 Wolja received the first direct letter from Ado for more than two years. Dated 1 July 1945, it took over two months to arrive. Ado expresses his relief that with the resumption of normal postal services he can write in French as it is very hard for him to write in English. After two years they have a lot of catching up to do and writing directly, Ado feels able to tell Wolja about his experiences during the war in a way he was not willing to do via an intermediary:

We were subjected to a regime of extreme tyranny and terror, every moment in danger of being deported, and in the first few days of the Legionnaires Rebellion in January 1941, - while Éta was still alive – we just escaped being shot. Then last year we experienced months of anxiety during the bombardments...I can tell you that I am well and that only the ardent desire to see you all again as soon as possible torments me...Might it be possible, now that the war is over, to obtain permission for me to come to you?

'Only One of Many Suffering Millions'

Perhaps triggered by the receipt of this letter, on 5 September 1945 Wolja made a new application to the Home Office: '... for permission to be granted, on compassionate grounds, for my father, Avram Saraga... of Roumanian nationality, 61 years of age, to come to this country and live with me. I am willing and fully able to support him adequately...' In making the case Wolja outlined his own history and current situation and described Ado's experiences during the war. As in his application for release from internment, Wolja tried to argue logically, appeal for sympathy and to cover all possibilities, whilst at the same time denying that he was making a special case:

> I would add that my father is a business man with wide experience and knowledge of European commerce and trade of which use could conceivably be made in this country's drive for exports. My application is however based on the purely compassionate grounds stated above and I would undertake that he should not seek any work here unless especially authorised by the authorities concerned.
>
> I very much appreciate that my father is only one of many suffering millions in Europe today and that for many there will be no relief or solution of their unhappiness for a long while to come. My father is however one of the few for whom there is a practical means of rescue in that I am fully able and willing to maintain him. I hope therefore that he will be allowed to take advantage of this possibility, and that my application can be granted.

On 7 September Wolja replied in English to Ado's letter:

> I hope that you are really well and do not say so in your letter in order to reassure me. What about your hernia? Did you ever do anything against it? Does it not disturb you? Two years ago I received permission to send you some photographs of little Peter. Did you ever receive them?

[He tells him about the application he has made, whilst preparing him for a negative response.]

> You know yourself what an application is, and that the answer may be negative. In that case I shall try again, and again. I shall definitely not stop before you are here. But you must have patience. It sounds very cruel when I write this, since obviously, for me with Lotte and Peter it is easier to wait than for you who is alone and with the memory of our dear Eti who has left us. Still I cannot do anything else than try as hard and as intelligently as possible to get the permission. I have made the application on purely compassionate grounds...

[He outlines the arguments he has used in the application, asks Ado a series of questions, passes on news of family and friends from around the world, and asks for news of Eti's sisters who escaped to Russia when the Nazis invaded Poland.]

What you are writing about the dangers in which you and our Eti were, of deportations, of execution and of bombs, that was no surprise for me. I lived in continual fear for you, since the outbreak of war, since I heard what the Nazi-murderers did in Poland. I remember the time of the earthquake, the time of the Iron Guard rebellion, the time of the German occupation, the Allied air raids on Bucharest, the bombing by the Germans. It was good that you could send me a telegram very soon after that...

Dear, dear Ado, I kiss you a thousand times, I hope very much to be able to do it without the help of a letter as an intermediary very soon.

In writing to his father, Wolja tried to balance his desire to encourage him, with being realistic about the possibilities of success. How he was actually feeling is revealed in a letter written on the same day to Sergeant Rowell:

To be quite frank, I am not too hopeful that this application will be successful. These things are very difficult and need time. If my application is rejected I shall have to try again, and my father must not lose courage. I have not lost any time in making the application; before the end of the war it was absolutely useless to try. I am quite sure in the end we shall succeed.

Wolja's application for a visa for Ado was rejected nine days after it was submitted, on 14 September. No reason was given. He started networking straight away. One of his contacts, P. Friedman, wrote to Wolja on 8 October 1945 enclosing a letter from his friend, Florence M. Morris, who worked at the Board of Trade:

I have just had a long talk with the Aliens' Dept of the Home Office and I am afraid I can hold out no hope that Mr. Saraga will be allowed to bring his old father over here. I am told that there are thousands in Europe in the same position as Mr. Saraga & therefore they (the Home Office) can make no exception to their rule. It is very very sad but I am afraid there is nothing to be done at the moment...

This 'old father' was 61. The underlining of 'at the moment', perhaps offered a bit of hope for Wolja.

The final letter from 'Mr. Rowell' was written on 27 November 1945 from an address in Coventry:

I left instructions with the young lady to hand the letters to my Corporal who would send them to me to pass on to you, but I have not received any up to the present. I will drop him a line today to contact her and to see your Father about some letter as you are anxious to know about him. I hope you, your wife and Son are all very well and wish you all the very best in life. If you have anything or letters you want to send to your Father, you forward them on to me and it will give me the greatest of pleasure to forward them to your Father.

He was very keen to return to Romania to take some form of employment and asked Wolja for advice on obtaining passports and visas. I have no record of Wolja's reply.

Notes

1. https://en.wikipedia.org/wiki/Legionnaires%27_rebellion_and_Bucharest_pogrom (Accessed 14 August 2018).
2. The conflict began on 22 June 1941. See https://en.wikipedia.org/wiki/Eastern_Front_(World_War_II) (Accessed 18 May 2013).
3. Letter to Mr. Storey on 5 March 1943.
4. D. Porat, *The Blue and Yellow Stars of David. The Zionist Leadership in Palestine and the Holocaust, 1939-1945* (Cambridge, MA: Harvard University Press, 1990), p.17. See also D. Porat, *Israeli Society, the Holocaust and its Survivors* (London and Portland, OR: Vallentine Mitchell, 2008).
5. See http://en.wikipedia.org/wiki/V-mail (Accessed 18 May 2013).
6. http://www.legislation.gov.uk/ukpga/Geo6/2-3/89 (Accessed 4 November 2018).

7

'Convinced Ultimate Success'

On 13 November 1945, in response to a Private Notice, The Secretary of State for the Home Department (Mr. Ede) made a statement on 'DISTRESSED PERSONS, EUROPE (ADMISSION TO UNITED KINGDOM)' to the House of Commons, outlining

> ...which of the classes of distressed persons among the countless cases calling for sympathy have special claims to join relatives in the United Kingdom... a visa may be granted (subject to considerations of public health and character) if the applicant falls into one of the following categories:
>
> (1) the wife of a man who is in the United Kingdom and any of his children under 21. If the result of bringing the wife and any children under 21 to the United Kingdom would be to leave alone and in distressed circumstances one daughter over 21 who is unmarried or widowed and without children, she also may be allowed to come;
> (2) the husband of a woman who is in the United Kingdom, if he is incapacitated, infirm or too old to support his wife abroad;
> (3) females under 21 with their children, if any, and males under 18, who have no relatives to look after them abroad but have a relative in the United Kingdom able and willing to take them into his household;
> (4) the mother or grandmother of a person in the United Kingdom if she is widowed and in need of filial care;
> (5) the father or grandfather of a person in the United Kingdom if widowed and in need of special care owing to age or infirmity.
> (6) Where both man and wife are living together abroad, such couples may be admitted if because of age or infirmity, or other special circumstances, they are unable to look after and support one another, and are offered hospitality by a child or grandchild in this country...

It is not possible to give a numerical estimate of the persons likely to be admitted under this scheme and its operation will be carefully watched. The difficulties are obvious which would be caused by large-scale additions to our foreign population at the present time…but it will, I think, be the general desire of the British people that, despite these difficulties…the utmost should be done to maintain this country's historic tradition of affording asylum to the distressed. It is to be hoped that other countries will share the task with this straitened island.[1]

The language of this statement seems remarkably contemporary in its reference to Britain's 'historic tradition' coupled with concern about the impact of too many foreigners in British society. But the explicit assumptions about age, gender and family embedded within the policy place it in a different era: men were expected to support women; young women were more vulnerable than young men, being eligible for help until 21 rather than 18 and a mother or grandmother had to require 'filial care', a father or grandfather 'special care'. By contrast, at the time of writing in 2014, a young woman was treated by the courts as an adult because she was 19 and deported to Mauritius without her family.[2]

An annotated copy of this statement was amongst the papers. The first thing I noticed was its date, 13 November 1945, the day of my birth. Wolja had told me he had a telephone call from the nursing home during the night and woke Peter to tell him that he had a baby sister. In his diary, he has written ESTHER! I imagine that he was doubly excited that day, as this statement offered him great hope that he could soon be reunited with his father who would qualify for a visa under category 5. He acted immediately; on 15 November he sought clarification about the application process from the Home Office; on 4 December he drafted a telegram to Ado:

> Visa Applications~~now possible~~ from~~by~~ father of person in united kingdom if widowed and ~~in~~needing ~~of~~special care owing to age or infirmity ~~now possible~~. You must apply ~~to~~British Mission Bucharest stop. Maintenance accommodation here available Love Wolja Saraga 42 words'.

Ado replied by telegram one week later: 'RECEIVED TELEGRAM APPLIED BRITISH MISSION LOVE AVRAM SARAGA'.

Through its crossings out and amendments Wolja's draft telegram seems to convey great emotion. In line with his mother's last wish, Wolja could soon be reunited with his father. Or so I thought. The application was to be turned down twice before finally being granted in August 1946.

In her letter to Wolja in October 1945 Florence Morris had written '...I am afraid there is nothing to be done <u>at the moment</u>...' This way in which the door seemed to be kept slightly open was to be characteristic of many of the responses he received over the next nine months. During this time difficult official and personal negotiations – with the Home Office and with Ado – had to be conducted in a context of unreliable and slow communication suffused with feelings of hope, despair, fear and longing. They tried to speed things up by sending lots of telegrams, but sometimes this added to the confusion as they had to keep telling each other which letters and telegrams had been received. Sometimes Ado re-sent letters when he had not received a reply to his questions. I imagine my feelings and confusion confronted with this correspondence mirrored those experienced by Ado and Wolja at the time.

Sufficient Room in the House

In January 1946 Wolja wrote to the Home Office, confirming that he had sufficient room in the house for his father, but the application was rejected even before his letter was acknowledged. He was then advised that the decision depended on the authorities in Bucharest. He should write to them enclosing a confirmation from his bank that he had sufficient means to support Ado and a certificate from a neighbour or friend that he had sufficient room in his house to accommodate him, without depriving anyone else of accommodation.

These two enclosures should have been straightforward. Wolja was employed with a good salary and towards the end of July 1945 they had bought a three bedroom semi-detached house in Petts Wood, the house in which we found all these papers. But a completely different set of papers, concerned with events occurring between September 1945 and August 1946, events that are not mentioned at all in the correspondence about the visa, complicated the situation that Wolja was in. He had even more to juggle and manage than I had imagined.

On 25 September 1945 Lotte wrote to their friends the Bikermans, from whom they had bought their furniture:

> ...our family has increased beyond expectations. We are now living together with a young English couple, he is a sergeant in the RAF. We know them only for a very short time. The girl started as Wolja's assistant, until she found out that she was going to have a baby. She

has already one child of just a year. They have no home and decided they should move in here. She has already been staying with us for three weeks and we are getting on very well together. Although we shall be fearfully crowded it will make things easier for both of us and it will help us financially. Wolja has applied for his father to come here, but, so far, the answer has been a sympathetic 'no'. It is very upsetting.

The 'young English couple' were Mr and Mrs Clarke. Ten letters written between 17 June and 26 August 1946 and a 22 page statement that Wolja prepared for lawyers are concerned with Lotte and Wolja's attempts to get the Clarkes to leave their house. What had been planned as an informal arrangement, helping a friend and providing some company and support for Lotte, turned into a nightmare. Mr Clarke lived there far more than had been anticipated and increasingly they behaved as if they were tenants, buying new kitchen utensils and taking over part of the kitchen and the small bedroom while Lotte and Wolja were away and behaving in an offensive manner. When they finally managed to talk to the Clarkes, it became a shouting match, which the Clarkes subsequently used against them. Lotte's attempt to reassert herself in the kitchen turned into a verbal and physical fight, during which Lotte shouted at Mrs Clarke 'I know now why you had to leave your mother and your friend' and Mrs Clarke replied 'I know now why you had to leave Germany'. Mrs Clarke called in the police, who once they had heard Lotte and Wolja's side of the story 'became more friendly', telling Mrs Clarke that she was in someone else's house and had to behave accordingly. They told her she must not say things like 'We let these people into this country'.

In his statement Wolja described in great detail every aspect of the house and how they lived, in an effort to prove that this was not 'a commercial transaction'. He knew that the Clarkes could not suddenly be asked to leave, because of the housing shortage and the house would not be 'overcrowded' until the babies started to crawl. In a style with which I have now become familiar, he tried to anticipate the arguments that the Clarkes would put forward and then counter them, arguing that the Clarkes contributed to household expenses, but did not pay rent, and that it was an arrangement for the time that Mr Clarke was in the RAF and not after he was demobbed. Wolja had not wanted to buy a house as he was trying to find a different job and might have to move. Indeed Mrs Clarke had helped him to draft an application for a research post in Australia.

I had bought a house in spite of great financial difficulties and in spite of an inflated price, because at our previous address we had lived in a furnished bungalow and were therefore not protected…as foreigners, we had little hope of finding a house to rent…they knew all the time that I would never knowingly enter any arrangement which involved losing my freedom of action, apart from the fact that I would have never converted a recently bought house with 'vacant possession' into the opposite, after having paid an inflated price for the 'vacant possession'.

Mr Clarke did not intend to leave. He told Wolja he would need an eviction order to get them out and this could only be obtained for three reasons – non-payment of rent, being objectionable, or overcrowding. Such an order could only be obtained through going to court, which Wolja might not wish to do while he was applying for naturalization. Wolja believed that the Clarkes wanted to establish their rights, claiming 'they want nothing else but a roof over their heads' and to show 'how unreasonable we, as foreigners, are'. Whatever happened, the Clarkes would win. If it went to court and Wolja lost, the Clarkes could stay; If Wolja won, the Clarkes would have to be re-housed.

Having lived in this house throughout my childhood, it is hard to imagine so many people living there. In Wolja's long statement no mention is made of the effect on the children. To live in this tension cannot have been easy, yet they never mentioned the Clarkes living with them in any of their letters to family and friends during this time, apart from the one letter of Lotte's already cited. The reason for this becomes clear in Wolja's letter to the solicitors on 27 June 1946, when he told them of his application for a visa for Ado:

> In the course of my endeavours to get my father who is very ill over to this country (I made my first application on the 5th September 1945 i.e. before the Clarkes moved in and I told them about it) I had – in March this year, i.e. after they moved in, to make a declaration to the Home Office that I could provide accommodation for my father in my house without depriving anyone else of accommodation. This is perfectly true, since whether the Clarkes stay with us or not, my father can sleep in our living room where a spare divan is available for him and as a member of the family will have no separate requirements from us. However, out of spite, Mr Clarke may during the proceedings say that my real motive for trying to get rid of them is to provide room for my father. I should like to emphasize that the problem of getting my father over here is of utmost importance to me and I do not wish to do anything which could make the Home Office refuse my

application on account of my proceedings against Mr and Mrs Clarke. I do not wish to mention my father's case in the proceedings concerned with the house, but I should like to have your confirmation that in case it is brought up by Mr Clarke we have the means to deal with it. In particular I am afraid that if we win the Home Office may say that we did deprive somebody of accommodation in order to find room for him, and if we loose but mention that the house is overcrowded the Home Office may say that there is obviously no room for my father. Therefore in my opinion we have to use the argument of overcrowding only in conjunction with the great number of very young children, the fact that there are two different families and two housewives sharing the kitchen and the fact that the personal relations are as bad as possible.

The Clarkes were first formally asked to leave on 16 May. Following a 'notice to quit' issued on 22 July, they did leave on 2 August, taking their keys with them to make the point that they had the right to stay until Monday 5 August, and with many outstanding debts. On 26 August Lotte told the solicitor: 'you cannot imagine what a relief it is for us to be rid of them.' To recover the money they were owed would have required suing the Clarkes. There is no further correspondence, so I imagine Lotte and Wolja had to cut their losses.

This new information shows how delicate Wolja's negotiations with the Home Office had to be and it offers a glimpse of some everyday experiences of refugees. The Clarkes behaviour reflected the widespread anti-foreigner sentiment, which it was good to see was not endorsed by the police.[3]

Distressed, Destitute, Homeless

Before I diverted into the episode of the Clarkes, I had reached the point at which in January 1946 Wolja had written to the Home Office and to the British Mission in Bucharest. On 20 January Ado wrote a long letter in English to Tom Rowell in Coventry. The letter must have been forwarded to Wolja. He described in great detail his personal and professional history and his experiences during the war, which he had put into his application.

At the Mission I was told to come for informations at the beginning of February. Now I am waiting the decision. I hope that it will be positive. In this case, I don't believe to be able to start before Spring. Will this dream of my life come to a reality?

[The second half of the letter expressed a different anxiety. He was worried that he would be a burden to Lotte and Wolja. He owned very little and his health had]

> ...suffered much through the different shocks I had during the last 10 years and that I got recently a cardiac-insufficience which decreased my force. I am not invalid, but I am no longer so vigorous as before. I thought it is my duty to tell you the whole truth about my situation, before you make up your mind. I, surely, should be very sorry, if we could not be again together as soon as possible; our destiny is not in our hands; who knows how long I shall live, and I should not like to leave my life like our poor Esther, without seeing you and Lotte and my nephews and without embracing you all. – But the truth firstly! I should not like to build the happiness of my last years on a mystification, and especially with you. My sincerity will perhaps seem to you a little hard, please excuse it.

If this was the quality of Ado's English, I am astounded that he was described as not speaking the language! But I imagine that he translated *Kraft* as 'force' rather than 'strength', *Täuschung* as 'mystification' rather than 'deception' and *Offenheit* as 'sincerity' rather than 'candour'.

On 10 February Ado sent a telegram: '*LETTERS ONTHEWAY APPLICATION DECLINED DESOLATED LOVE=SARAGA.*' The confirmation from the British Mission is dated 19 February: 'I regret that he does not appear to come within the special passport Control Regulations of 15th November 1945...' Again no reason was given, but the use of the word 'appear' seems once more to leave open the possibility of changing the decision.

A letter of 21 February to Mr Friedman, asking whether his friend could again make enquiries at the Home Office about the reasons for the decision, expresses Wolja's despair.

> ... in view of his ill health I am terribly worried and depressed... though I know I must help my father I just don't know what to do and where to start. I could understand the first refusal, since at that time the declared policy of the British Government was against the admission of distressed persons. Now officially the policy has changed and I as well as my father fulfil all necessary conditions, and in spite of this a blank refusal. I am sure there must be some misunderstanding and if I could find out the reasons for the refusal it would be most likely possible to get a reversal of the decision...

Writing to Ado on the same day Wolja tried to reassure him: 'I am quite certain that we shall obtain the visa in the end. You and I both fulfil all conditions for the visa...' He wondered whether Ado had not included his ill health in the application or stated his wish not to be a burden, thus giving the impression he would seek work. 'I am taking active steps to find out the reasons from this end and to get the decision reversed.'

He also responded to Ado's concerns about being a burden:

> You must not write nor think that it is any 'sacrifice' or 'burden' for me to have you for me. Since our unhappy separation through Nazism and war I have always suffered deeply through my physical inability to translate into reality my great and deep wish to have you and Eti – and since her death at least you – with me. The day you arrive will be a great day for me. And you must help me to make the day arrive by taking care of your health.

In a third letter written on 21 February Wolja made a complaint to the Home Secretary. We shall see that later he decided that 'complaining' was not the best strategy. He tried to anticipate what the grounds for refusal might be:

> My father is 61, Jewish, an educated person (see his letter of January 1946), ill (heart disease) a widower, destitute, has no one to look after him and I am his only child. I am a scientist, for seven years employed with the same firm and earning £700 a year. Some Government Department, not necessarily the Home Office, seem to do everything in their power to prevent your statement as made in November 1945 from becoming reality. With that aim in view it is of course easy to elicit some adverse statement from an old man, such as e.g. he would not like to become a burden on his son and try to make a living and thus confuse him.

A letter to Ado[4] from the British Mission spelled out the reason for the refusal:

> With reference to your letter of 24th January asking for an entry visa into Great Britain to join your son, I regret I am unable to grant it on the information so far provided. The entry of certain categories of persons into the United Kingdom is intended to extend solely to cases of destitution and homelessness. I will, if you wish me to do so, submit your case for consideration in London, but I do not foresee a favourable decision.

By referring to 'the information so far provided', yet again the door was left slightly open. Both Ado and Wolja lodged appeals against the decision.

In a letter to Ado in English on 3 March Wolja explained his understanding of the reasons for the refusal:

> ...the regulations apply to distressed persons, and in the first instance to survivors of concentration camps, to persons who have been in hiding from the Gestapo, and to persons who for various other reasons are in need of in special care. Preference will be given, particularly in the case of former enemy nationals, to persons who have suffered from Nazi persecution. I have not been able to read these regulations in detail since they are not shown to the public, but I have been told the above mentioned contents by an official of the Passport Control Office in London. He also assured me that the words destitution and homelessness do not occur in these regulations as conditions for a visa. However, this does not mean that we can say to the British Mission that they are inventing conditions which do not exist. It is possible – though not necessary – to interpret the word distressed as meaning destitute and homeless. In general distressed is used in a wider sense covering mental and spiritual distress, but the original meaning is physical. Therefore, as I wrote to you before, it is necessary that you tell them everything about your heart disease and your rupture and your need of special care, particularly filial care, which you cannot get in Rumania, not from your brothers (if you have not mentioned your brothers, do not mention them now!) especially if you should become seriously ill. As I see from your letter of January 20th, you have already given them the facts showing how your and my life has been affected in every aspect and how our family life has been broken up by Nazi persecution, and how your livelihood has been destroyed twice, in Germany and in Rumania and that you and Eti were prisoners of the Iron Guard (do not mention the bombing again, this is no reason in the eyes of officials of this much bombed island). You say in your letter of the 20th of January that you have no occupation, and in your letter of the 10th of February that you are actually destitute. You have never written to me before about your life, and therefore I do not mention this fact in my applications. You, however, if you can prove this fact, you must of course stress it very much. With regard to distress you must of course mention – as you have done – Eti's death, my being your only son, and the fact that being reunited with me is the only remaining purpose of your life. The reuniting of families is one of the purposes of the new regulations!

> I am very optimistic but we must be prepared to experience further difficulties before final success. It is of course possible that the British Mission will decide your second application before my letter arrives. In this case, if the decision should again be negative I shall have to appeal in London…

The following day Wolja wrote to the British Mission, repeating the information about his own position, the house, his work and his salary.

> … I do not know whether or not he is in fact destitute or homeless, since in the few letters which I have had from him since the end of the war he has written very little about his conditions of life. I have, however, made enquiries from the Passport Control Office in London and understand that the condition of destitution and homelessness is not stated specifically in the regulations. In these circumstances I hope that the information given above will clarify my father's position in this respect.

He told them his application for naturalization was supported by his employers. Since he had been engaged on war work, he was optimistic that it would be granted. 'I am owner of a house at the above address, and I am therefore able to provide the necessary accommodation for my father without depriving anybody else of accommodation.' This letter was written shortly before the Clarkes were asked to leave the house.

If Wolja was right that the decision could be reversed, then it was vital that he and Ado were telling exactly the same story, something that was very difficult to clarify with such unreliable post. In their letters they asked each other the same questions again and again and repeated information from previous letters, in particular what they had said to the British Mission. Ado tried to follow Wolja's advice, but on 15 March he told Wolja 'I have been advised not to stress my illness.' He repeated this two weeks later on 27 March, when he told Wolja that he had been ill again with 'a new heart congestion like last year which caused me a cardiac insufficiency'. He also wrote about the practical difficulties of travelling and asked what household and other goods it would be useful to bring with him. Wolja did not answer this question, which Ado repeated on 10 May, asking what it was absolutely necessary to bring.

On 15 April he wrote, in French, that he had prepared evidence on the state of his health and the treatment he needed, but not handed it in as he was advised for the second time by the secretary at the Consulate that it would have a negative effect on his application.

But you advised me exactly the opposite. I am totally confused. It is very possible that I have made a big mistake in not handing this letter to the Consul; but I can't change this now, because as I have already told you the Consul refuses to accept responsibility for the decision and shifted the centre of gravity of the affair to London, where only you are in a position to intervene if necessary.

In their letters they also exchanged family news. Ado asked whether Wolja has collaborated on any research related to the atomic bomb and wanted to know if Wolja had been granted citizenship. 'Peter and Eti are English citizens by right of birth; it is just that their parents should be too!' On 26 April Wolja told Ado he had written to the Home Office asking for the procedure to be speeded up on health grounds.

Unfortunately my powers are limited. I have interested a number of people with some influence in your case, but everything takes time, particularly in this country. In spite of all reasons which would justify a positive decision, we must even be prepared for a renewed refusal. This must not, if it should happen, depress you. I shall at once, if this does happen, renew my application, and shall ask some people for their help who do not want to intervene unless our application has been definitely rejected.

He emphasized that Ado must keep him informed about his health. If it were to become a matter of life and death, they might be able to get an immediate decision. He also asked Ado about his financial situation. 'I have not got enough money to send you some if you do not need it...On the other hand, if you do need it for your life now or for your journey, you must let me know and I shall try to get the permission to send it to you.'

I remind myself that these complicated and delicate negotiations were going on while Lotte and Wolja were coping with the Clarkes refusing to leave their house.

'This Waiting is Dreadful'

Amongst the papers are a letter to Tom Cook MP and a letter of introduction to Percy Collick MP, though there is no evidence that Wolja followed up the latter. Both were Labour MPs – Tom Cook for Dundee and Percy Collick for Birkenhead. There is no evidence from Hansard that either MP had a particular interest in refugee matters; I imagine Wolja was introduced to them via one of his friends or contacts.

When writing to Tom Cook in April 1946, Wolja enclosed copies of the relevant correspondence, information about himself and his father and a 'summary of the steps so far taken' for which I am very grateful; it allowed me to check my understanding of the sequence of events. On this occasion, he reassured him that he did not want to make a complaint. He had just learned how ill Ado had become and been advised that a Member of Parliament showing a 'friendly interest' might have a positive effect. At the same time Wolja was actively pursuing his application for naturalization. On 6 April 1946 he accepted an offer from SPSL to be included in a list of people who should be considered as priorities for naturalization, because of their useful war contribution. He took the opportunity to also ask for 'a great favour in a personal matter' – his visa application for Ado.

> I do not want to bother you with the details of the case...but I feel that if you are in a position to write a letter to the Home Office...saying that you know me and wish to support my application...this might be of very great help. I hope you will...forgive me for taking the liberty to ask for your intervention in a question outside the Society's normal functions. I shall perfectly understand if you tell me that it is impossible for you to do anything at all in this matter. On the other hand I am so worried about my father that I do not want to leave anything untried.[5]

On 9 April 1946, in her response[6] to the 'more personal question', Ilse Ursell explained that a supporting letter from one of the Bloomsbury House Committees would be more valuable than from SPSL, since they were now involved in advising the Home Office in relation to the Distressed Persons Scheme.[7] As a result, by the end of April Ruth Fellner of the Jewish Refugees Committee had taken responsibility for supporting Wolja's application for Ado. Although this was obviously helpful, it also created difficulties. Neither Wolja nor his personal contacts, like Mr Friedman and his friend Florence Morris wanted to do anything that would interfere with the close relationship between the Committee and the Home Office. At the same time, they were never quite sure what Miss Fellner was doing and whether she had all the relevant information, in particular the advice to Ado not to leave his medical certificates at the British Consulate. She was so overworked they were unable to speak to her or see her.

Wolja advised Ado to submit the certificates again and to send photocopies to him in London, but before Ado received this request the British Mission had asked him for the medical certificates to send to London. 'If you absolutely need them, I'll try to get copies from my doctors' (10 May

1946). A postscript, added twelve days later, told Wolja that after three weeks the British Mission had returned his certificates and said he should send them to Wolja to submit.

Wolja wondered whether Ado had been advised not to mention his health because they thought he had an infectious disease.

> In the meantime, waiting for your certificates, I could not do anything else. This waiting is dreadful. I think I told you in my last letter that I have also written to the Home Office. But no reply yet. Nobody can say how long it will take until you will be here. So far I have heard of only two people who obtained the British visa in Bucharest.

On the carbon copy of this letter, he has crossed out another version of the last sentence: 'I have spoken a few days ago to Mr.Weisselberg, a man of 75 years who came from Rumania in March. He has got a son here and he got the visa without any difficulties. He is neither homeless nor destitute nor ill. However his son is a big business man. It seems we have had very bad luck.'(19 May 1946).

I am reminded of the way Wolja felt in internment – not important enough even to be visited by the representatives of Bloomsbury House – and the way in which most histories of these events emphasize the eminence of the refugees.

On 21 May Wolja sent Ado a telegram asking for the certificates. The following day Ado confirmed by telegram that they were on the way. Sent with certified translations on 20 May by special courier, they did not arrive until 8 July. Whilst waiting for them, Lotte wrote to Mr Friedman, anxious that the Home Office should know about Ado's health and the difficulty of obtaining the appropriate medicine in Romania before making a negative decision. 'He fears the visa may come too late for his father'. When he replied on 28 May Mr Friedman told him that Miss Morris had spoken at length to Miss Fellner and was now hopeful that something favourable would happen in the next day or two. If not, she would contact other people. 'She is now really aroused in the matter, and I am sure that if it is at all possible to do something about it she will do so.' In early June a postcard from the MP Tom Cook acknowledged Wolja's letter of 14 April. On 25 June Wolja wrote to him again, concerned that if he now intervened it might not co-ordinate with Miss Fellner.

'Convinced Ultimate Success'

As with other sets of correspondence, I found myself becoming very emotionally involved with the day to day progress, or lack of progress. I began to fear reading the next letter, waiting for the next rejection. Dated 13 June 1946, it came initially in a letter from Miss Fellner, who had heard from the Home Office: '…it is indicated that the Secretary of State, after having carefully and sympathetically considered our representations, regrets that he is not prepared to authorize facilities for your father's journey to this country, as it does not appear that he qualifies under the scheme for the admission of distressed relatives in Europe.'

The official refusal from Bucharest, dated 20 June and postmarked 24 June, states that the 'competent authorities' in London had refused the request. No reasons were given. Miss Fellner did not understand the decision. Once again the word 'appear' was used and she wondered whether Ado was living with or supported by other relatives. In his reply on 15 June, Wolja confirmed that Ado was not living with relatives. His three married brothers all had sick wives and were also maintaining a widowed sister with no children. Ruth Fellner described Wolja's explanation as 'indeed most valuable… I cannot do better but to send your communication to the Home Office with a request that your father's case should be reconsidered.'

On 21 June Wolja sent a telegram and a letter to Ado, both of which illustrate how problematic the post still was: 'Heartiest congratulations birthday received your letters tenth twenty second thirty first May 4th June but not yet certificates Unfortunately visa decision again unfavourable but I have already appealed convinced ultimate success…' In the letter he told Ado he had just received

> …a letter of the 7th of March which was posted in London so that I assume that you sent it by somebody travelling from Bucarest to this country…it took three months so that it is not much good to use this particular way again. I have not yet received the certificates though the first letter in which you wrote me that you had sent them 'par voie speciale' arrived here more than two weeks ago (this was your letter with the postscript). I hope that this special way that you have sent it will not take another three months. I shall send you a telegram as soon as I receive the certificates. Thus you can decide yourself whether you want to send me duplicates, if you do not get a telegram from me announcing their arrival. …I do not yet know what the reasons for the refusal are, and I am very active not only to find out what they are, but also to refute them.

[He wondered whether the British Mission had not informed the Home Office about Ado's destitution and poor health. The Home Office would not act without confirmation from their representative in Bucharest. They may also think that Ado's brothers can maintain him.]

> ...it seems that we must have more patience. I know how easy it is to say such a thing and how difficult to act accordingly, and I do not forget for a single moment that in view of the state of your heart every delay may mean the worst. But unfortunately I have not invented the Atomic Bomb and my influence is very limited. I am absolutely convinced that we shall win in the end, but we must have patience...

[He tried to explain to Ado some differences between German and British officials.]

> I have noted what you write me about the unfriendliness of the officials at the British Mission. It is difficult for me from a distance to say why they are like that. They may of course be snobs who are interested in rich people only, or anti-Semites. But in general British Officials are very friendly and helpful and even if they appear to act in a different way, it is always best to appeal to them for help. It is no good at all to complain to or about them, the German concept of *sich beschweren* does not exist in English. There is another aspect to it: their reports concerning you form the basis of the Home Office's decision. It is therefore absolutely necessary to be on good terms with them...On the other hand, nothing in England is final. The fact that your application has been refused again does not mean that it is less likely to be granted the next time, but on the contrary that the next time they may feel that this time they must say yes. You must keep that in mind, and not hesitate to get in touch with them again, if you can think of any new circumstance which they may have misunderstood or not properly appreciated. Even if you had a disagreement with them - I hope not – you must try to establish friendly relations again.

Because Wolja describes *sich beschweren,* translated as 'to complain', as a 'German concept', I wondered for a while whether there was a particular linguistic meaning that I did not understand. There is not. Once again, Wolja is describing what he has learned about German/British differences in behaviour, in this case in relation to officials: in order to get things done, Germans complain, in contrast to the British who believe it is better to be polite and 'appeal for help'.[8] I recognize how hard Wolja tries to conform to what he understands as British ways of doing things and to explain the differences to Lotte and to his father.

He advised Ado to find someone who could make a recommendation to the Consular adviser, preferably in person. 'Rabbis and medical Doctors are recognised in English Custom and in British Law as persons which are particularly competent to give guarantees to officials concerning patients or members of their communities...because doctors as well priests are regarded as persons which...can be relied upon to speak the truth.'

At the beginning of July the certificates arrived. Wolja forwarded them immediately to Ruth Fellner, who in turn sent them straight on to the Home Office. On 25 July Wolja repeated his earlier advice to Ado about finding someone who might be able to influence the Mission in Bucharest

> ...because it is apparently they who have informed the Home Office in such a way that the Home Office has come to a negative decision. If they change their opinion everything will become much simpler. The fact that they have said 'no' twice does not matter, Englishmen are empirical in their outlook, they learn by mistakes, they do not stand on principle.

Ado had already followed Wolja's earlier advice.

> ...I thought about it a great deal and in the end I decided to approach the British Mission again, with a new more detailed medical certificate, which I enclose for you, and supported by an influential person to show that the decision...is unjust as my case fulfils all the conditions for a visa...this time the atmosphere was a bit more favourable for me and...I have a bit of hope, but only a little bit. I think that in a few days I shall be able to give you the result of this initiative or at least to be able to give you more precise information. (20 July)

On 2 August he did receive better news:

> I have been told that the Br. Mission has asked London by telegram for a visa for me. I immediately sent you a telegram...At last a first success. I understand of course that this is not yet finished, but I now have lots of hope and I think there will be a successful conclusion. My God, it is true that my dream of seeing you again and embracing you before I die will come true. It's almost impossible to believe, what a joy! I sent you a telegram to let you know and in case you can intervene with the Home Office. They told me at the British Mission

that they think that they will be able to give me the H. Off. decision after 8 days.

Wolja did receive this news by telegram on 4 August and wrote immediately to Ruth Fellner, hoping that she might be able to speed up the process. He repeated his familiar statements about his salary and having room in the house for Ado. The Clarkes had moved out two days earlier on 2 August.

'Nothing is Absolutely Necessary'

On 5 August 1946 Wolja wrote a long letter to Ado, telling him he was 'terribly happy'. Although it had finally been agreed that Ado met the criteria, it might still take some time to receive the visa. Ado would then need a passport, exit permit, and the necessary transit visas as well as organising his transport. Wolja also felt able now to answer Ado's questions in his letters of 27 March and 10 May.

> ...you asked me which of your things I regard as absolutely essential in view of the high cost of transport and the low limits of weight for luggage. I have discussed it with Lotte. It is very difficult to give you a definite reply as we do not know whether you will come by boat or by air plane. Therefore I think I will not give you just a brief list of things which you should take with you but rather my comments to your questions and you will have to decide for yourself.
>
> 1) Nothing is absolutely necessary, except you yourself.
> 2) 'Binocles'.[9] I think you should bring them, as we shall not be able to buy any here (we never got the other ones out of Germany), and they represent very little weight per value.
> 3) Linge de corps et de ménage. I think you should bring everything along. All these things are strictly rationed and very expensive here. Also all your suits etc. If you have any money left you may even get yourself a new suit as at the moment these things are very expensive and the famous good English material is only for millionaires or for export. The average Englishman is quite satisfied if his suit keeps one year only.
> 4) Eta's old dresses. I think I should try to sell them as they will probably not fit Lotte and therefore it would be a waste of space which you could use for other things.
> 5) Coussins, plumeaux, tapis would be very useful indeed, but on the other hand it will be difficult to transport. If you can manage

it, it would be good, as it is terribly cold here for half a year. It is of course not as cold as in Germany or in Rumania during the winter, but the houses are very badly built, only suitable for the summer, there is in our house of course no central heating and the open coal fires are a study in uselessness and inefficiency. Therefore it is also necessary that you take all your woollen *linge de corps* with you. But do not misunderstand me. Even if you cannot bring with you a single blanket, we have got enough for the beginning, and we shall arrange everything.

6) Portable type writer. My old Remington is still alright, but it may be useful to have another one if you consider it likely that you will use yours often, since Lotte and I are using ours very often.

7) Ulvir.[10] As I have still got my Ulvir lamp, I think you should leave yours in Rumania, but take all electrodes with you as it is impossible to get replacements.

8) Electric Iron. We have got a small one and I think it is not worth your effort to take it with you since it is very heavy.

9) *Pots, sérvice de Café.* Though very useful, I think it takes too much space to take it along.

In general it may be best to sell everything which you cannot easily take with you or send here and try to buy new things like suits. You cannot take new things into this country without paying very much customs duty and purchase tax.

My dear Ado, you must not let the decision what to take and what to leave worry you. Even if you make a mistake, it does not matter...

Perhaps you would like to know a few details about our life here, and our house. Petts Wood has the character of Dahlem. Our street has plenty of trees. Each family lives in a separate house. Some houses are 'fully detached' (completely separate), some are 'semi-detached' which means that two houses are built together. We are living in such a semi-detached house. It has a ground floor, first floor, and a loft, that is a room for storing in the roof. We also have a garage (without a car) which we also use for storing. There is a small front garden with flowers, a grass lawn and a few trees, and a larger back garden with two apple trees. One could grow a lot of things in the back garden, but as you can imagine I am a very bad gardener. In the ground floor are two big rooms and the kitchen. In the first floor are two big rooms, one small room, a lavatory and a bath room. We are thinking to make one of the big first floor rooms your room. The other big room in the first floor will become Peter's and Eti's room (until now little Eti slept in our room and Peter in the small room). The small room in the first floor will become my study. Lotte and I will sleep downstairs in the ground floor in the room facing the garden, and the room downstairs facing the [front] garden will become a common living room and dining room. We had some friends staying with us for some months, so we have to rearrange all the rooms now, and I am terribly happy that we can now plan for you too...

I was fascinated by this letter for what it revealed about Wolja's view of England and the English. My father at this time had clearly not understood the significance of the open fire, the hearth, for the English home![11] This critical view of English heating systems reflects Wolja's more general critical view of British industry and services in comparison with those of (post-war) Germany – another family theme. I was also struck by the number of possessions that Ado did have, the use of the house, the description of the rooms as large, and the way the Clarkes were referred to as 'friends'. They certainly did use the loft and the garage 'for storing'; it was in these two places that we found most of the papers.

For nearly a month they heard nothing more about the visa and Ado began to despair again: 'My hopes are beginning to diminish!...one has to go on having patience, still!' (25 August). In fact the decision had been made by mid-August. A letter confirming this, dated 15 August, from George Oliver at the Home Office, was sent on to Wolja by the MP Tom Cook on 29 August 1946.

The Language of Goethe

While waiting for news, Ado tried to find out more about the journey – possible routes and how to pay for tickets. On 25 August 1946, writing in French, he told Wolja that he would like to have the hernia operation before he came, if his heart allowed, as it was a very easy operation, requiring only a few days recovery and did not cost a lot. 'But all this is still in the realm of speculation, *Zukunftsmusik* [dreams of the future].By the way: do you think we could now correspond in the language of Goethe?!' He allowed himself to start imagining life in England. He liked Wolja's description of the house, was proud that he would be the neighbour of his friends Peter and Eti, but at the same time worried that he would not be able to talk to them as he did not speak English and they had no German. Perhaps because he was fluent in four languages, he thought that his English was not very good; but he seems to have understood Wolja's letters and written in English himself.

> In relation to the garden of your bungalow, don't be concerned, I shall take on the responsibility for taking care of it, on the condition that Peter is my assistant gardener and that he will help me construct a little holy corner surrounded by flowers, where I would like to bury the urn which contains the ashes of my beloved Eta, if, as I hope, I obtain permission to bring them and if you allow me this little corner of the garden.

[He asked what he could bring for Eti and Peter]

> I ask myself whether I really have the right to turn your lives upside down, to upset your routines in your domestic arrangements, in your relationships with your friends, in a word to enter into your lives, and all this to satisfy the egoistical desire of an old sick person to live close to you, without thinking about the sacrifices this desire means for you; and whether it would be better to give up the journey and stay here. If I were younger, if I had perfect health, if I were rich, or if at least I had the possibility of earning my own living over there, it would be a completely different matter. On the other hand my life is so sad, I find it very hard to be completely alone, my soul needs a little love, a warm friendly atmosphere, which I lack totally here. I have no-one in the world except you and my heart tells me that it is with you that I will be able to find a little love and happiness; and I think you would not refuse me this, especially as it was one of the last wishes of our beloved Eta, that I should live the last years of my life near you. I promise you that I will try not only to be agreeable to you, but also to become useful, you know that I have multiple domestic talents! and especially I shall try to earn my living in some way or other, perhaps as a correspondent for a Romanian newspaper. I ask you my dear ones to understand and to forgive my worries and not to be cross with me for my anguish.
> ...I find myself in a feverish mood waiting for the decision of the Home Office and waiting to see you again.

Finally, on 2 September, Wolja was able to send a telegram to Ado: 'Home Office writing consular adviser Home Office agrees visa love Saraga.' On 6 September 1946 Ado heard directly from the British Mission, who 'will grant the visa as soon as I present a valid passport for England and permission to leave. I am drunk with happiness.'

I imagined that from this point on, it would be straightforward, but the correspondence shows that it was not. Ado needed a passport and exit visa, to work out the best way to travel, travel insurance for himself and for his luggage and to pay for a ticket. All these arrangements became even more complicated, because of the difficulty of communication with Ado, and because of the involvement of the Jewish Committee in London. They were very helpful, but, as Wolja told Ado on 21 November, 'The Jewish Committee here works very closely with the Home Office and they do lots of things without informing the people concerned what they are doing.' Ado also had lots of preparation to do: selling goods he could not take with him, sending luggage he could not carry, repairing and washing his linen, making himself a suit. He thought he would need at least 4 to 6 weeks. Wolja advised against the hernia operation, as did the doctors in Romania, so Ado cancelled it. He also responded to Ado's idea about bringing Eti's ashes, offered him the same good advice he had given Lotte when arriving in England and tried to reassure Ado about disrupting their lives.

> Before you bring the urn with the ashes of our beloved Eti, you must also ask the Consular Adviser whether you are allowed to bring them to England, without further formalities. I do not think it will be possible to place them in our garden, that is probably not allowed, and it is also very difficult, because of the neighbours. We shall probably have to put them in a cemetery, but I will find out about this. Please believe me that I fully understand your wishes and you know how dear to me Eti is. But we must respect the laws and customs of the land in which we live...
>
> And when you land in England you must tell the customs officers everything that you have. Otherwise later you may have great problems when we apply for an extension of your stay. You will probably only get a residence permit for one or two months to start with. You do not need to worry about this. This is usual practice here and you can be absolutely sure that the permit will always be extended when you have been given a visa for this purpose. But this has nothing to do with the official at the port, who only has the right and duty to give you a short term permit...
>
> Dear Ado, dear Papi, you must not have such silly thoughts that you will disturb us. Since the outbreak of the war I have suffered so much from the thought that if I had only pushed you more, you would have been here before the war and I would have seen my Eti again. Since her death, I have only had one thought; I must succeed in getting

you here. The only difficulty that could exist when you live with us is that you will always be anxious that you are a burden and therefore unconsciously look for signs of our discontent and then decide that you have discovered some. I cannot say anything else. It is so obvious that you must live with us and you must believe this.

Replying on 29 September in German, Ado told Wolja he was of course right about the ashes: 'it was just a silly sentimental idea of mine; I had already reconsidered it, but too late, it was after I had already put the letter into the postbox.' If he was allowed to bring them he would like to place them in a crematorium, so that his ashes could be placed next to Eta's. Dated 22 November 1946 is a letter in Romanian authorising the transport of the ashes.

After this there are very long gaps in the correspondence and some letters may be missing. Wolja received contradictory information from Ado himself and from the Jewish Committee about how and when Ado was travelling. Wolja's letters show how anxious this made him. On 16 November he advised Ado to dress warmly for the journey.

Many trains are still not heated and England is the coldest country in the world. Peter is standing next to me and says that he hopes that next year you will go away with us. He asks me if I know when you are coming. When I say, soon, but I don't know when, then he says in a hopeful way, perhaps next Friday.

By late November Wolja seemed more confident that at last Ado would arrive, as indicated by the various thank you letters that he and Lotte wrote to Dr Rabinovitch, Ruth Fellner and to the MP, Tom Cook. He appears to think the MP's role was crucial: 'I am quite certain that your intervention was decisive as, before you took an interest in my case, complete deadlock seemed to have been reached.' (24 November 1946) Or perhaps he was being polite. My own reading of the correspondence suggests that Ado himself, following Wolja's advice, may have taken the crucial step when he involved 'an influential person'.

This was a story of delays and hiccups, which continued until Ado finally arrived in England. A telegram dated 29 January came from Zurich: '*ARRIVE THURSDAY FOLKESTONE 13.05 LONDON VICTORIA 15.36 WAIT FOR ME FOLKESTONE = SARAGA*. Once again they achieved a successful outcome because of the connections they had, their capacity to network and their sheer persistence. Their letters show that they had a very good understanding of how such processes worked and the need to involve 'people of influence', especially as Wolja 'had not invented the atomic bomb'.

Historical context

Two sources of information helped me to put Wolja's experience into context. In January 1946 in the first edition of AJR Information, the editor described the Home Secretary's November 1945 statement as 'a noble statement in a noble spirit!' Together with the resumption of naturalization, it had 'given new hope to Jewish refugees in this country.'[12] But in later issues, when they reported the numbers of distressed relatives who had been admitted, they became increasingly negative. By 13 January 1946 only 109 distressed persons had arrived, by 9 May 790 people and by 31 May the numbers were still less than 1000.[13]

Under the heading 'AN ELEMENTARY HUMAN RIGHT' they expressed concerns about the admission of 160,000 Polish soldiers into Britain on their demobilisation, which was seen as uncontroversial by the press in comparison with the less than 50,000 Jewish refugees from Germany and Austria, whose 'presence in this country has in the course of the last seven years given vent to not infrequent inimical attacks in newspapers and at meetings, and it was only after prolonged anxiety that naturalisation was resumed, which, we hope, will absorb most of them into British life.'[14] In January 1947 they expressed disappointment that the numbers 'may not be far below 3000'.[15]

More recently, Louise London described the Distressed Relatives Scheme as a concession to humanitarian pressure, aimed at concentration camp survivors, which took no risks over finance. 'The government acknowledged that the limited nature of the scheme would lead to refusals in cases where strong compassionate grounds existed.' She makes a comparison with the development of European Volunteer Worker schemes which 'hastily recruited from displaced persons' camps to work in Britain's understaffed industries and hospitals.' Jews and ex-enemy nationals were excluded from such schemes.[16]

Wolja's' understanding of the difficulties with which he was struggling seems to have been an accurate one.

The Death of a Distinguished Author

As with Lotte's arrival in London, I feel frustrated not to know more. From letters from Ado's brothers in Romania, I learned that in March he was already very ill. A very cold winter spell had started on 21 January 1947, nine days before he arrived. After Lotte's death, her friend and neighbour Mary told me how devotedly Lotte had cared for Ado, insisting on keeping him at home. A Ministry of Fuel and Power Certificate for additional heating on

Ado when he arrived in England. Photo in the possession of the author.

medical grounds – 'by reason of heart trouble, confined to room' – is dated 1 May 1947.

On 26 May 1947 Wolja wrote belatedly to thank Ruth Fellner for all her help:

> Unfortunately, he had one breakdown during the journey and then a complete breakdown two days after his arrival...My father's health has improved a bit since he is with us but he is still an invalid and unable to leave his room and it is doubtful whether he will improve any more. We are however, very happy that he is at least able to be together with us and to see his two grandchildren who make him very happy.

Replying in her usual warm personal style on 30 May, Ruth Fellner expressed her gratitude for Wolja's 'kind remarks', and her sorrow at Ado's state of health. On 4 July Wolja wrote to the Aliens' Department, requesting an extension for Ado's permit to remain, telling them that in the meantime he had become a naturalized British subject.

Suddenly, it was all over. Ado died on 10 November 1947 and I am left with many condolence letters, a funeral address and an invoice from the South London Liberal Jewish Synagogue for Ado's funeral – on 14 November - for 5 guineas and 12/6 for the cost of the 'Cosycar'. On 22 November, S.M. Rich, Minister and Hon. Sec. at South London Liberal Jewish Synagogue, sent Wolja a copy of what he said at the service.

> 'They were lovely in their lives, and in their deaths they were not divided.' These words from an ancient Jewish elegy are appropriate to this ceremony – when we bid farewell to the earthly habitations of Ado and Esther Saraga, two loving souls, now united in the peace of God. This joint disposal of their mortal remains is a symbol of their joint lives, in which they shared many joys and many sorrows. The love that united them enhanced the sweetness of their joys – and helped to lighten the burden of their sorrows. Because the later years of their lives were passed during a period of special tribulation and danger for many Jews, their sorrows were increased and intensified on that account. But the power of mutual love to overcome the burdens that beset our lives is infinite. Love can even conquer death itself, for it builds a bridge uniting the living with those who have cast off the burden of earth and have passed on still in the presence of God, to the future adventures that await the soul. Though they have departed from us, the influence for good that they initiated and exerted still remains, and continues to bear fruit. The enthusiasm of Esther Saraga for social betterment, her passion for social justice that found expression in her active membership of the Jewish Bund must have awakened similar enthusiasms in others, extending and continuing her influence on humanity. Ado: through the devotion of his son and daughter in law was spared to end his earthly pilgrimage surrounded by love, tended with every possible amelioration of his illness by his family in this dear land, watching with loving eyes and expanding heart the development of his grandchildren, Peter and the little Esther who bears the name of her, his life's companion and helpmeet with whose ashes his own are soon to be comingled as a symbol of their soul's unity. And so we pray...

Ado's final wish about his ashes was therefore granted.

I have no idea whether Ado had wanted a Jewish funeral in a synagogue or whether there was really no other alternative at that time. The correspondence shows that Wolja was put in touch with Samuel Rich through his friend Aaron Emanuel, a liberal English Jew. Shortly before I completed the book, Tony Kushner told me[17] that Samuel Rich's daily diaries were in the archive in Southampton University.

> He was a week off 70 when he did the service. He was a leading force in the liberal Judaism movement and a man of letters. It would have been a liberal service as orthodox would not have done a cremation... He was for many years a teacher at the Jews Free School in the East End and his diaries show both a support of the Anglicizing policies of the school as well as a strong empathy with individual East European origin immigrant children he taught. Rich became comfortably middle class and was closely allied with the older, richer elite of Anglo-Jewry, adhering to the 'Englishman of the Hebrew persuasion' model. But he was not very wealthy himself.

The relevant entries[18] show, in Tony Kushner's view 'an interesting interaction between a very assimilated English Jew and a refugee.'

> 10 November 1947
> Aaron Emanuel rang abt. a death at Orpington, father of a friend of his (Farada) who wants a cremation. Srefugee.do it for 5 guis - etc. They want the ashes of the mother brt [brought] into it somehow – She died in Roumania – much laughter by Amy [his wife], Helen & Willie abt. this 'mingling' of ashes. We tried the Canadian Whiskey & found it good.

> 11 November 1947
> ... Then came Wolja Saraja, 43, Kingsway PW (but by Aaron Emanuel), who wants me to conduct a cremation at 10.40 on Friday of his father Adolph (Ado) – Roumanian refugees. Son now a British subject. Ig took to them both.

> 12 November 1947
> ....'answered calls by the Saraga family abt Friday's cremation

> 13 November 1947
> Before writing my 'piece' for tomorrow's cremation, I wasted a little time looking for a special copy of the LJS Burial Service – By lunch time (early) I finished it.

14 November 1947
A hard day. Post fr. HGS who likesvNo.80 of the Bulletin, EJF and
RenebCumin, who wrote w. sympathy abtSIHaaltho' she'd never seen
him!...Before the cosycar called for me I wrote my speech for the Mem
Service in the evening.Did the cremation of Ado and Esther Saraga –
back by 11.15. Rain made me all nerves & Amy too. Then to Given after
early lunch for the child's Hebrew lesson. Arranged w.Her to get me 2
tongues and 1 lb smoke salmon for my party delivered on Thurs 27th.

21 November 1947
No fee has come fr. Saraga

22 November 1947
Banked cheque for W.Saraga of PW.

I was amused by his comment on 21 November: No fee has come fr. Saraga.'
The letter with the invoice is dated 17 November; he obviously expected to
be paid by return of post. Not something Wolja would have been good at,
even at the best of times. The laughter about the mingling of the ashes
shocked me, but I was moved by his statement that he 'took to them'. The
'piece' he wrote for the cremation service shows that he took great care to
find out about Eti and Ado. It does not betray his earlier response and his
letter thanking Wolja for the cheque, in our collection, is also very warm:
'Looking forward to meeting you again in happier circumstances.' He adds
a handwritten note sending greetings to Mrs Saraga and hoping she will
contact his daughter who it turns out also lives in Petts Wood. As Tony
Kushner comments '...having shown a negative side Rich does redeem
himself when meeting Wolja. In the short references it almost encapsulates
the tensions and ambivalence towards refugees from the elite.'

As with his encounters with establishment figures in SPSL, when he
first arrived in the UK, I was struck by the way that Wolja clearly made a
good impression on people, who I presume may not have expected to find
it so easy to like a refugee. Tony Kushner added an additional possible
explanation – that his response to Wolja was '...also I suspect on hearing
that he had become naturalized which Rich would have much approved
of.'[19]

On 11 December 1947 the Alien's Registration Office informed Wolja
that Ado's name had been removed from the Register of Aliens. On 19 Nov
1947, an obituary appeared in a Romanian newspaper *Adeverul*. It was sent
with a translation to Wolja by Bibi, his cousin, now in living in Milan. He
received it from his father, Lascar, Ado's brother in Bucarest. Written on the

side is: 'private translation for Wolja'. Only two of Ado's brothers are mentioned, both quite prominent citizens, omitting his third brother and his sisters.

> A cable from London is announcing the death of A.S., distinguished author, born in Jassy capital of Moldova, a direct victim of Nazi brutality. Born in 1884, son of Elias Saraga, publisher and bookseller, he was a member of the early Jassy group of Marxists, led by Ghelerter, etc etc. Living in Berlin, he studied there economics and social sciences. He translated in German the work of Kogatniceanu, 'The agrarian problem in Rumania' thereafter published by the Archiv für Sozialpolitik und Sozialwissenschaft. He held an important position in the leadership of soviet commercial representation in Berlin, until the Nazis took over, when he had to come back in Romani. His only son, Wolja, doctor of eng. of Berlin University and assistant of Heinrich Hertz Institute for radiations went in England as a refugee where he held an important position in the science world. After a long parting from his son, suffering of heart disease, after losing his wife too, he went over in England, some months ago, where he is dead. This son of the old family Saraga from Iasi was the brother of Mr. Achille Saraga, MP & Lascar Saraga, Chancellor of the Rumanian Bar Association.

Postscript: The Ashes

There is one final set of letters relating to Ado's death - correspondence with Golders Green Crematorium in the 1970s about Eti and Ado's ashes.

At the beginning of the book, I referred to the notes that Lotte used to leave on the mantelpiece when she went away. In addition to telling us where to find their wills and apologising for the mess, she tried to protect us from getting a shock when we found an urn containing Eti and Ado's ashes in the sideboard. By the time Lotte spoke to me about this, the ashes were safely lodged under a rose bush at Golders Green. I have no idea whether Wolja or Lotte ever visited the crematorium but, when Wolja died, I suggested we should put his ashes with those of his parents. Lotte must have organized it. I have a vague memory of discussing a new inscription with her. But my next very clear memory is going to Golders Green crematorium for the funeral of a work colleague. I could not be there without looking at the memorial. With some trepidation, I went to the office and they told me where to find it. Two colleagues came with me.

When Lotte died we put her ashes there too, and the gardens of the crematorium became an important place of refuge for me. I would go and find the rose bush, never at first quite remembering where it was, and cry a lot. Then I would walk round the gardens, and perhaps sit for a while in one of the pagodas at the far end, before returning to the little café for a cup of tea. Peter had done all the paper work after Lotte died – part of his share of our division of labour when we were caring for Lotte in those last years; he did the practical and financial work and I did the emotional. I remember some years later we agreed to renew. Then Peter moved. I presumed we had paid for two periods of 10 years, which took us to 2005. At some point I would go there; I had plenty of time.

On a sunny day in May 2004, while driving down the M1 from Milton Keynes after work, the thought came into my head to go to the crematorium on my way home – a thought that would not go away. The gardens were closed, but the office was open. I explained the situation. I did not know the number of the memorial, but the name was quite unusual. The woman in the office could not find it due for renewal in 2005 at all, so she searched elsewhere. Eventually she found it; it should have been renewed in June 2003. They had written to Peter several times, but had no reply. I became very anxious. Had they removed the ashes and the plaque? No. They usually keep them for a year hoping that someone will turn up, as I had done, just in time. And now I understood that the renewal periods were related to the initial disposition, which was 14 June 1973. I paid the arrears, and gave her my address.

I do not know what made me go to Golders Green that day. I had not yet read the correspondence with Ado about the ashes. For it to have ended because of our neglect would have felt very bad. We renewed for a 20 year period.

Notes

1. Hansard, 'DISTRESSED PERSONS, EUROPE (ADMISSION TO UNITED KINGDOM)' *HC Deb 13* (November 1945) vol. 415 cc1922-7.
2. http://www.bbc.co.uk/news/uk-england-london-26856434 (Accessed 10 May 2014).
3. See, for example, A. Karpf, 'We've been here before', *The Guardian*, Saturday 8 June 2002.
4. The text of this letter appears in Wolja's later summary prepared for the MP Tom Cook. No date is given.
5. B338/389.
6. B338/391. Also available in our own collection.
7. Reported in *AJR Information*, April 1946, p. 30.
8. Thanks to my German teacher, Anya Buchele, for helping me to understand this.
9. Translated as 'pince nez', but perhaps just a pair of glasses.
10. A sun lamp.
11. An interesting observation made to me by Gail Lewis.
12. *AJR Information*, January 1946, p.1.

13. *AJR Information*, March 1946, p. 22; June 1946, p.46.
14. *AJR Information*, July 1946, p.49.
15. *AJR Information*, January 1947, p.3.
16. L. London, *Whitehall and the Jews 1933-1948* (Cambridge: Cambridge University Press, 2000), pp. 266, 268, 269.
17. Email to the author, Tony Kushner, 30 November 2018.
18. MS 168 AJ 217/43, University of Southampton archives, Samuel Rich diary for 1947. https://archiveshub.jisc.ac.uk/data/gb738-ms168. Abbreviations as in the original. I am very grateful to Tony Kushner for alerting me to the existence of this archive and for sending me these extracts.
19. Emails to the author, Tony Kushner, 30 November 2018 and 4 December 2018.

8

All Their Worldly Possessions

10 June 2010

It's summer 1955 and we're on holiday in North Wales with Lotte's sister, Mara, and her son Uri. Lotte and Mara are drawing pictures in the sand, trying to reconstruct their parents' apartment in Berlin and the furniture in it. It's the first time Lotte has seen her sister since Mara and her husband fled from Berlin to Prague with their baby son (Uri's older brother) in 1938 and also the first time I have experienced having a 'family', other than Peter and my parents. It is also my first memory of my parents making claims for 'restitution'.

The possessions about which Lotte and Wolja had argued in 1938 never arrived. As a result we lived with the very heavy German furniture that Lotte and Wolja had bought from their friends, the Bikermanns, when they emigrated to the USA. It was dark and oppressive and much too large for the small rooms of our suburban semi. It was also completely different from the furniture in my friends' houses, which did not help with my desire to conform to suburban Englishness. I disliked it intensely and happily let Peter have it when Lotte died, even though at that time I was living in a house with rooms large enough to accommodate it.

In their letters in 1938 their negotiations about their possessions seemed to become the carriers of their emotions - fears, anxieties and desires for the future. When their goods did not arrive, they lost more than a material link to their past. At the time of reflecting on the meaning of this loss, I was reading a novel by Irene Nemirovsky, *All our Worldly Goods*. In one scene the residents of a French village, Saint Elme, have to flee from the advancing German army in 1914. Madame Hardelot, a bourgeois woman, is in despair

> ...I'm losing my mind. Just imagine everything we have to leave behind, our furniture, our linen, our family momentos...I'm just throwing together what I can at random...I want to take everything, she said as she picked up a variety of objects and pressed them close

to her heart before putting them down again: a photo of Pierre as a child, a silver sugar bowl, a damask and lace table cloth.[1]

I wonder whether Lotte and Mara's pictures in the sand were a relatively safe way of both acknowledging their losses and re-living something of that past together. Perhaps a focus on spaces and objects was less painful than talking directly about the death of their mother.

Amongst our collection of papers we found three solicitor's files and two envelopes of material, partly sorted by Lotte, concerned with claims for compensation from Germany. They contain literally hundreds of letters, certificates, testimonials and affidavits relating to their losses of possessions, education, qualifications and employment, as well as applications for pensions for Lotte and Wolja. Many of the papers are drafts in various stages of completion including *Lebensläufe* [curriculum vitae] for Lotte and Wolja and also for Wolja's parents, Esther and Ado. Once again I was amazed by the documents that they had kept, including the records of all the lectures that Esther had attended as a medical student in Bern (1901 -1905) and later in Berlin (1905 - 1908).

One of the envelopes of material, labelled 'German, Restitution Lotte, Old material', includes the correspondence in 1938 and 1939 with Schenker, the firm paid by Lotte to transport her furniture, as well as correspondence between Lotte and Schenker in 1947, when she tried to locate the lost furniture after the war. The second envelope, labelled 'Cromwell, Lotte, Furniture', starts three years later, in 1950, once formal legal processes for restitution had been established by the German Federal Republic. The correspondence in this collection continues until the end of 1968, and includes Lotte's claims for compensation for loss of the furniture as well as other restitution claims to which I shall return in the next chapter.

Sometimes the sums of money claimed or received are expressed in Reichsmarks (Germany currency 1924 to 1948) or Deutsche Marks (after 1948 until replaced by the Euro) and others in Pounds Sterling. £1 was equivalent to approximately 12.4 Marks in 1938 and 11.71 in 1960.[2]

'Every Trick in the Book'

On 8 July 1938 Lotte wrote to Wolja that she had chosen the removal firm Schenker because they 'are first class, very respectable and not more expensive, and where in particular I can leave everything without worrying'. An itemised bill from Schenker, dated 27 August 1938, gives a total cost for her transport of RM 558, including delivery to an address in London within the 5 mile zone, and up to a third storey, as well as storage for 4 months at a cost of RM 10 per month. It also included a tip for the removal men of RM 8. Lotte paid this bill immediately, two days before she left Germany, telling Schenker that any further inquiries should be addressed to her lawyer Paul Schidwigowski. She left money with her aunt Gertrude for any additional charges that might arise for her mother's goods.

Two of Lotte's last letters to Wolja in August 1938 tell a very different story: '...the most important things I still have to do: I have to deal with the Schenker business for Mutti and for myself; for Mutti because the notification from the exchange control office has been delayed, I don't know whether it is possible to get it before the end of the week...'(23 August) and 'As always, everything goes wrong at the last minute. In particular the business with the carrier for Mutti's and my transport is dreadful and having a terrible cost on my nerves. Hopefully I'll be able to sort it out in time.' (27 August)

Lotte arrived in England on 31 August 1938. Her efforts during 1938 and 1939 to persuade Schenker to ship her goods are described in forty five letters in German between Lotte, Paul Schidwigowski and Schenker. On several occasions she thought the problems had been solved, but each time she was let down when Schenker came up with yet another reason why the goods could not be sent. Between 1947 and 1965 Lotte herself, and later Mr Cromwell, attempted successively to track down the furniture, to sue Schenker and, when that failed, to claim for compensation in line with the developing laws on reparations. The correspondence is very extensive and detailed, but my task is facilitated by a summary of the pre-war correspondence that Lotte prepared for Cromwell, telling him 'the letters show without a doubt that Schenker, using every trick in the book, sabotaged this process'.

A letter of complaint to Schenker dated 14 June 1939, offers a clear picture of the hoops through which emigrating Jews had to leap and the way in which Schenker behaved both towards Lotte and her lawyer. She began by describing their service as 'extremely negligent, shoddy and indifferent' and telling them she was prepared to sue for damages, reserving the right to hold them fully legally responsible. They had been recommended by her employer, the Banca d'Italia and she in turn had recommended them to other people. She reminded them that she had paid the bill in full in advance before she left Germany, having been reassured by Schenker that they would continue to represent her interests. Between September and December 1938 she was presented with a series of bureaucratic obstacles and difficulties and demands for more money – all of which her lawyer had managed to resolve, despite Schenker's lack of help.

> ... you made Dr Schidwigowski's task more difficult in every way, since the person responsible could never be reached by telephone,

never rang when he promised to, and did not answer any letters if he could help it. This behaviour is absolutely typical of the handling of my transportation. Because of the delays in your conduct of my business, which can be attributed to the indifference of your firm, further difficulties arose in respect of the payment in Reichmarks of the transport costs in England, which of course I had already settled.

Here too Dr Schidwigowski resolved the problem – a currency exchange permit was obtained on 14 December. Despite this

> …you sent me an estimate of costs of RM 890 for the transport of my goods in a container to the port of London. On 13 December…my solicitor…was – completely incomprehensibly – told that it was not known if the deposit which had been left with your firm would be enough for the carriage of the goods. As is clear from all the papers in your possession, the payment which I made to you is not a deposit; rather, I had already paid an itemised account for the transportation… nothing had changed in the conditions of the transportation. In your letter of 9 January, that is three weeks later, you finally declared yourself ready to meet your obligations and to carry out the transportation in accordance with the agreed conditions.

In a letter to Paul Schidwigowski on 29 March Schenker had claimed that for over two months they were unable to find an official to deal with the necessary customs clearance. Lotte challenged this. Other people's consignments, for which clearance permission had been applied much later, arrived every day in London. Paul Schidwigowski reminded Schenker again on 4 May, but his letter 'as usual remained unanswered'.

> I must say that before I had this terrible experience, I would have considered it impossible for a large removal firm to behave in this way. I know no-one else who has had such difficulties with their company.
>
> I must now urgently request that you give me, by the 25th of this month, a firm date within the next 4 weeks on which the goods will leave Berlin. If I do not receive this confirmation within this time limit I shall regretfully be obliged to engage a lawyer to take all necessary measures against you in order to gain possession of my goods. I hope however that it will be possible to persuade a firm with your reputation to fulfil your contractual obligations without recourse to such measures.
>
> Furthermore I urgently request that you immediately take all necessary steps to enable the dispatch of the few items of silver in the

consignment, since they should have been sent a long time before the new regulations concerning the transportation of valuable goods, and it is your responsibility that they are still in Berlin. I also ask you to check carefully that the consignment is complete. You will recall that in the consignment of my mother, Mrs Erna Isenburg, the most valuable items, a wooden chest with bed and table linen, were missing. I assume that in view of the negligent treatment of the transportation up to now, you will exercise particular care with this final shipment.

I expect confirmation from you by return of post, as I cannot possibly manage without the goods any longer, and I am also not willing to do so.

Lotte's worry about the silver was not unfounded. Writing from Bucharest on 25 June 1939, Ado told them: 'Our things are at last underway after nearly a year of exasperation and irritation and should arrive any day. The silver is not amongst it, but following an intervention from the Rumanian consulate in Berlin, the confiscated silver was released, but only after the consignment had been loaded. The silver will be sent later...'

Lotte also visited the Head Office of Schenker in London, hoping they might be able to put pressure on the Berlin office, but to no avail. When Schenker Berlin finally replied on 13 July 1939, they claimed that crucial papers had been mislaid in going from one official to another. A week later they informed Lotte that her permit had expired and she would have to make a completely new application. Following the intervention of her mother's cousin Herr Silberstein, who knew someone who worked for Schenker, the old approval was extended and the goods were expected to be sent off that week. On 18 August 1939 Schenker said they were awaiting further papers and would then send the goods. Lotte replied very politely on 22 August: 'I thank you very much for your letter of 18 August and your efforts in this matter. I hope that now I will receive the goods very shortly.'

But she did not receive them, and not surprisingly there was no more direct correspondence with Schenker, as twelve days later Britain declared war on Germany.

Lotte did not give up. There are three letters in the file, between 11 December 1939 and 25 January 1940 from a Dutch shipping company, Scheuer Brothers (London) Limited. Lotte asked them to try to get the goods from Schenker, but nothing came of it. The process was very complicated and Schenker very unhelpful.

***

In 1947 Lotte tried to locate her possessions. Communication with Germany was now possible, Ado had finally joined them, and discussions about German reparations were beginning. She wrote to Schenker on 26 June asking whether they could let her know the whereabouts of her goods. She had all the paperwork if this would help. They replied on 21 July: 'We regret we are unable to give you any information about your furniture, as all our offices and warehouses, including inventories and documents were destroyed in the war. We understand that you should address your claim for damages to the Magistrat of the Stadt Berlin. We regret we are unable to give you a favourable response.' This polite but blanket dismissal of Lotte's questions and concerns was to characterize all her subsequent dealings with Schenker.

'The Prospects Look Dimmer Than Ever'

The story of the 'lost furniture' had turned out to be much more complicated than I had imagined. Schenker were clearly very obstructive, taking no responsibility at all for failing to fulfil their contract. This was Nazi Germany in 1938/39, yet Lotte demanded her rights and threatened to sue, appealing to Schenker's desire to preserve their good reputation. Paul Schidwigowski, a Jewish lawyer acting for a Jewish client, similarly expected to be treated properly. I was curious about the role he had played and found myself becoming more and more concerned about why he was still in Berlin?

During my first encounter with these letters in 2002, when I simply sorted them into date order, I was unprepared for the impact of physically handling them. The headed notepaper used by Paul Schidwigowski and his colleague Alfred Traube is shown on the facing page.

All subsequent letters from Paul Schidwigowski were the same. From July 1939 the formal letters came from another lawyer, Alfred Traube, at the same address. The additional name 'Israel' was now printed on his headed paper.

That all Jews without a recognizable Jewish name (listed by the Nazis) were required to take on the name 'Sara' if a woman and 'Israel' if a man, was something I already knew. The shock came from handling a piece of paper on which Paul Schidwigowski had inserted 'Israel' by hand. How did Lotte feel when she received it? In checking the facts of this new law, I discovered that it was passed on 17 August 1938, two weeks before she left, but came into effect on 1 January 1939.[3] Once again, I was faced with the knowledge of how late she had escaped.

When I returned to these letters in 2008, my wondering about the fate of these two lawyers turned to increasing concern as the dates of the letters moved closer and closer to the outbreak of war and the closing of all borders

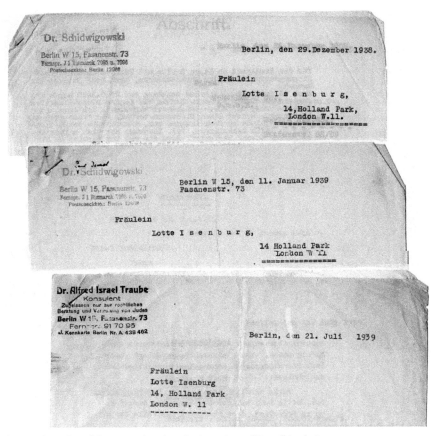

Letters from Lotte's lawyers, showing the insertion of 'Israel' in their names.

and possibilities of escape. What had happened to them? Why were they still in Germany? How was it they could still work? How well did Lotte know them? I went back to the letters to see whether they offered any answers to these questions.

Although Lotte wrote to Paul Schidwigowksi quite formally, they clearly had mutual friends, including Max who appeared in Lotte's letters to Wolja. Their letters always include personal good wishes and enquiries about each other's situation. As a result I feel I can refer to him as Paul.

On 19 October 1938 Paul wrote: 'I can answer your enquiry about my situation with a gentle reference to the law that has in the meantime been passed concerning Jewish lawyers. Nevertheless I am holding my head up'.[4]

On 30 October Lotte replied: 'I don't find your personal news very exciting. But for that very reason I wish you again sincerely all the very very best and hope to hear better news from you soon.'

On 13 December when he told Lotte that he had successfully persuaded the exchange office to drop the extra charge, leading her to believe the problems had been solved, he added: 'My partner Dr. Traube is allowed to continue as a so-called consultant. I have been appointed by the president of the regional court as a member of his staff, so I am able to continue to work professionally.' In her reply three days later, Lotte addressed him as 'lieber Herr Doktor', rather than the more formal form of address 'Sehr geehrter Herr Doktor' that she normally used.

> Please excuse the familiar form, but I was so happy to get your last letter, not least because of your personal news. I thank you so very very much for your great help. Without your support, I would have probably had to wait another two years for these things, because of Schenker's dreadful actions…Please write to me when I can somehow here return the favour for all your troubles.

This last sentence made me wonder whether and how Lotte was paying Paul for his services; there is no record amongst the letters of fees, but perhaps she left money with him before she left. There is also no indication in the letters of a response from Lotte to the insertion of 'Israel' into Paul Schidwigowski's name in January 1939. It may have been dangerous for him if she were to do so or perhaps, as with all previous regulations, they just accepted them. But her letters continued to express concern for his situation alongside further requests for his help. On 26 March 1939 she wrote: 'I am so sorry that you still have no further prospects. Hopefully you will also soon be successful in this respect. I am still well.' But on 6 April he replied: 'In my own affairs, I have not moved one step further forward.'

On 4 May 1939 he regretted he could tell her nothing positive about her furniture, but 'I shall continue to make every effort that I can and hope if I can achieve anything it will be to successfully make Schenker send your goods to you.' And on 2 June 1939:

> I am somewhat restricted in what I can do, as I am no longer able to carry out legal services in my own name. I could of course get my partner Dr.Traube to write again to Schenker and threaten legal proceedings. I have not so far chosen this route as Dr.Traube had to dissolve his business as a consultant, and there is no money available to pay him.

On 30 June he wrote: 'I hope things still go well for you. We can –
unfortunately – not tell you anything new.' Despite the earlier comment about
payment, the formal correspondence was taken over by Alfred Traube at this
point. But Lotte did hear from Paul again on 8 August, after she had asked
Dr. Traube whether Paul still had a copy of the receipt from Schenker.
Enclosing the receipt, Paul was delighted that it looked as though Lotte would
finally get her goods. 'I hope everything is still going as planned for you...I
have got no further with my own plans. The prospects at the moment look
dimmer than ever.' This was the last letter Lotte received from Paul
Schidwigowski.

By reading these letters one by one and making notes, I lived once again
through a series of emotions – anger, anxiety, fear and expectation. It helped
me to imagine how Lotte may have felt. In relation to the furniture I already
knew the final outcome. But I did not know what had happened to Paul. On
1 November 2008 when I had finished reading this correspondence I tried
to find out. I found him in a list of murdered lawyers:[5]

> **Schidwigowski, Dr. Paul**, Berlin / * 27. August 1895 Gadderbaum/
> Westfalen , † 25. Mai 1943 / Tod im Lager Auschwitz in Polen /
> Tafel 7

I wrote in my notebook:

> I feel in shock...how lucky Lotte and Wolja were – but why didn't he
> leave – he went on helping others...did Lotte know? Alfred Traube
> was not on this list, but I found a later mention of his name, which
> suggests that he did survive...[6] The shock of learning what happened
> to Paul is clouding my reading of all the subsequent material.

Making Good Again

The early 1950s saw the passing of successive reparation laws which
distinguished between different kinds of claims – in particular between
Rückerstattung [restitution] for the return of identifiable material property
and *Entschädigung* [compensation or indemnification] for personal losses of
goods or damage to health, freedom and professional career.[7] It was in this
context that Lotte and Cromwell began their fifteen years of making claims,
first directly against Schenker and later for compensation for her possessions.

The letters, written in English and German, begin on 30 May 1950 with
an apology from Lotte to Cromwell for the delay in replying to his letter in
February. '...but it was really very difficult...I know it is a long time...I also

hope that I am forgiven.' I imagine it was difficult emotionally as well as practically. Lotte and Wolja had estimated a total of RM 5,000-6,000 for the goods, but Cromwell suggested they claim 10,000.

As in the pre-war correspondence there were many setbacks, but they did not give up on the claims themselves nor on the level of amount of compensation. Other on-going features of the correspondence include: Schenker's refusal to be helpful for fear of accepting some liability and Cromwell's refusal in turn to let them off the hook; the ever changing laws, which required new claims and new arguments; Lotte's profuse apologies for delays in replying to Cromwell's letters, usually blaming illness; and her insistence that the claims go beyond the legal criteria to acknowledge the persecution she experienced.

The references in the correspondence to Paul Schidwigowski caused me to wonder again whether Lotte knew about his fate or whether she tried to find out. If she did know, did it make her even more determined to get something out of Schenker?

Lotte's case did not fit the criteria for restitution, which referred to the return of identifiable goods to their rightful owner. Nevertheless Cromwell decided to approach Schenker directly, stating his intention to make a restitution claim against them, as restitution claimants only paid the fees of their own lawyers. The alternative, to sue Schenker in the civil court, would be very expensive. In his letter of 31 May 1950 Cromwell made it clear to Schenker that he considered them responsible for the loss, arguing that after December 1938 they had no reason for not shipping the goods.

> This you did not do. Instead you put forward a completely new bill. You had to withdraw it after vigorous legal action, but you delayed the furniture still more, apparently because of the bad faith of your employee who had had to withdraw the new invoice. It was delayed so long, that it was no longer possible to send it…Under these circumstances you are responsible for the failure to send the goods. The value of the furniture is DM 10,000. A list is enclosed. The correspondence that my client has speaks for itself.

Schenker's reply on 8 June repeated almost word for word what they said to Lotte three years earlier. However, perhaps now because a lawyer was involved, they wrote more extensively - concerned to protect their reputation, to have a clean record from the Nazi period, and to appear to be helpful:

> …you can be reassured that as one of the largest world renowned carrier services, …[we] have always fully looked after the interests of

our customers independently of any political situation, so long as we were not going against official orders. It is therefore completely impossible that this transport was delayed wantonly by one of our employees. It is however the case that after the outbreak of war, there was a great reduction in traffic and in this way there were delays.

[They acknowledged that some goods were confiscated by the Gestapo, but insisted]

We are however not responsible for any loss that has occurred, as the handing over of the goods happened because of state directives, which we could do nothing about. We are therefore not liable for damages.

Replying on 15 June 1950 Cromwell acknowledged their 'generally very good name', but challenged their claim of non-responsibility:

I can only explain what happened in terms of the relevant official losing interest - once again putting it mildly - after the failed attempt to impose an extra payment... Irrespective of the reason, after...13 December 1938 – you were in breach of contract, and...[it was] totally foreseeable that emigrating Jews would lose their possessions, if they were not transported with judicious haste.

On 21 June Lotte told Cromwell 'I enjoyed your answer very much...'

Victims of the Nazis

Cromwell's next step was to make the claim for restitution. On 29 August 1950 Schenker repeated their assertion that they had no responsibility, but if this action was being taken against them, they wanted to see the 'proof' and certified copies of the correspondence. It took Lotte nearly seven months, until 15 March 1951, to send the information to Cromwell:

...and I can't even offer a satisfactory excuse, apart from the fact that I overlooked your remark that you were awaiting my instructions and that I was submerged in household, children, ailments and so on. As I do not want to take your time with an analysis of my rather weak character, I only want to say that I am resolved to put first things first and I hope you will forgive me and find an excuse for the delay in the reply to Schenker.

On 19 May 1951 Lotte's case was passed to the *Wiedergutmachungsamt* [the office dealing with restitution claims]. Six months later, on 1 November 1951, Lotte asked Cromwell whether anything could be done, 'a) as a matter of principle, b) we could more than do it with it'. By the end of February 1952 the case had been prepared and on 8 May Schenker formally rejected it. Another six months passed before Cromwell told Lotte, on 6 October, that the case had been referred to a court. Replying three weeks later, Lotte apologized once again for the delay – citing on this occasion 'the winter ailments of septic throats etc'. She was very pleased to hear that things were moving and wondered whether anything needed to be prepared for the hearing. Cromwell doubted whether they had a restitution case, but he hoped if possible to move Schenker towards a settlement.

On 7 January 1953 Lotte made some important amendments to the affidavit Cromwell had prepared for the court:

> I think it would be psychologically good to explain why I left Germany before the arrangements for the transport had been finalized… Considering our ambiguous situation (civil rights claim or restitution) I think it is important in the affidavit to suggest that Schenker's attitude can only be explained in terms of the Nazi racial policies, and that the company would never have treated a non-Jewish customer or lawyer in the same way…I don't know whether it would also be useful to point out that I found the German authorities at the time very helpful (see the approval from the *Oberfinanzspräsident* [regional finance minister], which I mention in the statement.) This approval is itself the 'turning point' of the whole thing and that is why I refer to it. But I want to emphasize again most strongly that Schenker's holding back of my goods can only be explained on racial policy grounds – they seem to have been more catholic than the Pope in this respect – and therefore my claim is not a civil rights case. Is there a way of explaining to the Compensation Office that the loss of the furniture made our exile in England 100% harder? And precisely because of this loss, and the fact that we had to buy furniture later at inflated prices, we are not in a position to take a civil claim out against Schenker, that in the end it must be recognized that we would not have emigrated if it had not been for the Nazis, but I would have continued with my medical studies, and therefore in this sense in the true meaning of the word we were victims of the Nazis.

This letter was written in German, but Lotte used the English phrase 'turning point'. 'Victim of persecution' was a legal category into which Lotte had to fit,[8] but in her insistence that Schenker's behaviour should be recognized for what it was, a direct expression of Nazi policy, I felt I was reading for the first time Lotte's own expression of her feelings of persecution. I am relieved that she did not always deny or diminish her experiences. Perhaps Schenker provided a clear focus for her feelings.

Cromwell continued to try to get Schenker to settle the case in advance of court proceedings. He told Lachotski, his representative in Berlin, '...the burden of proof is on Schenker. If Schenker did nothing for all the time after December 1938, despite numerous demands, it happened because Schenker could afford to do this to a Jewish woman who was abroad.' On 23 January 1953 the court ruled that it was not a restitution case. There was no evidence to show whether the goods were confiscated by the former Deutsche Reich or lost because of the war and they were not able to make a judgement on the reasons for Schenker's actions. There were no costs to pay.

'Explore Every Avenue'

Lotte's loss was not disputed; it was a material loss which could be identified and given a monetary value, but it could not be compensated for, as it did not fit the criteria of a particular law. In addition both Lotte and Cromwell wanted to use arguments that the law would not consider, demanding recognition of the persecution that led to the loss, its consequences and its symbolic value.

Nothing more happened for sixteen months. The only remaining legal option was to sue Schenker and Cromwell believed their case was promising. But even to start the process required a security deposit of more than 1000 Marks. Lotte and Wolja failed to make a decision about it, but they did continue to do their own research from the AJR supplements. They annotated an article about a new law of 18 September 1953, and on 13 May 1954 Lotte wrote to Cromwell to ask when he could

> ...spare some time to talk over the unhappy affair of my furniture and Schenker...In the meantime we had unfortunately a tremendous lot of illnesses of quite a serious nature, the culprits being my daughter and I, so that I really could not make up my mind one way or another. In the meantime so much new legislation, I think, has come out that I think it will be necessary to talk the whole matter over before deciding. I would also like to know whether the compensation law would apply in my case. Anyhow, I would be grateful if we could 'explore every avenue'.

Lotte cited illness so often it is difficult not to see it as an excuse for her procrastination; it was perhaps easier than acknowledging the emotional difficulty of dealing with the issues. But on this occasion I am able to verify that I did have two 'illnesses of quite a serious nature', scarlet fever and pneumonia. As a result of the scarlet fever in April 1953, I was in quarantine in my bedroom for three weeks; only my mother, wearing a white coat, was allowed to come in. She would sometimes sit on the spare bed near the door, reading a particular book, *The Family from One End Street.* Published originally in 1937, it appeared as one of the first Puffin books in 1942. It became a classic children's book and 'was regarded as innovative and ground breaking for its portrayal of a working class family at a time when children's books were dominated by stories about middle-class children'.[9] Peter listened from the other side of the door, sitting on a trunk on the landing. After I had recovered, my room had to be fumigated. I fell ill with pneumonia on Christmas day 1953, not returning to school until early March 1954.

At last it seemed that the loss of Lotte's possessions was covered by the law. On 7 June 1954 Cromwell submitted a compensation claim for Confiscation or Loss of Furniture. But a new law meant that the claim had to be rewritten to fit in with its criteria and it required evidence. The same day Cromwell approached Schenker, suggesting:

> If you were able to support me in my search for evidence, then I could avoid bringing a case against you. In order to help you I am giving you copies of your correspondence, from which you can presumably tell where the goods were stored…It can be assumed that there must have been some dealings with the authorities who confiscated them.

But a week later, 14 June 1954, Schenker dismissed his request in a single sentence, using virtually the same words as in the letter to Lotte in 1947.

Over the next three years Lotte filled in forms, prepared affidavits (several different versions exist) and went to London to the German Embassy to get them sworn. The forms include claims for different kinds of compensation, to which I shall return in the next chapter. Some of the forms include the ages of her children, allowing me to date those left undated.

In 1956 the law changed again, so a new form dated 2 October 1957 was completed. On 11 October Lotte told Cromwell 'hope or no hope against Schenker, I think I shall continue to prod as long as I can'. At this point offers started to be made for Lotte's other claims, but Schenker did not go away. On 28 March 1958 Lotte told Cromwell: 'As for Schenker, we have to get down to it after Easter'. But nothing happened until 2 August, when Lotte asked Cromwell whether paragraphs §51 and §56 in the law might apply to her Schenker claim: 'Possessions abandoned because of emigration to escape drastic Nazi measures, which can be proved by showing one belongs to a group that was persecuted by the Nazis.' On 11 August Cromwell told her:

> Your notes on paragraphs 51 and 56 work like a refresher course on me. The point is whether the furniture has been stolen by the Government or its associates or whether it has perished owing to circumstances connected with persecution or if it has perished independently of persecution. In cases of this kind §51 is not applicable but the *Bundesrueckerstattungsgesetz* [Federal restitution law] would be applicable if the government had at any stage taken possession.

He approached Schenker again on the same day:

> ...if from your experience, you can state reliably that following the general confiscation of Jewish property of emigrants in November 1941, the state instructed you to treat all goods in your warehouses as belonging to the state, then the claim in question can be made effectively as *Eigentumsschaden* [damage to property] against the main culprit. The difference between this and previous attempts is that evidence of a general experience with the goods of emigrants would be enough, and the proof of what happened to these particular goods would not be needed.

Later I learned that under the Eleventh Ordinance to the Reich Citizenship Law of 25 November 1941, all Jews living outside Germany lost their citizenship and their property was legally confiscated.[10]

Schenker replied promptly on 21 August 1958. After a first paragraph that repeated for the fourth time that they did not have any records, they appeared to offer something which, without implicating them in any way, might nevertheless be helpful.

> We can only state in general, that – in the meantime we have ascertained – in January 1941 carriers and warehouses were told by the Reich Traffic Handling Division that on the orders of the Head of Reich Security in Berlin, the public sale of Jewish goods in warehouses would take place. We know for example that this took place in Hamburg and it is possible that this happened to all German freight carriers.

But their help was of no consequence. A month later they refused to sign a statement based on this letter. Nevertheless Cromwell and Lotte continued to complete all the forms. The signed affidavits, sworn at the German embassy, are dated 27 November 1958. Seven months later, on 18 July 1959, Lotte's claim for her household goods was formally acknowledged and another six months passed before Cromwell was informed on 20 January 1960 that within three months they must send a long list of further items of information, all as sworn affidavits. These included proof that Lotte belonged to one of the groups persecuted on religious, racial or political grounds and an exact description of the goods and their purchase price, with evidence from receipts, or affidavits, so that a replacement cost could be established.

For once they acted quite quickly; the answers were all in the Schenker file. They sent the information on 8 March 1960. In the reply on 18 May 1960 from the compensation office Lotte is referred to as 'the deported and expatriated person'. Their headed notepaper includes the word '*Ostsektor*' and they say they can find no information about her – she is not mentioned in the papers from the former *Oberfinanzspräsidenten* Berlin-Brandenburg.

There was an unexplained delay. On 15 September 1960 Cromwell wrote back:

> In the matter of Lotte Saraga, I have never claimed that the claimant was deported. As an emigrating Jew she comes under the 11.-DV Reichsbürgergesetz. Recently there have been different interpretations of this law. It would be rather extraordinary if the state confiscated all the possessions of emigrating Jews, and then in individual cases demanded proof that the state had seized the possessions that had disappeared...The claimant lived in the West (the comment 'Ostsektor' has no basis).

Cromwell's concern about proof in individual cases was not unusual. Many people had their compensation refused on this basis.[11]

'Then I Can Go and Swear'

It was now twenty two years since the possessions were lost and over ten years since they had started to claim for compensation. Suddenly, at the beginning of 1961, there was a completely unexpected development in the form of a letter dated 2 January 1961 from *Der Senator für Finanzen Sondervermögens* [Senator for Special Financial Funds] to the *Wiedergutmachungsämter* [Reparation Offices]. Referring to his letter of

24 November 1960 (which is not amongst our papers) he described Lotte's goods as 'missing because of the war'. 'From the reports on furniture that are still available, it is stated that on 10 March 1942 a sum of RM 742.50 was collected for the sale of removal goods. Since the files have been destroyed, it is not possible to ascertain exactly which items were included in the sale.'

Without further proof, he was willing to offer DM 1,850 – the usual two and a half times the sale price. If they rejected this offer, they would have to provide a statement under oath from the claimant in which she described the goods in more detail, and if possible the purchase dates and costs. This would have to be backed up by a specialist report endorsing them.

It was a shock to read this myself; how did Lotte feel finally knowing what had happened to her possessions? Was she relieved or angry? To read that they were 'missing because of the war' seems insulting. There was no acknowledgement that Schencker and the Nazi state bore any responsibility. I know the Nazis kept records, but I am amazed that Lotte's possessions could be identified in this way.

The sum offered was derisory, but the hoops they would have to jump through if they appealed were enormous. Nevertheless I feel very relieved that they did appeal. I was fifteen years old when they got this news; I don't remember being poor, though also not wealthy. How could there be any sense of closure if they accepted this offer?

A list of items in the transport already existed. On 22 February 1961 Cromwell asked them for further information about Wolja's books and also the scientific worth of the Trautonium, an electronic musical instrument. On 15 April 1961 Lotte sent the information needed for the affidavit, starting with the usual kinds of apologies:

> I was quite ill when your letter came…At last we have discussed the book question… By the way I don't know any more how much we calculated in total, but I hope that we asked for an overall sum of about 10,000 or not less than 8,000, as some of the items were old family possessions, like the table silver, carpet and the 'bottom drawer'. And perhaps in the price we can indirectly take account of the higher rents and difficulties we had as a result of the loss of the furniture.

How possible is it to reconstruct such lists after this length of time? I understand why Lotte discussed the furniture with her sister a few years earlier, sitting on the beach in Wales. It is also not surprising that when they went through the list of books in detail they realized there were far more than previously remembered. Their handwritten notes, found amongst the papers, are further testimony to the amount of time and effort devoted to this activity.

On 2 May 1961 Cromwell sent Lotte a draft affidavit and a statement for Wolja to sign. She replied six weeks later: 'We are definitely agreed with all your points. It is too long ago to remember things in detail. This is as much as we can reconstruct. We are going on holiday now and shall be back on 5 July. Then I can go and swear.' (15 June 1961) This last sentence, in a style that is by now quite familiar from her personal letters, seems to express very succinctly how Lotte must have been feeling.

The claim was Lotte's – she had made all the arrangements and signed the contract with Schencker – but some of the goods had belonged to Wolja, and the compensation office insisted that Wolja was an independent claimant, who had to sign his own affidavit. Wolja's part in this final stage of the claim became very significant and another cause of delays.

A copy of Lotte's sworn affidavit, witnessed at the German Embassy, is dated 9 August 1961. The lists of possessions offer an insight into how my parents and grandparents lived. She explains that:

> ...Until the inflation my parents were comfortably off and had a well-furnished 5-room flat, 27 Hohenzollerndamm, until about 1930. When I emigrated, I was engaged to be married and my mother wanted as far as she was able to help us to furnish our new home. As she was closing down her flat, the possessions in good condition, which were less useful for her or my emigration, were put up for sale.

Amongst the possessions belonging to 'my then fiancé, now husband' were a desk, couch and two 'bookcases up to the ceiling'; two oriental covers likely to be valuable Turkish handicraft, and a list of books

> The books were of great importance and high value. Apart from books of little value, mainly paperbacks or lightly bound books, like Inselbuecher,[12] it was a full library.
>
> All the classics, the Gundolf edition of Shakespeare; very many philosophy books: Kant, Nietzsche, Hegel et al. Sociology: Max Weber, Mannheim et al. History: Roman History by [gap here], Jewish history, Graetz; Psychology: works of Freud, Jung, Köhler; Russian literature: Tolstoy, Dostoyevsky, Chekov, and many others. French literature, for example Romain Rolland, Racine, Corneille, Anatole France and many others. In addition the full complement of German writers Thomas Mann, Heinrich Mann, Hauptmann et al. can be mentioned.

A rough estimate is that there were about 300 books, not counting the small books. The average price on 1 April 1956 cannot be less than RM 5 per item.

Amongst Wolja's possessions was also a Trautonium, acquired after 1933. She explains:

> This was an electrical musical instrument developed by Professor Trautwein. My husband was and is a physicist and had amongst other things worked in this field, and had himself developed something. At that time Telefunken, for collegial reasons in recognition of his work, gave him the Trautonium for a nominal price of RM 50. It was worth not less than RM 400 and as a focus of study at that time it would have been useful in emigration. Today it has a scientific rarity value as an object from a particular stage of development of electrical music.

Lotte's personal possessions included furniture, lamps, 'an Axminster carpet and bed linen and table linen, all acquired in the last few years and as good as new' and a number of items of considerable value:

> …our family silver, partly marriage gifts and partly silver wedding presents to my parents. The value is hard to estimate…the Mokka service and the Limoges and other cups were particularly fine and expensive bone china, more for display than for using. Fruit plates: hand painted. Rosenthal. The white wine and red wine glasses, about a dozen of each, were similarly valuable. The daily tableware was Hutschenreuter.

The final item was a radio – Nora Rienzi. Lotte comments that 'It was a good radio and could have been made use of here in London where there are 3 local radio stations.'

These lists reflected Lotte and Wolja's well-off, middle-class backgrounds. As a child our house was different from those of many of my friends; but I felt different in so many ways, that I did not think about lacking 'old family possessions', matching sets of crockery and cutlery or beautiful linen. In July 2010 when I visited the Freud Museum, in which Freud's study was reconstructed for him in London, I was moved to see that it was full of 'bookcases up to the ceiling', more than the two that Wolja's parents had. The list of books feels like a rich cultural heritage that we didn't live up to; and it certainly does not fit with my memories of my father, who only read crime stories. On the other hand books were highly valued in our family and on

Christmas Day my father would produce a small suitcase of books – novels and non-fiction (either politics or science). None were wrapped; we took it in turns to choose one until they were all gone and sometimes our choices surprised him.

The affidavit was finally sent off on 18 August 1961, but only after Lotte and Wolja had been contacted by Cromwell's secretary: 'there is an author missing on page 2 – for "Roman History"; should it be Mommsen?…could you phone after 11am in the morning to give me the name, or send it to me'. It seems extraordinary that such minute details were needed about this one book, but Lotte and Wolja had left a space for an author, suggesting it might be a book of value. And indeed if it was by Mommsen, it was a three-volume work, published between 1854 and 1856, which led to him becoming the second person to win the Nobel Prize for literature in 1902 with the commendation 'the greatest living master of the art of historical writing'.[13]

In his accompanying letter, Cromwell argued that it was unlikely that the public auction involved all the goods – they would have been looted many times before they came to be sold. Further letters from the Senator's office reminded Cromwell that he had not responded formally to the original offer of January 1961. Replying on 8 February 1962 Cromwell again tried to move beyond the narrow legal arguments: 'One should not forget that we are dealing with a situation in which young people lost all their worldly possessions through persecution, and not fob them off with an amount that does not even cover a fraction of their loss…The estimates from the claimant are not presumptuous and her descriptions useful.'

'We Have to Come to Terms with It'

Cromwell's letter seems to have done the trick. On 16 March 1962 an increased offer was made, double the previous amount – a joint payment of 4,500 DM. They were given two months to appeal the decision. It was still less than half their original claim, but Cromwell recommended acceptance. Nevertheless it took a further fifteen months for the process to be completed. Some of this was due to bureaucratic processes and some due to Cromwell; but most of the delay seems to have arisen from Lotte and Wolja's resistance and avoidance. Several times Cromwell wrote to Lotte asking whether she had already accepted the offer, which he was willing to accept on her behalf if she simply telephoned his office.

The bureaucratic processes included the need for them both to fill in questionnaires for the German authorities. Despite a request from Cromwell's secretary, Lotte and Wolja did not complete all the sections on Wolja's form, and as the months passed their resistance was expressed by their refusal to accept it as a joint claim. Cromwell explained that it was needed because some of Wolja's books were in the transport.

Wolja must have queried the decision to accept the offer, as there is a reply from Cromwell, dated 27 June 1962, in which he repeats his view that they would not get more than DM 4,500 for their furniture. At the same time he offered them a bit of consolation; having now received the files from Berlin, he was reminded that they had claimed RM 580 for the transport and storage costs. They should now make a claim for these and for the cost of their journeys. Finally in a letter to Cromwell dated 17 July they gave up the fight. '…of course we leave the decision to you. If you think it is not possible to get more than DM 4,500, then we have to come to terms with it.'

But the money was still not paid. Cromwell chased it up in early January 1963. In their reply six weeks later, the Berlin authorities told him they needed the completed questionnaire from Wolja Saraga, for which they had asked twice. It took Cromwell two weeks to pass this on to Lotte and another three weeks for her to reply – on 2 April 1963 – with apologies for the delay: 'it has been such chaos, with so many visitors and I did not feel well, so that I procrastinated with everything. As you know the restitution claim and the furniture transport have been only in my name. It was also all paid by me, the petition to the Exchange control was also only from me.'

After such a long time, was Lotte reluctant to accept such a low offer and to lose control of a process in which she had invested so much time, energy and emotion? I wonder whether, if their roles had been reversed and Wolja had been claiming for Lotte's possessions, her signature would have been required. I am reminded of the occasion on which Peter and I registered Lotte's death. As a married woman her certificate had to include Wolja's occupation. The reverse had not been true when we registered Wolja's death five years earlier. My outrage was tempered by the pleasure I had in Peter telling the registrar that he had spelled 'physicist' incorrectly.

On 6 April 1963 Cromwell explained patiently once again why Wolja had to fill in the form. To avoid further questions coming back, he made it clear that the money would be paid into a 'joint account'. But the difficulties continued. On 25 June 1963 Cromwell's secretary sent Wolja an authorization to be signed and sent directly to Cromwell in Germany. The absence of any further information in the file suggests that the money did then get paid, fifteen months after the offer had been received, and almost twenty-five years after Lotte had handed over her goods to Schenker.

But the story was still not over. Another year later, on 15 June 1964, they received an offer of DM 150 for the transport and emigration costs, which Cromwell suggested was fair. But at this stage Lotte became completely unable to respond. Between 3 August 1964 and 27 January 1965 the

Compensation Office sent six identical postcards to Cromwell, asking for a reply to the letter of 15 June: 'please respond or tell us the reason for the delay'.

Cromwell wrote to Lotte in October and November 1964. On the second occasion he enclosed a letter for the Compensation Office, in which he accepted the offer on Lotte's behalf, asking her to send it on. Following the fifth reminder postcard on 9 December 1964, still not having heard from Lotte, Cromwell wrote to the Compensation Office three days later: 'In the matter concerning Lotte Saraga, I regret the delay. I am getting no response from my clients. They are very proper and educated people. From my experience, I think this may be a question of nerves. I have written to Mrs Saraga to say that if I don't hear to the contrary I will accept your proposed offer.'

Five days after receiving the sixth reminder postcard on 27 January 1965 Cromwell did accept the offer. The official papers for the settlement of 150 DM were signed on 11 February 1965 in Nürnberg, by Cromwell and on 17 February 1965 in Berlin by the *Entschädigungsamt*. Finally on 23 April 1965 there was a letter from Lotte, written in a mixture of German and English. 'At first I must very humbly apologise for not writing. I was not very well at the time, and I am feeling rather bad about it. I hope you will forgive me. Thank you very much for the cheque. It isn't a very big sum, but it bought my daughter a frock and gave some spending money to Peter.'

I was relieved to reach the end of this claim, but distressed by the state that Lotte was in. At the time they started this process, they really needed the money, but throughout they were also concerned with justice. As the years went by they seemed to be motivated more and more by issues of principle. If I am right, it would have been very hard after twenty-five years to settle for so little money, without any apology or recognition of wrong doing or of persecution. But these are my speculations. I was away at university at the time and I have no memories of any of this.

Silver Spoons

In 2010, while working in detail on these papers, Liz and I were involved in our own compensation claim, arising from the redevelopment of the house next door to us in London. I was struck by the parallels of an unsatisfactory financial settlement which does not acknowledge any responsibility for the damage done and which offers no apology. I wrote in my notebook:

> There is no dispute that our house has been considerably damaged but the legal processes take no account at all of how it feels to live for

18 months with the noise, dirt and ever widening cracks in the walls of our beautiful house – the law allows only for the costs of repairs. We have had to pester all the way to have the extent of the damage acknowledged and appropriate costs paid, and in the end we have been awarded less than we think is due to us.

Of course this situation is very different from Lotte and Wolja's claims for compensation; yet it gave me an understanding of the sense of injustice aroused, when you are entirely the injured party, but made to feel almost greedy for wanting more money than originally offered.

These papers also offer insights into the significance of possessions. It is a common experience to have emotional attachment to 'things' for nostalgic, historical or symbolic reasons that may often bear little relationship to the intrinsic characteristic or value of the objects themselves. In 1938 Lotte and Wolja's household goods were the focus of their fear, hopes and anxieties; twenty years later they became the focus of their anger at the persecution they experienced from the Nazis as well as of their desire for acknowledgement and justice. My sadness about not owning anything that had been passed down from my grandparents became very clear when I met Uri, my Israeli cousin, in 2008, after a gap of eighteen years. He did not know about Lotte's stolen furniture. I did not know, but could have guessed, that he now owns many of our grandmother's possessions – the ones that did get to Palestine. I felt very envious.

Lotte had told her colleagues at the Further Education college where she taught, that she had never owned a set of matching saucepans, so when she retired they bought her a set of heavy red cast iron pans – not an ideal present for a woman of 65 who had had two breast cancer operations, but she was delighted by them. After her death, Peter and I divided them between us. We both wanted the skillet, but I let him have it and felt deprived for a long time. Why? It was not its monetary value, nor its practical use – I had other frying pans and could afford to buy my own skillet. Somehow it acquired a symbolic value, or more likely it became a focus for feelings of sibling rivalry, as we had divided all the other possessions with no difficulty.

In her list of the missing goods, Lotte referred to 'family silver'. In the middle-class suburb in which we lived, several families had silver cutlery. When I was about five years old Peter and I stayed with some very close English friends, John and Liss Dowman and their two children, while our parents were away. My father knew John through work. When I came home I complained to my mother that we didn't have 'silver spoons' like the Dowmans did. Whenever we visited them later Liss would tease me, waving the silver spoons at me and saying 'look, silver spoons!' But all came right for me in the end. I am now in a relationship with Liz who has a silver canteen, one that she bought with money that her mother had put into a Co-Op savings account for her. This is an important part of Liz's family history. Her great grandmother saved for her grandmother and this saved the family from destitution in the 1930s; in turn her grandmother saved for her mother, who used the money to buy household goods. For Liz, the money was less essential, but it felt important to her to buy something special with it.

'Not Just a Refugee'

It would be easy to explain Lotte's difficulties in responding to Cromwell, which became acute during the last few years, in terms of her experiences as a Jewish refugee, reliving the persecution and having to come to terms with an inadequate solution. But I have to complicate this account; as their daughter, I know about other significant events in her life which are also likely to have affected her.

In 1963, between school and university, I decided to go to Israel for four months. I persuaded my mother to come with me for the first few weeks, to visit her sister, whom she had not seen since Mara's visit with Uri in 1955. She came for six weeks and by the time she returned home, Wolja had started an affair, one that was to last for seventeen years until his death. Lotte told me later that he had had other affairs before this, and it made sense of many experiences of my childhood. Amongst the papers is a collection of letters from a previous lover. They are in an envelope on which Lotte has written 'Wolja – private – to be thrown away'.

Shortly after my return to England I started at university. I only knew for certain about the affair two years later, when I asked Lotte directly about my suspicions. Lotte and Wolja never separated, but he lived a very complicated life, which both of them found very hard. On one of the rare occasions when I spoke to Wolja about it, he told me he still loved Lotte and wanted to be with her, but he wanted to be with Winifred as well. Being with Lotte was difficult as she was rarely nice to him; I think he wanted my advice on what to do. When I told Lotte what he had said, she told me that if they had good times together now, it reminded her of how things once were, and that was even more painful.

These memories test my boundaries about what I should put into the public domain. They are particularly difficult because of my feelings of guilt that I had persuaded Lotte to go to Israel, and because I so often acted as a mediator – a role I am perhaps continuing here. But they are important because they show how easy it would be to interpret everything one dimensionally – to see Lotte and Wolja's lives as determined by their experiences as German Jewish refugees. The circumstances of Wolja's affair affected Lotte's mental health, and this is consistent with Cromwell's surmise about the reasons for Lotte's failure to be in touch with him.

I imagine that their experiences as refugees and their personal circumstances are inextricably linked in a way that profoundly affected the meaning of this claim for Lotte. It may have been therapeutic to revive memories of persecution, to work through their feelings; but it also took her back to a time when their lives were so entwined, a time at which it was their love and the strength of their relationship that seemed to keep them going through all the difficulties. No wonder she could not take the final step.

Schenker

In 2010, to give myself some closure on this part of the story, I tried to find out what had happened to the firm Schenker. From the internet I learned: 'DB Schenker is a division of the German rail operator Deutsche Bahn AG that focuses on logistics. The company, created by reorganisation and rebranding of Deutsche Bahn subsidiaries, comprises a logistics division encompassing air, land, and sea freight, and a rail division made up from European rail freight companies.'[14] The history section on their website starts with the company's founding in 1872, but it jumps from 1931 to 1945, omitting the period of the Nazi regime entirely.[15]

Notes

1. I. Némirovsky, translated from French by S. Smith, *All our Worldly Goods* (London: Vintage, 2009), p.60.
2. It is difficult to obtain accurate figures. The ones I have used can be found in http://www.history.ucsb.edu/faculty/marcuse/projects/currency.htm (Accessed 16 March 2019).
3. 'Law on Alteration of Family and Personal Names', https://www.ushmm.org/learn/timeline-of-events/1933-1938 (Accessed 8 December 2018). See also S. Friedländer, *Nazi Germany and the Jews. The Years of Persecution 1933–39* (London: Weidenfeld & Nicolson, 1997), pp. 254-255.
4. See Friedländer, *Nazi Germany and the Jews*, pp.28-29, 259 and footnote 87 on p.385 for information on the laws relating to Jewish lawyers.
5. https://anwaltverein.de/de/service/erinnerung/mahnmal Alphabetische-namensliste-mit-biographischen-angaben.pdf. (Accessed 12 June 2018).
6. On 11 May 1945 his name appeared in Aufbau in a list of bereaved people, who have just learned of the deaths of family members in Theresienstadt in 1943: http://freepages.genealogy.rootsweb.ancestry.com/~alcalz/aufbau/1945/1945pdf/j11a19s 18.pdf. (Accessed 20 August 2011).
7. See, for example, C. Pross, trans. B. Cooper, *Paying for the Past: The Struggle over Reparations for Surviving Victims of the Nazi Terror* (Baltimore, MD: John Hopkins

University Press, 1998) and 'Bundesentschådigungsgesetz', https://de.wikipedia.org/wiki/Bundesentschädigungsgesetz (Accessed 24 November 2018). The German reparation laws are discussed further in the next chapter.

8. M. Roseman, *The Past in Hiding* (London: Penguin Books, 2001), p. 416.

9. E. Garnett, *The Family from One End Street* (London: Puffin Books, 1942) See also https://en.wikipedia.org/wiki/The_Family_from_One_End_Street (Accessed 4 November 2018).

10. https://www.theholocaustexplained.org/events-in-the-history-of-the-holocaust-1933-to-1939 (Accessed 24 November 2018).

11. See, for example, H.G.Hockerts, 'Wiedergutmachung in Germany: Balancing historical accounts 1945-2000', in D. Diner and G. Wunberg (eds), *Restitution and Memory: Material Restoration in Europe* (New York and Oxford: Berghahn, 2007), pp. 323–372, p. 335. See also Roseman, *The Past in Hiding*, p. 469.

12. A series of relatively inexpensive books or smaller-format books.

13. http://en.wikipedia.org/wiki/History_of_Rome_(Mommsen) (Accessed 21 June 2018).

14. https://en.wikipedia.org/wiki/DB_Schenker (Accessed 21 June 2018).

15. https://www.dbschenker.com/global/about/history (Accessed 21 June 2018).

9

'A Long-Lost and Nearly Forgotten Acquaintance with the Continent'

19th March 1980

Dear Dr Davies

Thank you very much for your letter. I am enclosing a cheque for £30...as you know, death brings not only bereavement, but involves a considerable amount of work. As most of our possessions were in joint name, I am getting on with it on my own. It keeps me out of mischief, but it needs a clear head and a lot of time.

I shall visit my sister, who lives in Israel and is now 73. We are very good friends and it will take care of part of the critical period ahead. I shall be away from the 24th April until the end of May.

In view of my absence, and because BUPA is very tight fisted as far as my - what they call – my 'psychiatric trouble' is concerned I had a talk with Dr Moss, who is willing to prescribe for me, and I assured him that you would raise no objections and that I could always come back to you if it should be necessary. Was I right?

I want to be off Marplan before I set off on my pilgrimage (it won't be anything like that, but I love Jerusalem) because it would be more than inconvenient if I had to avoid eating cheese. The price of meat in Israel is astronomical and their cheeses are excellent.

Dr Moss will help me to do that and perhaps will put me on a mild antidepressant, if he thinks it is necessary. He will most likely keep me on the Inderal, because I want to avoid the state of anxiety and tension, which prevents me from coping efficiently or makes it much more difficult. Personally I trace these periods of tension, (which I used to have from time to time, usually when I was run down) back to the Hitler period when, like so many others I had some very frightening and sad experiences and the news which came out after the war from the concentration camps, which have left a scar on many of us.

Lotte suffered from anxiety and depression for many years, taking a variety of drugs prescribed by her GP, Dr Moss. As a life-long socialist, she did not really approve of using BUPA, but she was a member through Wolja's employment and it allowed her to see a psychiatrist very quickly.

I accompanied Lotte on her first visit to see Dr Davies in October 1979 and at her request sat in on the session. He talked with Lotte about the main events of her life, identifying many of the losses she had experienced including the death of her father when she was 21, saying goodbye to her mother at 24 and never seeing her again, her own forced migration and her two breast cancer operations. Each time he acknowledged the loss, saying something like 'that must have been hard for you' or 'that must have been very painful'. And each time Lotte would seem to deny or diminish it, suggesting 'it wasn't so bad' or 'I've got over it'. Finally he said: 'it's very difficult for you to acknowledge that you have suffered isn't it?' Her letter to him, written one month after Wolja died, shows that she did feel that her experiences in Nazi Germany had had long-term consequences for her.

His sympathetic understanding did not extend to her adult life in Britain, living in the suburbs. He presumed she had been 'a very conscientious housewife' and once again did not believe her denials. This time Lotte insisted: 'I hated housework and was no good at it.' She turned to me: 'you tell him' and I did.

Like many refugee families we rarely if ever spoke about what later came to be called 'the Holocaust' and I have no memories of either of my parents speaking about the impact of the news of the concentration camps. I wonder whether she is making a general reference in the letter, or was she thinking of people she knew, like Paul Schidwigowski?

Lotte suffered very greatly from Wolja's death. Writing to her friend Ruth in Israel a year later, she sympathized with Ruth's depression and described her own feelings.

> At that time I took tablets, but then Wolja became ill and in face of catastrophe, I freeze up completely. Now I am paying for it; at the moment I swallow far too much and not the right tablets…I am now completely aware what I have lost with Wolja. I miss him with every step I take and life without him has little meaning. In addition I am incapable of making any decisions…I do hope to get myself out of this state.

Her past experiences surfaced again during 1984, the last year of her life. I was involved in a court case arising out of student protests about the presence of a National Front student at the Polytechnic where I worked, the events that Esther Simpson referred to when she wrote to me after Lotte's death. While this case was on-going Lotte was admitted to a local hospital, having fallen out of bed in the night. The L-Dopa prescribed to treat her recently diagnosed Parkinson's disease triggered a temporary paranoid psychotic episode, during which she was convinced that she would be put on trial by the National Front and denied NHS treatment, while I would lose my job.

In 2016 I felt able for the first time to read some notes Lotte had written during this difficult time. Although the source of her fears was recognized by the medical staff and her condition could be treated relatively easily with drugs, these notes reveal the extent to which her fears persisted. She continued to believe that she was behaving badly, that the social worker did not want to have anything to do with her and that she always said the wrong things to people. There are three drafts of a letter to the social worker, in which she tells him that the psychiatrist came to see her again sooner than she had expected so that she was not prepared. Nevertheless, she thinks she emerged 'whiter than white', but underplayed her depression and phobias. She believes that a 'dossier' is being kept on her, and that the staff want to be rid of her, they 'now have a "Now out" campaign.' She also has to see another consultant, who '…has I think been asked for the "final solution".' Her use of this phrase was of course chilling, but it reinforced my understanding of the way her personal history was so intertwined with her current problems.

At the time we did our best to support and care for her. Now it made me reflect on my childhood experiences – what messages did we receive about their German pasts? The predominant message was that we lived in England and should learn to be English, complicated by our parents' wish for us to avoid what they saw as a narrow Englishness. Apart from learning to dislike Volkswagen cars and Wagner, I had no sense that they or we should avoid contact with Germany or the Germans. As most 'foreigners' living in the UK will probably testify, people continue to be seen in terms of where they are from. When people heard Lotte's German accent for the first time they would frequently ask how long she had lived in Great Britain. Her answer was usually 'longer than I was there'. I am reminded of a comment made by Joseph Roth in his book *The Wandering Jews*: 'Oh – the whole world thinks in such tired, worn, traditional clichés. It never asks the wanderer where he's going, only ever where he's come from. And what matters to the wanderer is his destination, not his point of departure.'[1]

Both my parents spoke very good English and made a point a doing so. Lotte was scathing about old friends who spoke German with her and she invited English people to call her Lottie. I have now learned that their attitudes were very much in line with that of the Association of Jewish

Refugees which, unlike other Jewish organizations in Britain, '... distinguished scrupulously between National Socialism and German culture as a whole, refusing to see the latter as inevitably tainted by association with the Hitler regime...[2]

Wolja re-established contact with some German non-Jewish friends soon after the war and developed an on-going professional relationship with post-war Germany, often comparing German industry's attitude to scientific research favourably to that in Britain. In April 1956 he gave a paper at a conference in Stuttgart and met up with Peter who was staying with Wolja's old friend Werner in Hamburg. In 1960 I stayed in Munich with the family of a German man, Herr Saal, who Wolja knew through his work, a man young enough to have fought in the German army. Inviting me to stay was I think a gesture of reparation to Wolja and my parents seemed happy to accept. I wonder now whether my mother had some ambivalence about this. Later, when she met Frau Saal, she commented that it was inappropriate for her to talk about her own hardship during the war. Two years later I stayed with the family of another old friend of Wolja's near Frankfurt. At the time I did not question any of this. Peter has suggested that Lotte and Wolja had happy memories of their life in pre-Nazi Germany and believed that these visits would give us a broader continental outlook on life.

One of the sorted envelopes contained postcards to Peter and me from Lotte and Wolja in 1950. They were on holiday in Switzerland, while we were looked after by Dora, a close family friend. Too young at that time to think about the meaning of this trip, I can imagine it now. It was the first time they were back on the 'Continent', as we called it, and the first time for twelve years that they were again in a German speaking country, though not of course in Germany. On 21 June 1950 Lotte wrote to Cromwell, enclosing an authorization for him to act for her in relation to Schenker. 'We had a few nice days in Zurich with Wolja's relatives and are renewing a long lost and nearly forgotten acquaintance with the Continent.' In this simple phrase, she seems to express competing and perhaps contradictory feelings – the desire both to reclaim what has been lost as well as to put it into the past.

Reading the Schenker papers had forced me to recognize that Lotte and Wolja had not put the past as firmly behind them as I had imagined. Would the rest of what I called the 'Restitution Papers' tell me more? They include a series of claims for compensation for Lotte, Wolja and Wolja's parents, as well as claims for pensions for Lotte and Wolja.

When I first looked at these papers, they seemed boring, dry and unemotional in comparison to the personal letters. I skim-read them, making notes. They were useful for factual information such as addresses, dates and places of work, but nothing more. By now I had learned the importance of reading again in great detail. I did this solidly for three weeks in July 2010 and lived forty five years of anger and frustration with them. I learned that Lotte's claims had to be fought for, challenged and appealed over many years. Ultimately, they were all successful, if sometimes financially derisory. By contrast all Wolja's claims were unsuccessful, although he did receive some money on behalf of his parents. Later I discovered that Lotte and Wolja were not alone in spending 'years and years and years and years and years' on restitution claims.[3]

I now recognized that I had a rich resource, offering Lotte and Wolja's own stories, something I lacked and longed for. At the same time I had to recognize, as Mark Roseman says, that 'statements…made in the context of restitution…may not quite be what they seem.'[4] I had only ever thought of their claims in terms of money and this is how I remember them talking about it. Lotte in particular worried rather obsessively, and unnecessarily, about money as she got older. They had lost a lot – not only their possessions but also opportunities for study, work and careers. It seemed very reasonable that they should be compensated financially. Now I wanted to ask questions about what the claims meant to them emotionally. Were they also seeking some form of justice, or at least acknowledgement of the persecution they had experienced? Mark Roseman describes the 'biggest challenge' of restitution claims as 'the mix of moral, emotional and psychological problems interlaced with the purely legal complexities.'[5] Could I use my papers to explore questions about the emotional consequences of turning personal experiences of loss into a legal claim for compensation? Is it psychologically damaging or healing, hanging on to the past or coming to terms with it? If a claim is accepted, does this constitute an acknowledgement of the persecution? If it is rejected, is the persecution denied? Does this make it harder to let go? And does a focus on claims for compensation avoid the pain of coming to terms with the losses those legal processes cannot deal with?

Wiedergutmachung

First I needed to know more about the processes of restitution and reparation established by the post-war German government. Most historical analyses are not concerned with the claims of individuals, but with the politics of restitution and compensation, in particular with the demands of the Allies after the war that Germany make reparation, and the desire of the post-war West German government for rehabilitation – to establish itself as non-Nazi and anti-fascist in the context of the Cold War and growing European integration. Such historical accounts emphasize the ambivalence of Germany and the Germans, the widespread public reluctance to debate the past and the resistance from German officials who had acquired confiscated property. Often the Jews were seen as 'money grabbing' for wanting financial compensation and reparations were also often described as money making charters for greedy lawyers.[6]

The German word used to describe the process of restitution itself, as opposed to particular legal categories for claiming, is *Wiedergutmachung*, a complex German noun translated in the dictionary as 'compensation, atonement, reparation or restitution'. If it is broken down into its component parts, *Wiedergutmachung* means 'making good again'. It is not surprising that the use of this term has been controversial.[7] On the one hand it is argued that unlike 'reparation', it recognizes that the victims of Nazism wanted more than money – they wanted symbolic gestures too, in particular recognition of what had happened to them and an acceptance of guilt and responsibility by the perpetrators. Others have suggested that the 'making good again' was aimed primarily at the rehabilitation of the German perpetrators and as a way of promoting democracy in the new West German state.[8]

There have been a few explorations of the personal dimensions of such compensation claims, which describe the range of very different views expressed about claiming compensation from Germany. Some people did not want to be beholden to 'the Germans' or imply some kind of forgiveness for what had happened; they did not want 'blood money', or they accepted it with 'gritted teeth'. Others saw it as an entitlement, as justice, since the Germans had stolen it in the first place. Some supported *Wiedergutmachung* as an opportunity for the Germans to show repentance. Many needed the money; they had limited opportunities for re-establishing careers or starting new ones, or they were old and needed pensions. For others reparation and compensation procedures were important for establishing their pre-Nazi identity for restoring some sense of achievement, or as an acknowledgement of what they had suffered.[9]

Often the legal arguments used against claims and the demands for detailed proof felt like administrative harassment and many people found it psychologically damaging and exhausting.[10] In this respect claiming for compensation from Germany was no different from any other insurance or compensation claim – the onus is on the individual to prove that their claim is not false and that they themselves are not responsible for their own losses. German has a word for this – *Selbstschuld*. To be eligible for compensation you have to be an 'innocent victim'.

Legal processes require definitions of persecution and of victims. Criteria for eligibility included racial, religious and political persecution but, despite the acceptance of Nazi persecution and crimes against Jews and settlements of collective compensation to Jewish organizations and to Israel, individual claimants were often expected to prove that they personally had been persecuted. They also require proof – that is documentary evidence of loss or damage. They therefore cope better with material losses such as property, income or employment than with less tangible losses of health, freedom and potential professional success, let alone losses such as language, landscape or national identity. Claims were rejected if they could not be substantiated in ways that conformed to the criteria within the law. Although claims could also be made for loss of life, it had to be directly caused by the Nazi regime, rather than hastened by it, as may well have been the case for Lotte and Wolja's parents. And of course Lotte could not make a claim for the losses she experienced through her termination and miscarriage, even though such losses remain as painful trauma.

Legal processes also set up 'ideal' scenarios of what has happened to people. Your life gets broken down into a series of discrete events. When the circumstances don't quite fit, the boxes can't be ticked. Schrafstetter suggests that 'the history of Wiedergutmachung is also a history treating millions of dead and injured as abstract categories defined by the perpetrators.'[11] Rather than giving their own account of events, Lotte and Wolja, with help from lawyers, had to try to fit their experiences into the categories the laws allowed. The existence of different drafts of many of the letters and personal statements, often with handwritten annotations on them, shows how hard they worked on the presentation of their stories.

'I Would Like to have the Original Back'

We have already seen the way that Wolja had actively acquired many documents in the period after 1933, often shortly before he left Germany. He needed these to establish his qualifications and experience as well as his statelessness. Now they both needed documents as evidence of loss. For Wolja's claims what they had were not sufficient and they went to great lengths to try to find further evidence for their losses.

Once again the story is characterized by Lotte and Wolja's procrastination and Lotte's excuses about illness. Lotte did most of the work and she continued to study the new laws, to make carbon copies of everything she sent and to ask the lawyers for copies of everything they wrote or received. Some documents had to be officially translated and then, together with the affidavits, be officially authenticated by the German Embassy. The documents became very valuable to Lotte. On 11 October 1957, when she sent Cromwell the original of her testimonial from the Banca d'Italia in Italian, together with a translation in German, she wrote: 'I would like, however, to have the original back, just for the fun of it. Would it be possible to send a photostat to the Entschädigungsamt?' On 20 July 1965, shortly after receiving the final cheque for her claim for her goods and the cost of the transport, Lotte told Cromwell: 'I do not know whether it would be wise to destroy the papers, if you have not enough room I would be very willing to keep them at home.' Once again I am grateful to her.

Some claims were more straightforward than others; most were either rejected or offered at a low level of compensation the first time they were submitted, requiring difficult decisions about whether to appeal, knowing this would involve yet more work. But neither the lawyers nor Lotte and Wolja ever wanted to give up; even when there seemed to be little chance of success, they usually had one more go.

'Eine glatte Erfindung'

I started with Lotte's claims, trying to focus my reading and interpretations on the psychological meaning and consequences of the process. On 7 June 1954, at the same time as making the claim against Schenker, Cromwell registered two separate but related claims for Lotte, one for loss of education and one for loss of professional earnings.

1. My client had studied medicine and was excluded as a Jew from the university, 'because of political activities', although as the daughter of a front soldier she was entitled to continue studying. She had excellent qualifications but no opportunity to continue her medical studies.
2. The claimant was eventually successful in finding a job with an Italian government agency of the Banca d'Italia in Berlin, where she earned about 2000 Marks. In August 1938 she was forced to emigrate. From that time until July 1939 she had a position in London in a household, where she earned 15/- a week with free board and lodging. In July 1939 she married, and since then has not earned anything.

Lotte spoke proudly about being thrown out of university. She told us she had to appear before a student tribunal who accused her of having communist friends. Defiantly she asked who they would like her to be friends with – Nazis? Perhaps it felt better to be expelled for beliefs you were proud of than for characteristics over which you have no control. Fourteen years later, in 1968, when Cromwell was investigating Lotte's eligibility for a pension, the reason for her expulsion became significant. 'I note that the failure to finish her education was certainly due to persecution, as can be easily verified. It was not only the general persecution on racial grounds, but also an individual expulsion because of communist activity – *eine glatte*

Erfindung' [an outright fabrication].' In the early post-war years, in the context of the developing Cold War, there were many debates about whether people persecuted by the Nazis for communist activity should be ineligible for compensation because they were enemies of the liberal democratic order and promoting an alternative totalitarian regime. Roma and Sinti were seen as 'asocial' and therefore 'undeserving', and homosexuals excluded since homosexuality was at that time a criminal offence in the German Federal Republic.[12] Later, in line with political developments in Germany in the 1980s and 1990s, these restrictions against the 'forgotten victims' were lifted.[13]

The file contains several different versions of an affidavit which accompanied the claims, showing once again how much work went into getting it right. These affidavits were the first full account of Lotte's story that I had read. The version I have translated gives both a factual account of her education and employment in Germany and subsequently in London, and also an argument about the professional status and earnings she could have expected to have enjoyed if she had not been persecuted. It was sworn at the Germany Embassy in London on 8 August 1957.

I was born on 4 September 1913 as the daughter of business man Hermann Isenburg and his wife Erna née Putzig. My parents and grandparents were also of German origin. My father was a front soldier in the 1914-18 war. I passed my Abitur in 1932 at the Cecilien School, Nikolsburgerplatz, Berlin and in April 1932 I began to study medicine at Berlin University. In the summer semester 1933 I had to give up my studies because of the National Socialist laws. Otherwise I would have completed my studies in 1937 and been licensed to practice as a doctor in 1938.

After my exclusion from the university, I worked as a dental assistant for Dr P. Oppler in Berlin, until 1 July 1934. In August 1934 I went to Italy hoping that I might at some point to be able to progress my medical studies there. At first I supported myself through giving lessons in German, and then I took a position as governess in a family. However in May 1935, after the death of my father, I returned to my mother in Berlin.

From July 1935 to 31 July 1938 I worked as a shorthand typist and correspondence clerk as described in the enclosed employment book. On 31 August 1938 I emigrated to England where I worked from October 1 1938 as a domestic help for a weekly wage of 15/-and free board and lodging.

I got married on 15 July 1939 and stopped working as at that time there were no work permits for anything except domestic work. My husband's income was very small. After the work permits were extended for foreigners, I worked as a clerk for a brush firm in Hendon in 1941, at first full time and then, after our move to Orpington, on a casual basis. I estimate that my total earnings during this time, which finished in April 1942, were approximately £60-70. I had to give up work when my son was born (22.9.42). In 1947, together with my husband, I acquired British Nationality.

For financial reasons, I was not able to pick up my medical studies again. But if I had been able to finish my studies in Germany, with German qualifications I would have been able to work during and after the war and, as a result of this work, like all German doctors with unblemished records, I would have been able to register as a doctor. That means that from 1946 I would have been a fully qualified doctor and from 1 July 1948 licensed to work in the National Health Service. I would of course not have given up this work following the birth of my children as the earning capacity of a doctor is high enough to afford domestic help...

In his accompanying letter on 14 October 1957 Cromwell argued that Lotte's claim for professional damages was not subsumed by the claim for educational damages as she was also prevented from pursuing alternative careers. She had trained at commercial school and was

...an expert in the English, French and Italian languages. The loss of any significant earned income after March 1938, the expected date of completion of her medical training, qualifies her for damages for loss of profession, in other words on the basis of an independent position as a doctor, or at the very least based on a skilled language or commercial position.

Eight further documents were enclosed, including Lotte's birth certificate, proof of her matriculation and job testimonials. As proof of her address before emigration Cromwell gave them the police notice of her departure, dated 27 August 1938, commenting: 'which at the same time shows factually, if not grammatically, that the claimant is Jewish.' Lotte told him: 'I liked the bit about "factually, if not grammatically"', showing once again how emotions – perhaps frustration and powerlessness – were expressed through language and style, in simple phrases or sentences.

Lotte's expulsion from university was a matter of record, so the claim for educational damages was settled quite quickly, April 1958, with a standard payment of DM 5,000. To claim the DM 10,000 they had originally asked for her she would have to specify it in greater detail and provide proof of her expenses and loss. They decided to accept the lower payment and pursue a separate claim of DM 12,000 for professional damages, even though the two categories were difficult to distinguish. The DM 5,000 was the first compensation payment Lotte had received. Did the money in any way acknowledge the extent of her loss? Writing and rewriting her case and reading her lawyer's statements were a constant reminder of what might have been, while the letter awarding the money did not explicitly endorse any of these statements.

In pursuing the claim for professional damages on 26 June 1958, Cromwell argued: 'The marriage did not constitute an alternative form of financial provision and was never intended to do so. Without the persecution this claimant would have been a very accomplished person, well positioned as a doctor, given that, since the changes in the arrangements in England since 1948, there is still a shortage of doctors'. Four years later an offer of 2,772 DM was made for Lotte's professional damage, covering the time period 1 August 1938 to 30 April 1942. Replying on 2 June 1962 Cromwell expressed his frustration: 'I thank you for your offer of 16 May. Your letter arrived on 1 June in an envelope stamped 21 May.' Although he was happy about the level of the settlement, he considered the time period used to be 'an undeserved harshness'. When the Compensation Office explained on 17 July 1962 that it was based on Lotte's statement in her affidavit that she was employed until April 1942, Cromwell's reply was almost despairing:

> I do not believe you have fully understood the meaning of my statement…I have tried to explain to you that the claimant could not find any suitable work in England, because there were restrictions for foreigners here, and because she did not have full English qualifications. The affidavit of 8 August 1957 does not say anything different. On the contrary. If she could never find appropriate employment, then it is irrelevant when the inappropriate employment ended, and it is also irrelevant that the pregnancy was the reason for this. Any possible doubt on this last point is taken into account in my counter suggestion. The question seems to me to be: what would this woman have done in Germany if she were not Jewish? And the answer: after 1942, she would, perhaps with the occasional break, have been profitably employed.

The Compensation Office asked for an affidavit from Lotte explaining why she gave up work in April 1942 and for the children's birth certificates. When he advised Lotte on how to answer these questions, Cromwell demonstrated the way such claims have to conform to legal categories rather than describe lived experience.

> As the reason for giving up your work, I would say childbirth. The birth certificates, they can have. Can you explain that after the first child, you would have definitely gone back to work if the immigration restrictions had not been there – and what these were? In order to reach a settlement, I would then give in on the birth of the second child.

Following reminders from the Compensation Office, Lotte drafted and redrafted her affidavit. It was not finalized until 2 May 1963:

> I gave up my position as a clerk in April 1942 as I was expecting a child in September, and the doctor looking after me advised that continuing work and the daily journey to London were inadvisable on medical grounds. After the birth of my son the circumstances of my emigration made it impossible to work, even though I would very much have liked to on economic and personal grounds. One of these circumstances was the isolation and separation from all members of the family who had migrated to all parts of the world, and therefore the loss of the family support and help that were necessary to enable a mother of a young child to work. Paid help was either impossible to find or too expensive, so that it would only have been possible to take a highly paid job, something I couldn't do because of the 1933 laws and my emigration in 1938. Apart from this the stress and difficulties before and after the emigration had damaged my capacity for work and my physical and nervous robustness so that, after the birth of my son, I could not build a career.
>
> In case the Entschädigungsamt is interested in 'the difficulties before my Emigration', here are a few details. I don't know any more whether they are in my CV or elsewhere.
>
> My father died in May 1935 from a heart attack. He was a front soldier in the First World War, Iron Cross second class, a member of the Reich Association of Jewish Front Soldiers and a proud German. The loss of his honour and the hopelessness of his existence absolutely broke his heart. My brother in law who was a general manager at the Iwria Bank was arrested by the Customs Investigation Office because of his position at the bank. My sister had at that time a baby of two

years old. They were forced to flee and to make an application for my mother to come to Palestine. These events did not contribute to a stable state of health.

This statement feels like one of the most important that I found. Most of these facts were in Lotte's original affidavit, but here they are imbued with great feeling. I have tried to convey in my translation the sense of anger, frustration, persecution and injustice that come across in the German, especially when she describes her father's broken heart.

The impact on Lotte of her father's death and her sister's flight were not relevant legally; no compensation could be claimed for them, but she wanted the compensation office to know how she felt. Lotte saw the consequences of her experiences primarily in terms of her health, something else that could not be claimed for. And I am discovering just how far back her mental health difficulties go.

In his accompanying letter to the *Entschädigungsamt*, on 10 May, Cromwell maintained that a sworn affidavit should not be needed.

...it is indeed true that the pregnancy and birth of her child were the reasons for stopping work. On its own, under other than circumstances of emigration, there would be no reason not to start work again after the birth of a child. Because of her husband's job the woman moved to live in a suburb of London, where there were very few German immigrants. As she rightly says, under the same circumstances in Germany she would have continued with her profession. The legal position is that in April 1942 this woman had not yet found a comparable livelihood. To deny her loss of her professional earnings for this reason is only possible if she is culpable by avoiding opportunities to work. This cannot be maintained... If this woman had not been persecuted, she would have been a doctor. That she didn't become a doctor has been settled with the damages for education. But the fact that with her knowledge of languages that she already had in Berlin, she did not become the head of a travel bureau has not been settled and is a direct result of her forced emigration. That a woman gives up work on the birth of her child is an exception, and was certainly exceptional during the war, as Frau Saraga correctly writes. This woman is also in fact very affected by her health and this is a reason for the slow response to your request.

Cromwell's arguments might seem convoluted, but he had to make a case on what might have been, rather than what was, to convince by argument rather than evidence. It is a testament to his skill and his patience with Lotte that he persisted, despite Lotte's frequent procrastinations.

Five weeks later, on 19 June 1963, they received a new offer of 6,330 DM, for damages until 30 June 1948. These claims for educational and professional losses had taken eleven years and the offers were once again lower than they wanted. At about the same time they had to decide whether to accept the low offer for their possessions – a double sense of injustice. The official form for professional damages was signed by Cromwell on 24 July in London and the *Entschädigungsamt* in Berlin on 30 July 1963.

But this claim was not still complete. On 23 April 1965 Lotte wrote to Cromwell:

> I have been told by friends that the Germans have decided to make a second payment on the lump sum of 5,000 DM for interrupted study. Everyone who receives this settlement should get another payment. I think it's another 5,000 DM. This isn't for professional loss, but simply for education, and should be paid in 1965. I don't know if it comes automatically or you have to apply. Could you let me know what you know about it, and could you do it for me?

And on 20 July 1965 she wrote in English: 'I hear that the *Endgesetz*[14] [final law] will not only give another DM 5,000 for *Ausbildungsschaden* [educational loss], but also an increase in its payment on *Berufsschaden* [professional damages]... I do not want to sound too greedy, but if there is a general supplement to these payments, it sounds very nice'. I have no information as to whether she received this extra money, but her last letter leaves me feeling slightly uncomfortable.

'The Biggest Loss was Purely Scientific'

Although there is no paperwork explicitly referring to the rejection of Wolja's restitution claims, it is clear from later letters that this is what happened. He first registered a claim, for loss of patent and loss of profession, in 1952, but without any documentation. Dated 14 October 1957 is a photostat copy of the first page of a letter to Mercker, his German lawyer, listing all the documents he was enclosing – everything that might help him to resume his promising scientific career. This photostat has only survived because Wolja sent it nearly twenty years later to Dr King who was representing him in a pension claim.

1. Birth certificate
2. German *Fremdenpass* [Alien's passport] together with a copy of the notification of the *Ausbürgerung* [expatriation]. (the original must have been given up when receiving the *Fremdenpass*)
3. *Belegebuch* [record book] of the University of Berlin and 2 student cards (Green stripes: foreigner before the naturalization, yellow stamp and card: German Jew, blue card: foreigner after the expatriation.) The *Belegebuch* is professionally important, so we ask you to send it back to us, as it will be needed for future English university examinations.
4. *Doktordiplom*
5. Certificate of attendance at Heinrich Hertz Institute (copy; attested photocopy will be sent later)
6. Testimonial from Prof. Leithäuser, HHI. (copy; attested copy will be sent later)
7. Photocopy of the expulsion from the Institute (attested version will be sent later)
8. Certificate of good conduct, 1938
9. Letter from the Swiss relief organisation for German Scholars: 8.11.35
10. Refusal of *Einreiseerlaubnis* [entry permit] by the Swiss authorities (the reason given: refusal because of statelessness)
11. Letter from the *Reichschriftstumkammer* 4.3.1935 (copy) (attested copy will be sent later)
12. Refusal of work permit 19.12.35
13. German naturalization certificate
14. Voluntary renunciation of Rumanian citizenship

(attested copies of 13 and 14 will be sent later) The originals of 5, 6, 7, 11, 13, 14 are in our possession.

The only documents still in my possession are those that were used again in Wolja's later claim for a pension. I am particularly sad that we don't have the German naturalization certificate given how rare it was to be able to be naturalized in Germany, nor the *Fremdenpass* with the notification of the *Ausbürgerung*, given its significance in Wolja's story. They would also have been very useful for my claim for German citizenship. The only other information about these claims comes from Wolja's affidavit for Eti and Ado, sworn ten years later in 1967, in which he states: 'My own claim for restitution is being dealt with at the office of restitution in Berlin under the Reg.Nr 75 256'.

A green application form for professional loss, full of crossings out, shows how difficult it was for Wolja to fit his experiences into the legal framework.

The categories on the form assumed that education or employment had been interrupted, although there was space for describing career expectations that could not be realized. Wolja included the interruption of his PhD studies, but had to add that he was nevertheless able to complete his PhD three years later. The fight to achieve this, described in Chapter 3, could not be documented on the form and it was hard to know where to put the fact that he was prevented from taking up work or continuing to write for scientific journals. He stated that he did subsequently teach in a Jewish school, but could not remember its name.

As the form was not helpful, he had to explain his experiences in his affidavit and CV. The many drafts we found are testimony to his struggle here too. The most complete version is four pages long. Although not dated it includes information about his salary up to 1957. The extracts I am presenting here are those in which Wolja describes the losses he incurred as a result of the delay in publication of his thesis:

> The biggest loss was purely scientific. In my thesis I described an analogy between electrical lowpass filters and electrical bandpass filters, which is very important for modern telecommunications engineering. In the English-American literature V.D. Landon is described as the discoverer of this analogy. His publication appeared in December 1936 that is after my doctorate exam in summer 1935, and even after my Promotion in summer 1936, which had to wait for the publication of my thesis. As a result of being forbidden to publish my thesis in a German scientific journal, my name is not associated today with this discovery. This fact is significant because such international recognition would certainly have influenced the development of my professional career...the same scientific-technical ideas led to a patent application in Germany with the title: Second Order circuits: No.S.124 751 VIII b/21d2., in which the firm Julius Pintsch showed great interest. Herr Dr Dällenbach, with whom I was conducting the negotiations suddenly broke them off, making it clear to me that to his great regret, because of the anti-Jewish laws, he was no longer able to finalize a contract with me. I was forced to let the application lapse in England, U.S.A. and Canada, where it had also been lodged, because of my total lack of money. I had been promised a down payment of RM 3,000 from the firm Pintsch, as well as the repayment of all my expenses. Instead I lost more than RM 1,000 for fees and other costs from this application.

There were two different versions of a final statement. I have combined the main points:

> As a result of my ideas and inventions I came to the attention of several professors very early in my studies, and through my work at the Heinrich Hertz Institute, my scientific publications, my lectures at the Radio Exhibition and my contributions to the radio engineering journal, I established very good relationships within scientific and technical circles...In Germany I would have had good prospects of developing either an academic career as a Professor, or in a leadership position in a scientific research institute. As a result of this interruption to my professional activity, and the difficulties of having to find a job in a foreign country, I have not been able pursue a scientific career. Admittedly I work as a development engineer, but I have not been able to use my scientific gifts.

As with the claim for Lotte's professional losses, Wolja was trying to claim for 'what might have been'. His case for the kind of academic success he would have been expected to achieve if the Nazis had not come to power seems strong, but claims could only be made for financial losses deriving from persecution, not for loss of status or unfulfilled ambitions.

His experience also shows how significant age and chance are. If he had been younger and failed to complete his PhD, it would have been easier to show what had been lost. If he had been just a few years older, he might have established his career sufficiently to substantiate the case he had made or, more likely, he would have been taken on in the UK in an academic post and developed the promised career anyway.

At the time at which he wrote his statement he had been with the Telephone Manufacturing Company (TMC) for nearly twenty years. Various papers in our collection provide evidence for his dissatisfaction there. They include letters expressing his reluctance to go back to TMC after his release from internment and his frustration with the attitudes of his managers who did not give him the opportunity to do research, but only routine 'bread and butter' work. Any longer-term research investigations were considered to be his private work and not a priority. His comment 'it is also difficult to carry out investigations if one is asked to guarantee success' contributed to his later negative opinion of British industry's attitude to research.

Wolja was offered other jobs, in universities, in Bangor in February 1941 and in Liverpool in September 1942, both of which he declined. Bangor seemed a very long way from friends and the refugee organizations in London, and the post in Liverpool involved a lot of teaching. He thought he should only give up his current post for 'more and more useful research'.

He was able to develop some research, though this may have been in his private time. In May 1943 he published an article in *The Wireless Engineer*.

By 4 May 1944 he was appointed at TMC as a member of a 'Long Term' development group. Nevertheless in August 1945 he wrote to Australia House about an advertisement he had seen in the journal *Nature* for a 'Research Physicist'. This is the application that Mrs Clarke had helped him to draft, but I have no evidence that he pursued it. By this time the war was over, Lotte was about to have her second child and Wolja was actively engaged in trying get a visa for his father.

After the war he started to teach evening classes and in 1947, after he had been naturalized, he was granted a patent. Towards the end of the war and in the early 1950s he also tried to pursue his research into electronic music. Letters in the Bodleian archive[15] also show that in 1947, while Ado was living with him, SPSL were helping Wolja to try to find other work, but clearly nothing came of this.

A letter from a former TMC colleague, Peter Eckersley, on 4 January 1958, confirms Wolja's view that his talents were wasted at TMC: '...your remarkable gifts decorate the organisation to which you belong but...you've had more fun with a long-term research environment than struggling with costs, routines and the sordid hurly burly of a festering commercialism. But as I said before, you can comfort yourself by a world recognition of your gifts and the undoubted admiration and affection of your staff.'

This context of his experiences with TMC is important for interpreting his statement of his professional losses in 1957. As a child I believed that he kept this job, which he didn't like, because he had to earn money to support us. It was therefore beholden on me to be 'good'. He continued to do theoretical work at home and worked all the time; he was happiest if he could work with us around him, though we were not supposed to interrupt him. If we wanted help with our maths or physics homework we could ask him, but it was something you thought about very carefully – he wouldn't just help with the bit you were stuck on, but insisted on starting again from first principles. It was futile to argue if the help was needed.

In 1958, a year after his statement of loss was written, Wolja changed his job; he joined Siemens (later the Associated Electrical Industries) at their Research Laboratories in Blackheath as a Research Scientist and Group Leader. He told Esther Simpson in November 1961 'I find the work very interesting and rewarding.' And his satisfaction is confirmed by a letter from Peter Eckersley in March 1963, who writes of the 'vicarious pleasure you gave me when telling me of your contentment with your life in general and particular'.

Further evidence comes from an obituary in the Proceedings of the Institute of Electrical Engineers in August 1981.[16]

It was in 1958 that he began a very successful and enjoyable period... It was here that Wolja's deep interest in filter design flourished, where a generation of industrially based circuit designers first learned their trade, and where many visitors, both national and international, converged to benefit from the stimulating environment that Saraga had created. Few of these visitors escaped – or indeed wanted to escape – the obligatory post-lunch walk to inspect the Greenwich Meridian and to stand, momentarily, with one foot in each hemisphere! It was during the 'Blackheath period', in 1962, that Saraga's key contributions were recognized by the award of the Fellowship of the Institute of Electrical and Electronics Engineers, 'for contributions to network theory and its application in communications'.

In 1968, just before he was 60, AEI was taken over by the General Electrical Company (GEC) and Wolja had to transfer to work in Wembley. I remember him saying that for the first time in his life he was too young for something – had he been 60, he could have retired and got his pension, and been free to do his own work. He continued to teach evening classes and spent 'one day a week giving postgraduate lectures and supervising research students at Imperial College, and he found this an increasingly rewarding experience'.[17] When he did retire in 1973 at 65 he was made a Visiting Professor by Imperial College. 'He found the atmosphere conducive to successful research in an increasingly broad range of topics. There cannot be many university research supervisors who commanded so much professional respect, and yet were held in such affectionate regard by their students...'[18]

I imagine that a statement of his professional losses written in 1972 would have been very different from the one he wrote in 1957.

Further clues to Wolja's feelings come from correspondence in German in 1962, when he wrote to his old Professor Leithäuser at the Heinrich Hertz Institute, on the occasion of his 80th birthday. Leithäuser was delighted to hear from him:

> ...you cannot believe how happy I was to get your good wishes. They came from one of my most treasured students, from a time when the development of radio engineering and electroacoustics were making such tumultuous progress. I have often recently heard about your work and I have been so pleased that with your diligent working methods you have achieved a great deal.

Replying, Wolja expressed his delight that Prof Leithäuser had seen some of his publications, enclosed information about his latest work which was about to be published and most significantly referred back to his time at the HHI: 'I often think about the wonderful time at the Heinrich-Hertz-Institute and about how you, esteemed Professor, supported and encouraged me in my scientific and technical ideas.'

'My Parents Sold It All Off Cheap'

Although Wolja's own claims for reparation were unsuccessful, he did receive some money for his parents' losses. Three applications were made: for losses associated with forced emigration including the sale of their furniture at rock bottom prices (in German described by one word – *Verschleuderung*) and for professional losses for both Ado and Eti. I wondered whether making these claims might have helped Wolja to come to terms with the failure to get his parents to this country before the war and with their untimely deaths. But this is speculation on my part.

I imagine that Mr Cromwell had retired; he would have been over 70 by now. Their lawyer for all these claims was Fanny Spitzer. She started with the furniture claim but, unlike Lotte, Wolja had no list of furniture to start from and no siblings to consult. In their attempt to provide evidence Lotte went to Berlin, in August 1966, to try to obtain an affidavit from Frau Harder, Eti and Ado's neighbour. It was Lotte's first trip back to Germany, twenty eight years after she was forced to leave. I found a postcard that she sent to me: 'Sweetpie, Here I am in Berlin. Just walked through old streets, where we used to live. Hewald Str., 9 where I left is still standing. Just eaten Pflaumenkuchen mit Schlagsahne [plum cake with whipped cream]. This afternoon, am going to see an old friend, knew her when I was 6. Best of luck, see you 29th. Kisses Lotte.'

Lotte had often talked about cafés on the Kurfurstendamm (Kudamm), the street on the photograph, as one of the few things she missed about Berlin. The card suggests that being in Berlin was both significant and a positive experience for her. It was the first evidence I had of Lotte being in contact with old friends in Germany. I do not know whether she made this trip 'on spec', or whether she knew that Frau Harder still lived in the block of apartments. Perhaps she needed such a significant reason to go back to Berlin for the first time.

Lotte did meet Frau Harder who agreed to provide written evidence, but it was not followed up until 11 April 1967 when she sent a brief written statement describing Eti and Ado's apartment in general terms as 'well furnished'. It took a further two years for her statement to be put together with an affidavit from Wolja, sworn at the German Embassy on 19 May 1969.

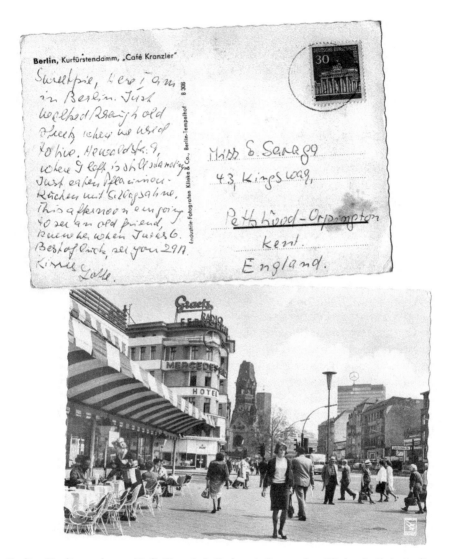

Berlin, Kurfürstendamm 'Café Kranzler'. (Industrie-Fotografen Klinke & Co.), Berlin-Tempelhof. Postcard from Lotte, August 1966.

My parents had furnished in the modern and very nice style, and nearly everything which was in the flat in Sven-Hedin-Street and had to be sold at give-away prices when they left, had been bought as new when they moved into this flat in 1932. I am no longer able, after so many years, to give information about the purchase and sale prices.

But they were very good items of furniture and carpets (even if the latter were not oriental) and in the end my parents took any price for them, since they had no other choice in view of their planned departure and the overabundant supply of furniture from emigrating Jews. In particular I remember that I occupied the smallest of the three rooms; that in each of the other two bigger rooms there was a wide divan, that we had some old wall-hangings, carpets, curtains, lamps – as usual – and in one room several armchairs, in the other a dining table with chairs, as well as other furnishings, a sideboard, cupboards, kitchen fittings, linen, porcelain, silver. My parents sold it all off cheap. They took none of their furnishing to Romania. I remember that we had a great deal of crystal, because my mother liked it.

On 9 July 1970 they received a very low offer – DM 2,100 – to cover both Eti and Ado's emigration costs and the sale of the furniture. It was assumed from Wolja's description that the furnishings were not very extensive or valuable. They knew that there was no point in appealing if they were unable to provide details of all the goods, so they accepted the offer and the money was given tax free. For the first time Wolja received some compensation.

On my trip to Berlin with Liz in 1995, we also went to a café on the Kudamm, where I ordered *Apfelkuchen mit Schlagsahne* [apple cake with whipped cream], because it represented my parents' German pasts for me. I had not yet read Lotte's postcard or I would have ordered *Pflaumenkuchen* instead. I went to look at the apartments in Sven Hedin Strasse. It made me understand why Wolja liked the suburbs so much. I looked at the names on the bells; one was Harder, I imagine the son of the Frau Harder of these letters. Liz asked me if I wanted to ring their bell, but I could not do it. I did not feel that my German was good enough to explain who I was. But this was not the real reason. I was frightened about how I would feel and how they would respond.

Thanks for 'bullying' us

The claim for Ado's loss of profession was very straightforward. With clear evidence that he was prevented by the Nazis from pursuing his very successful career as a business man, his case fitted into the legal categories. A good offer was made at the end of September 1970 – with interest £2,263. Fanny Spitzer's fee was 10%, but on 22 March 1971 Lotte sent her a cheque for £250: 'Once more many thanks for your help, patience and kindness, thanks for "bullying" us, and thanks for charming the Authorities on our behalf.' Two days later, Spitzer thanked her for 'your charming letter…your cheque for £250 – in settling my fees and making such a generous gesture of acknowledgment.'

Fanny Spitzer immediately started on the claim for Eti's loss of profession. On 24 March 1971 she told them the claim required evidence or witnesses to show that Eti had made serious attempts to find work after 1933. 'This is the point round which the whole problem revolves and on which it hinges.' Once again it was a claim for an absence or for what might have been. As a foreigner in Germany Eti had always been restricted in the work she could do as a doctor, but she had had a position in a children's clinic and later also developed an interest in nutrition. However in the 1920s she had to give up work because of ill health and by the time she was able to start again the Nazis were in power and she was excluded as a Jew.

Once more Lotte and Wolja procrastinated. Spitzer wrote them angry letters and the Berlin authorities imposed a final deadline of 30 June 1972 for the claim. Because she was ill, she was able to obtain a six-month extension. But I presume Lotte and Wolja still did not respond as she wrote them a very angry handwritten letter on 25 August 1972. It started in English:

> You will see from our correspondence how many times I have reminded you of the need to answer the enquiries I received from Berlin. You know yourselves that you have not co-operated, even when I pointed out I was very ill and had to speed matters up – I really have no time to write. You have yourselves received a direct communication from Berlin dated 15/8/72. I leave it to you to correspond directly with Berlin…I also enclose your documents…

She listed forty letters and documents with their dates and moved into German: 'In respect of the enormous amount of work I have done, despite the regrettable lack of support, I am requesting a fee of £12 to settle this matter.'

This time Lotte did reply. Her letter, written in English, seems very defensive.

> I meant to speak to you after receipt of your letter, but, on second thoughts, I decided to write. I am very sorry that we have caused you so much annoyance, and equally sorry that you are not well. In mitigating circumstances I can only say that, as far as your last reminder is concerned, that there must have been a misunderstanding on my part. I don't know whether you remember that I spoke to you on the telephone before you went on holiday. What I thought we arranged was that, if I found any written material I would get in touch with you – I mean send it – but that failing that you would let me know

when you came back and we would then discuss the matter. I know that we are the world's worst procrastinators, but this time we waited for you, knowing that you had been so ill, and that we should not over-burden you...

After nearly 40 years it is impossible to provide proof, other than a declaration on oath. I looked through old correspondence but could not find anything. If you do not feel too tired, I should be very grateful if you could let us know what we should do under the circumstances.

In the meantime I am enclosing a cheque of £12 for your professional services and wish to thank you very much for what you have done.

I do hope your health is better.

Given the anger and finality of Fanny Spitzer's letter, Lotte's reply astounded me. Having tried to justify her failure to reply in terms of not wanting to burden Fanny Spitzer, she nevertheless asked her for further advice. It seems very insensitive, given the levels of their procrastination. However I am in danger of judging with hindsight, as I know that Fanny Spitzer died three months later in November 1972. Lotte and Wolja tried to continue the claim alone, with an affidavit and later statement from Wolja in general terms, but they were not successful.

Lotte had had years of experience of working with Philip Cromwell who was always sympathetic and never cross. She could apologize and charm him. This strategy worked with Fanny Spitzer when working on Ado's claims but it could no longer work when the lawyer became so ill. Was it particularly hard for Wolja to deal with his mother's losses, given how painful the loss of his mother had been?

'The Cheek of These Things'

In the mid-1970s a new German law[19] allowed Lotte and Wolja to make claims for old age pensions if they could demonstrate that they had at any time paid social insurance contributions in Germany. If eligible for a pension they would also be offered the option of paying back contributions to increase the level of payments they would receive. Their claims were made by two lawyers they had not used before – first Dr King and later his colleague Dr Halpern – recommended by the Association of Jewish Refugees as specialists in social insurance law.

For Lotte the process was relatively straightforward. Cromwell had already established how many years should be allowed for her persecution and forced emigration and there was clear evidence of the years in which she had been employed. Lotte continued to be both fastidious in reading the small print of the new laws and regulations, concerned that she was being cheated or done down by low offers. This was perhaps not surprising, given her experiences with the earlier claims. Sometimes she was right and at other times Halpern explained patiently why she was wrong. But he did win her more money – a pension from her 65th birthday, paid at a higher level than originally offered, recognising that without the persecution, she would have been a high earner. This pension made an enormous difference to her financial situation when she retired, but it did not prevent her anxiety about money in her last few years. I wonder whether this was related to the earlier loss of all her personal possessions.

For Wolja the pension claim was much more complicated and ultimately unsuccessful, because there was no evidence that he had at any time paid into the German social insurance system. But Halpern persisted with it until 1982, two years after Wolja's death, by which time it had become a claim for a widow's pension for Lotte.

Before he would take on the case, King sent Wolja a standard letter:

> Due to the fact that many of my dear colleagues for health reasons, or because they have died, cannot process any more German cases, my colleagues Dr Halpern and I are too much in demand for work. However we feel a moral obligation to our co-refugees, to take on further cases. It is however possible, as we are all only human, that there will be flaws and mistakes in our work, and we must refuse to be responsible for such mistakes. We can therefore only take on your case if you sign the declaration below. Otherwise we regret we cannot represent you. (11 December 1975)

Wolja's signed acceptance that he would only hold him responsible for 'deliberate damage' and not for 'incorrect handling' of his case, appears at the bottom of the page. Far from the picture of greedy lawyers making money out of the restitution process, here were committed fellow refugees feeling an obligation to continue this work.

None of Wolja's many testimonials and certificates showed evidence of having paid social insurance contributions. In his attempts to remember names and events from nearly forty years earlier, he told Halpern that he had worked for three to six months as a consultant for a firm, whose name he could not remember, 'in the year in which the large Zeppelin (Hindenburg?) burst into flames on landing in the USA'. From the internet I learned that this happened on Thursday 6 May 1937. His work at the Heinrich Hertz Institute had been unpaid, but he hoped there might be records showing contributions from his time at Siemens or when he did some maths and physics teaching for a private Jewish School in Berlin.

All attempts failed. Every organization they consulted, including those in the DDR, replied very quickly and all tried to be helpful. But no-one had any relevant information. Siemens confirmed Wolja's dates, but information on earnings was no longer available. The Trade Union Federation regretted that in the archive of the former insurance office there was no insurance information available. Most people referred Halpern elsewhere, often to organizations he had already tried.

On 22 November 1977 Halpern asked Wolja for the originals of the statement from Siemens from 1927 and the one from the TH Berlin from 1935, papers from 50 and 42 years earlier. It seems extraordinary both that they would be expected to and did have them. On 3 December, apologising for the delay which she blamed on 'a winter infection', Lotte sent these documents and also another one from Samsonwerk from 1929. 'In addition we have suddenly found another document – *Abgangs-Bescheinigung* [leaving certificate] from Siemens dated 31.3.27. The cheek of these things, it had completely hidden itself in the file, through which we had always looked. Any chance?' This last certificate states that Wolja paid medical insurance contributions for five months.

All the relevant documents were verified by the German Embassy and on 4 January 1979 the pension claim was submitted, with a letter from Halpern stating that Wolja was a NS-*Verfolgter* [a National Socialist Persecutee – no simple term in English] and enclosing the various documents. The claim was acknowledged in a card dated 23.3.78. Seven months later he received the rejection, dated 15.2.79.

This date is exactly one year before Wolja's death. As with previous sets of correspondence I am living the week by week progress, or in this case lack of progress. The search was very painful and feels quite desperate. And I know the outcome of the claim and for Wolja and this made my anxiety increase as they continued with what I know was a futile search. Wolja clearly pinned his hopes on the Jewish School, though he could not remember its name. The Director might have been Dr Adler. Halpern appealed the decision and continued the search for evidence, in particular trying to locate the school. They tried several different archives. Once again everyone was very helpful, replying promptly and suggesting further organizations to contact. On 8 June 1979 Halpern sent Wolja a list of possible schools to look at. Wolja delayed in his reply, so Halpern asked for an extension of the deadline for an appeal, reminding Wolja that he needed a response.

On 1 July that year, Peter and I threw a surprise belated joint birthday party for Lotte and Wolja, to celebrate their 65th and 70th birthdays respectively. We couldn't do it at the right time as Lotte was receiving treatment for her second breast cancer. In August 1979 I had a five-week holiday in the USA, mainly in New York, and had an amazing experience. In a swimming pool I met by complete chance an old school friend of Lotte's, a woman Lotte presumed must have perished as she was active in the resistance. Two months after my return Wolja was very seriously ill, diagnosed with a malignant brain tumour.

Yet they continued with Wolja's pension claim. Writing to Halpern on 29 December 1979 Wolja identified one possible school from the addresses, but thought he may have misremembered the name of the Principal. He still believed that the letter refusing him permission to teach 'even if it does not contain details about the school, constitutes in itself first-class evidence about the matter in question.' His friend, Prof. H. Nathan, of Lansing University, Michigan, USA 'says that he remembers very well that I taught Mathematics and Physics (and possibly also Chemistry) at a Private Jewish School in Wilmersdorf, and he is very willing to confirm this in any way you might suggest (including a sworn affidavit)…'

In his reply on 4 January 1980 Halpern dashed their hopes about the value of the 'refusal of permission to teach'. He had had it for nine months; it did not mention the name of the school, and it was not clear that Wolja was already teaching. By this time Wolja was very ill and they knew that eventually the tumour would kill him. Hans Nathan wrote to Halpern on 17 January, very worried about Wolja's health. Unfortunately he only remembered that Wolja did some teaching in a Jewish school, but no details of the school or the dates of his employment.

The next item in the file is a copy of Wolja's death certificate. His brain tumour was inoperable but he received the latest laser treatment radiotherapy. He was fascinated by the technology involved. His consultant told us that he had known people with Wolja's condition live for any time between two and ten years, but he lived for three months, dying on 15 February 1980 aged 71 from a pulmonary embolism. He continued to work and died in bed with his work around him. Lotte told me later of her regrets that they never spoke about his dying. I wonder whether a lot of their emotion during these three months went into this claim, which may have felt even more urgent. It was something they could do together at such a difficult time, which focused them on Wolja's early life in Germany, rather than facing the pain of Wolja's imminent death.

On 25 February 1980, ten days after Wolja's death, Halpern informed the Social Insurance Office saying however: 'The action will continue.' Although with hindsight, it seems like a hopeless task, Halpern and Hans Nathan continued to search for the name of the Jewish school, but with no success.

Over the next eight months Halpern received three reminders from the Office, and each time he asked for a further extension. On 5 October 1980 after the third reminder he wrote to Lotte: 'You will remember that for many years we have tried to find evidence that your late husband had paid social insurance contributions. Unfortunately there seem to be no documents in existence. Sadly I see no possibility of achieving success, and I would be grateful if you would agree to withdraw the claim.'

But Lotte was clearly unwilling to give up. Halpern wrote again to the Social Insurance Office on 29 October: 'The widow of the claimant is making great efforts to look through old relevant papers. I shall get back to you by 28 February 1981.' On 7 January 1981 Halpern wrote to Lotte again, asking her to get back to him by the end of January. I imagine she did not do this as the deadline was extended again until 30 April 1981. When Halpern wrote to Lotte to tell her of the new deadline, he said that if he had not heard from her by 20 April he would assume her search for papers had been in vain. This time Lotte did get in touch. On 22 April Halpern wrote to the Social Insurance Office: 'The widow…wished to check in old papers for relevant documents. Unfortunately she is a sensitive and ill woman; this kind of search makes her very anxious. I ask for an extension until 30 June 1981.'

On 4 June Halpern wrote again: 'My continued requests to Mrs Saraga to look for relevant papers remain unanswered; I must therefore assume that she – as last year – is ill. I ask for a further extension.' Twenty years earlier when completing the claims for Lotte and her mother's emigration costs, the same thing happened – reminders from the officials, Lotte not responding, and ever more extensions being granted. In May 1963 Cromwell had explained that 'This woman is also in fact very affected by her health and this is a reason for the slow response to your request 'and in December 1964 he had explained 'from my experience, I think this may be a question of nerves.' And now Halpern had to explain that Lotte was 'a very sensitive and ill woman.' Indeed she was and trying to care for her and support her at that time was very hard.

There is a final letter from Halpern to Lotte on 9 November 1981, this time in English: 'Last spring you told me that you would go through old documents to find any trace of your husband having paid German social security contributions. I would appreciate if you would inform me whether you have had any success or whether we should let the matter rest.' On 15 April 1982 the Social Insurance Office gave them a final extension until 31 July 1982.

That's it! It feels so sad. I remember none of this, though of course I remember the terrible anxiety that Lotte suffered from after Wolja died, never forgiving herself that at the moment of his death she had turned away from him, because she could not bear to watch him die. She had had to let go of Wolja, but she could not take the decision herself to let go of his pension claim.

In Person

About a week after Wolja's death the following letter, dated 20 February 1980, arrived:

> Dear Wolja
> It is a great pleasure to inform you that your Transactions paper (co-authored with David G. Haigh and Robert G. Barker) entitled…has been chosen as recipient of the 1979 <u>Darlington Award</u>. On behalf of the members of the administrative committee and the awards committee, I would like to congratulate you and your co-authors for a well-deserved honor. Unlike the Guillemin-Cauer Award which is given annually, this award is given only when a truly outstanding <u>applications oriented</u> paper has been identified…
> The <u>Darlington Award</u> will be presented at the 1980 <u>International Symposium on Circuits and Systems</u> at Houston, Texas, April 28-30. I am looking forward to seeing you there and congratulating you in person.

But Wolja could not receive his award in person; he did not even know that he had won it. It seemed like another unfair blow for someone who had always felt his achievements were not recognized. It would have made him so happy. These thoughts added to our pain at his death. So much so, that when my mother expressed her sadness that Wolja did not know about the award, I tried to reassure her by saying 'he does, I know he does'. What on earth did I mean? I have no belief in an afterlife – I just couldn't bear to feel the pain myself.

Notes

1. J. Roth, trans. Michael Hofmann, *The Wandering Jews* (London: Granta Books, 2001), p.124.
2. A. Grenville, 'The Association of Jewish Refugees', in A. Grenville and A.Reiter (eds), *I Didn't Want to Float; I Wanted to Belong to Something* (Rodopi: Amsterdam, NY, 2008), p.100. See also M. Roseman, *The Past in Hiding* (London: Penguin Books, 2001), p.490, and M. Berghahn, *German-Jewish refugees in England. The Ambiguities of Assimilation* (London: Macmillan Press, 1984), p.206.
3. Roseman, *The Past in Hiding,* p.466.

4. Ibid.,p.165.
5. Ibid., p.468.
6. The three main sources I used were: C. Pross, trans. B. Cooper, *Paying for the Past : The Struggle Over Reparations for Surviving Victims of the Nazi Terror* (Baltimore, MD: John Hopkins Press, 1998); T. Winstel, 'Über die Bedeutung der Wiedergutmachung im Leben der jüdischen NS-Verfolgten. Erfahrungsgeschichtliche Annäherungen' in H.G.Hockerts and C. Kuller (eds), *Nach der Verfolgung. Wiedergutmachung nationalsozialistischen Unrechts in Deutschland* (Göttingen: Wallstein Verlag, 2003); T. Winstel, *Verhandelte Gerechtigkeit* (Oldenbourg Wissenschaftsverlag GmbH: Institut für Zeitgeschichte, 2006).
7. H.G. Hockerts, 'Wiedergutmachung. Ein umstrittener Begriff und ein weites Feld', in H.G. Hockerts and C. Kuller (eds), *Nach der Vervolgung*, pp. 9-13.
8. S. Schrafstetter, 'The Diplomacy of *Wiedergutmachung*: Memory, the Cold War, and the Western European Victims of Nazism, 1956-1964', *Holocaust and Genocide Studies*, 17, 3, (Winter 2003), pp.459-479.
9. Winstel, 'Über die Bedeutung', p. 203, T. Winstel, *Verhandelte Gerechtigkeit*, p.269. See also Berghahn, *German-Jewish Refugees in England*, p.208 and Roseman, *The Past in Hiding*, pp. 466-472.
10. Winstel, 'Über die Bedeutung', p.207, p.213.
11. Schrafstetter, 'The Diplomacy of *Wiergutmachung*', p.471.
12. https://de.wikipedia.org/wiki/Bundesentschädigungsgesetz (Accessed 24 November 2018).
13. C. Reimesch, *Vergessene Opfer des Nationalsozialismus?: Zur Entschädigung von Homosexuellen, Kriegsdienstverweigerern, Sinti und Roma und Kommunisten in der Bundesrepublik Deutschland* (Berlin: Verlag für Wissenschaft und Kultur, 2003). See also Pross, *Paying for the Past*, p.51; H.G. Hockerts, 'Wiedergutmachung', p.18; R. Ludi, 'The Vectors of Postwar Victim Reparations: Relief, Redress and Memory Politics', *Journal of Contemporary History*, 41, 3 (2006), pp. 421 -450, p. 442.
14. Lotte has used the wrong name here – in German it is the *Bundesentschädigungsgesetz*, BEG, *Schlussgesetz*.
15. B388/383 and 384.
16. 'Wolja Saraga (1908-1980)', *IEE Proceedings*, 128, 4 (August 1981), p.145.
17. Ibid.
18. Ibid.
19. See AJR Information, June 1975, p.2.

10

Afterword: 'Personal Letters – To Keep'

What is past cannot be mastered. It can be remembered, forgotten or repressed. It can be avenged, punished or atoned for and regretted. It can be repeated, consciously or unconsciously. Its consequences can be managed either to encourage or discourage their impact on the present or the future. But what is done is done. The past is unassailable and irrevocable. The word 'mastering' in its true sense applies to a task at hand that must be worked on and worked through, until it is completed. Then the task no longer exists as such. (Bernhard Schlink)[1]

How do I conclude a project that has absorbed me and structured my life for so long? Am I completing a task for my parents or for myself? Schlink's ideas on *Vergangenheitsbewältigung* [mastering the past], which were written in the context of German guilt about the past, nevertheless seem to give a name to what I have been engaged with for the last sixteen years.[2]

The discovery of the papers in 1985 felt like an amazing gift. They have introduced me to the grandparents I never met, and given me a greater knowledge and understanding of my parents, of their relationship with one another and with us, their children, and hence of myself. In the process of working with them, I have learned some German and British history and am (almost) fluent in German. I have made many new contacts and friends, including two very special German friends, both of whom sadly died before the book was completed.

The papers have also been a burden, encouraging me to focus on the past and my parents' lives rather than on my own life in the present. I have had to find ways of handling the painful emotions expressed in the letters and to recognize the many difficulties and losses each of my parents faced. But I have also been put in touch with their determination and courage and understood the significance of their educational and class background which contributed to their extraordinary capacity to network, without which they would not have succeeded in the way that they did.

I do not have an answer to the question of whether I have the right to use their personal letters in this way. My parents were not public figures, but

I feel responsible for the picture of them that I present and an obligation to be as 'truthful' as I can. From the beginning I felt voyeuristic reading the love letters between my parents. I still have not read the letters from one of his lovers, but I have also not thrown them away. To have ignored the impact of Wolja's affairs on Lotte would have been to present her only as a Nazi victim. Can I make a distinction between what is personal and what is private – a distinction Lotte herself made in labelling her envelopes?[3]

As I learned more about their experiences, it was hard at times not to think about what 'might have happened'. I neither want to see my parents only as victims nor to adopt Lotte's position that 'they didn't really suffer'. There is evidence in these papers of persecution and injustice that they never told us about and their losses were much greater than I had realized. But they came through it and reconstructed their lives and it is important to remember that, because of the war, many other people of their generation had similar kinds of professional losses, even though they did not experience persecution.

I wonder whether there is a danger of silencing people about the suffering and persecution they have experienced. A denial of what did happen may in turn deny people the possibility of working through their loss and grief. Is it not possible to hold the ambivalence and contradictions? They did suffer, they were persecuted, and they also survived and are grateful for the help they were given.

Given these reflections, I was surprised to find myself ending each of the last two chapters on such a sad note – Lotte's depression and Wolja dying before he knew he had won an international prize. More recent, unexpected events in 2015 and 2016 helped me to redress this balance.

Wolja

Peter worked in a similar field to Wolja and tells me that Wolja was internationally recognized; indeed nearly forty years after his death he is still referred to. In May 2015 I was contacted by Simon Crab, who has developed a website on the history of electronic music. He used the papers in our collection to develop his entry on Wolja,[4] helping me to identify a photograph of Wolja working on his 'Saraga Generator'.

Following this up, I learned that the Generator was exhibited at the International Radio Show in Berlin in 1932,[5] at which The Heinrich Hertz Orchestra of electrical instruments was playing. 'Daily lectures were given by Prof. Dr Gustav Leithauser and his assistant Wolja Saraga. Up to six performances took place per day during the 10-day show.'[6]

In 2016 Peter was contacted by Tony Davies, who contributed

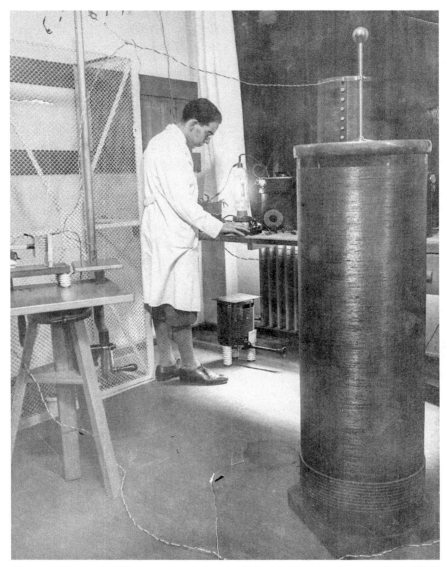

Wolja working on his 'Saraga generator' at the Heinrich Hertz Institute, Berlin in 1932. (Presse-Photo GES M.B.H. Berlin S.W.48)

three pages on Wolja to the 'In Memoriam' section of a book on the history of 'circuits and systems' in electrical engineering. Published by the IEEE (the Institute of Electrical and Electronics Engineers, the world's largest technical professional association, based in the USA), the book 'fills a gap in published literature by providing a record of the many outstanding scientists, mathematicians and engineers who laid the foundations of Circuit Theory and Filter Design from the mid-20th Century.[7]

Lotte

In December 2016 I received an email from a German journalist, Cristina Fischer. She had tracked me down through these two recent items on the internet about Wolja. But it was Lotte she was interested in. She was researching the stories of women and men who were part of the resistance, most of whom were murdered by the Nazis. She hoped that I might have further information on Lotte's communist activities, for which she had been thrown out of Berlin University in 1933. I explained that, as described in Chapter 9, Lotte had never been a communist, but had communist friends. Sadly I had no material from this time, but I was able to put her in touch with a friend, whose mother had been in a communist youth group. In May 2017 Cristina told me:

> Lotte Isenburg had the student number 3645/122 (*122* means the 'Rektorats' year when she inscribed for Medicine, = 1931/32) and was relegated on 12 of December 1933 together with Richard Freymann (med), Margarete Gottschalk (med), Bruno Lechner (med), Manfred Magner (med), Heinrich Metz (med) and Kurt Silbermann (med). It is to be supposed that all these students knew each other. But I have found no further information about them. The lists were made by Nazi students (in this case medicine students) who had watched their enemies when they distributed leaflets or flyers, discussed in groups and so on. In most cases these students were really members of communist or Marxist groups. Margarete Gottschalk was the only one whose relegation was cancelled. She made her thesis in medicine in 1937. So your mother was the only woman among the relegated medicine students of the December list. She was a Berlin student between winter 1931/32 and winter 1933. But perhaps she left long time before because Jews were often chased by Nazis and had to fear mobbing and violence.[8]

Lotte herself writes that she left the university in summer 1933. As part of my search for information, I came across a tiny student book for her two semesters at Berlin University, listing all the courses she attended.

The last date in this book seems to be June 1933, but a certificate from the *Physiologisch-Chemisches Institut der Universität Berlin* shows that she

Lotte's Berlin University book, 1932-33.

studied Chemistry from 8 May to 1 August 1933. Cristina's interest in Lotte as a politically active student put me back in touch with a different Lotte, someone who was competent and courageous in the face of multiple difficulties. I am reminded of an occasion in 1977 when I was arrested early one morning during a protest demonstration at Grunwicks. I was meeting Lotte for lunch and she had to wait for me until I was released from the police station. Her first words to me were: 'if I were younger I would join you'. But later, when I told her that I planned to return the next day, she tried to dissuade me: 'Can't you let history happen without you?'⁹

On 6 December 2018 I received the news that my application for German citizenship had been approved. It aroused very mixed emotions – I was delighted that Wolja had been recognized, but at the same time my 'certificate of naturalisation' feels like a tangible reminder of Lotte and Wolja's persecution.

Not Just a Personal Story

During my many years of working with these papers, I have been astounded how often contemporary events have resonated with Lotte and Wolja's experiences: the designation of refugees as 'enemy aliens' or bogus/illegal asylum seekers; assumptions of disloyalty or dangers of terrorism, which justify internment or detention; the difficulties of negotiating with the Home Office and the struggle to bring in a family member even when they meet the Home Office's own criteria.

Lotte and Wolja's letters help me to understand the emotional impact of such experiences, which are not specific to their particular circumstances. In 2002, when I read Ghada Karmi's autobiographical account of her middle-class family's expulsion and exile from Palestine in 1948,[10] the similarities with my parent's stories were remarkable. I had the same experience in 2017 when I watched the BBC TV series '70 Years On: Partition Stories', which marked the 70th anniversary of the Partition of India and Pakistan,[11] and this is often the case when I read the stories of the many refugees across the world today. Coming to the end of my project in 2018 coincided with the 'Windrush scandal' and I recognized again the crucial importance of having the 'right' documents and the fact that my father's papers were also destroyed, but in his case with no dire consequences.[12]

I am not suggesting direct parallels with today. Much has changed and the context and circumstances in which people have to flee are always important. This does not mean that connections cannot be made. However, Tony Kushner argues:

> The enormity of the Holocaust has led to a tendency to place it outside of history and therefore beyond comparison. In terms of Jewish refugees during the Nazi era, this has meant an emphasis on the impossibility of escape and, for those that did manage to do so, a failure to connect to other migratory movements, whether before, during or after.[13]

When writing the 'In memoriam' piece about Wolja mentioned earlier, I was surprised that Tony Davies did not, in his first draft, explicitly describe Wolja as Jewish. When I queried this Tony told me: 'I had avoided explicitly stating that Wolja was a Jew, because he never mentioned it and I never felt any awareness or significance of it in all the years during which I knew him.'[14] I am still surprised, but it makes me remember the way in which my parents described themselves, proudly, as 'refugees', and this strengthens my belief that theirs is not a Holocaust story, but is indeed a story of refugees.

In contrast to the way migrants and asylum seekers are discussed today, the dominant historical memory remains that Jewish refugees were welcomed to the UK in the 1930s as 'genuine' refugees and model immigrants, who made no demands on the welfare system, were willing to 'assimilate', and made great contributions to the social and cultural life of the UK.[15] Historical research shows a very different story. The UK government was very reluctant to admit them; many were refused and many more excluded than allowed in. It did not want permanent settlers in a country considered to be overcrowded and which had mass unemployment.[16]

In line with this, the British response to the situation of Jews attempting to flee from Nazi Germany has been characterized as either generous or restrictive. The 'generous' view, that it was a continuation of the tolerant, liberal tradition of welcoming those seeking asylum, is adopted by accounts that emphasize both the gratitude of the refugees and also their 'dazzling contribution' as an 'elite', or 'starry bunch'.[17] Given the events of the Holocaust from which they escaped, it is not surprising that victimhood is often frowned upon. Organizations representing Jewish refugees have also focused on gratitude, the most notable example being the 'Thank-you Britain' Fund, initiated by the AJR and others in 1964.[18] These sentiments were not universally shared, but it can be hard to speak against such a strong norm.[19]

I never had any sense of Lotte and Wolja feeling 'Thank-you Britain' and indeed in all their correspondence I have only found one letter, quoted in Chapter 4, in which Wolja, arguing that the Home Office should recognize him as stateless, writes 'I am very grateful to this country which has given me an opportunity to begin a new life', a sentiment he repeated in his draft application for release from internment. On the other hand both our archive and that of SPSL are full of letters from Wolja or Lotte thanking people individually and SPSL for their great kindness.

Tony Kushner suggests that 'no other country possess such a strong belief in its own tolerance and decency – past and present'.[20] And Louise London argues that the 'comfortable view has proved remarkably durable and is still adduced to support claims that Britain has always admitted genuine refugees, and the latest harsh measures against asylum seekers are merely designed to exclude bogus applicants'.[21] Distinctions are always made between deserving and undeserving migrants.[22] Wolja's files in the SPSL archive show the processes of selection at work. Given Makower's first view of Wolja's chances, 'prospects not good, though not impossible', it is hard to imagine that without the recommendation of Max von Laue and hence Sir William Bragg, the outcome would have been so positive. Makower himself died in 1939. He did not live long enough to write a post-war recollection or memoir, or to know what might have happened to individuals who were turned down. Yet many were refused and in his account of the AAC, Beveridge acknowledges the people he was unable to help. 'My personal files are full of desperately hard cases of such men and women, recommended to me often by university teachers in the same subjects; ...I could do nothing but pass such cases on to someone else, or occasionally make an appeal to an influential friend.'[23]

What I have learned about my parents' experiences and the social political context in which they took place, is precisely this set of contradictory positions, of help and hindrance.

As I was completing this book in 2018, the actual numbers trying to reach Europe had dropped considerably, but the anti-migrant rhetoric had been ratcheted up, with the European states and the USA seeming to be in a competition to develop the most restrictive policy. This leads me to end where I began, with Lotte's fears that the world is becoming ever more dangerous.

Notes

1. B. Schlink, *Guilt About the Past* (London: Beautiful Books, 2010), p.43.
2. See also M. Berghahn, *German Jewish Refugees in England. The Ambiguities of Assimilation* (London: Macmillan, 1984), p.206 and M. Roseman, *The Past in Hiding (London: Penguin Books, 2000)*, p.490.
3. For further discussion of some of these issues and dilemmas, see the 2017-2018 series of lectures on 'The Difficulties of Writing Family History' organized by the Leo Baeck Institute in London. They can be listened to on podcast from their website http://www.leobaeck.co.uk (Accessed 3 December 2018).
4. http://120years.net/saraga (Accessed 3 December 2018).
5. P. Donhauser, *Elektrische Klangmaschine. Die Pionierzeit in Deutschland und Österreich,* (Wien-Köln-Weimar: Böhlau Verlag, 2007), p.67.
6. https://archive.li/1wMEh. (Accessed 3 December 2018).
7. F. Maloberti & A.C. Davies (eds) *A Short History of Circuits and Systems,* (Aalborg & Delft: River Publishers, 2016). The section on Wolja is pp. 279-281. Quote is on the blurb.
8. Email to author, C. Fischer, 25 May 2017.
9. 'The Grunwick dispute was an industrial dispute involving trade union recognition at the Grunwick Film Processing Laboratories in...Dollis Hill in... London...that led to a two-year strike between 1976 and 1978...' https://en.wikipedia.org/wiki/Grunwick_ dispute. (Accessed 3 December 2018). I was acquitted of obstruction.
10. G. Karmi, *In search of Fatima: a Palestinian story* (London: Verso, 2002).
11. BBC 2 Series, '70 years on: Partition Stories'. https://www.bbc.co.uk/programmes/ p05b5fdg. (Accessed 3 December 2018).
12. See for example https://www.amnesty.org.uk/blogs/yes-minister-it-human-rights-issue/seventy-years-after-windrush. (Accessed 3 December 2018).

13. T. Kushner, *Journeys from the abyss. The Holocaust and forced migration from the 1880s to the present* (Liverpool: Liverpool University Press, 2017), p.306.

14. Email to the author, Tony Davies, 23 February 2016.

15. A. Kushner, 'Remembering to forget: racism and anti-racism in post-war Britain', in B. Cheyette & L. Marcus (eds), *Modernity, Culture and 'The Jew'* (Cambridge: Polity Press, 1998) pp.226-214, p.236.

16. L. London, *Whitehall and the Jews 1933-1948* (Cambridge, Cambridge University Press, 2000), T. Kushner, 'Clubland, Cricket Tests and Alien Internment, 1939-40', in D. Cesarani and T. Kushner (eds), *The Internment of aliens in twentieth century Britain* (London and Portland, OR: Frank Cass, 1993), pp.79-101.

17. See for example, Grenville, Anthony (2009), 'The rescue of refugee scholars', in *AJR journal* 9 (2) pp.1-2.

18. See *AJR Information*, XIX, 9 (September 1964), p.1.

19. See, for example, *AJR Information*, XX, 4 (April 1965), p.1., Kushner *Journeys from the Abyss*, p. 52.

20. Kushner, *Journeys from the Abyss*, p. 303.

21. London, *Whitehall and the Jews*, p.13.

22. J. Harding, *Border Vigils: keeping migrants out of the rich world* (London: Verso, 2012), p.x., T. Kushner, *Remembering refugees, then and now* (Manchester: Manchester University Press, 2006), p.32.

23. Lord Beveridge, *A Defence of Free Learning* (London: Oxford University Press, 1959), p.18.

Index

Page references to endnotes are followed by the letter 'n'.

Lightning Source UK Ltd.
Milton Keynes UK
UKHW021054300621
386327UK00017B/548